Architects of the Self

Architects of the Self

George Eliot, D. H. Lawrence,
and E. M. Forster

BY CALVIN BEDIENT

UNIVERSITY OF CALIFORNIA PRESS
BERKELEY · LOS ANGELES · LONDON
1972

University of California Press
Berkeley and Los Angeles, California

University of California Press, Ltd.
London, England

1SBN: 0-520-01873-7
Library of Congress Catalog Card Number: 70-142056
Printed in the United States of America

for Vanessa

Acknowledgments

For help and encouragement, I owe many thanks to Wayne Burns, E. E. Bostetter, and William H. Matchett, of the University of Washington, and to Walter Anderson, of the University of California, Los Angeles. My chief debt is to my wife, Vanessa, for her patience and perception.

I am grateful to *The Hudson Review* for permission to reprint, with some changes, Chapter III and Chapter VII.

Contents

CONTENTS

Introduction

Of the major English novelists since Jane Austen, the three who can tell us most—and who are most concerned to tell us—about the costs and rewards, the hazards and consequences of being one or another kind of self, are George Eliot, D. H. Lawrence, and E. M. Forster. All the important aspects of human beings—social, moral, personal, natural, cosmic—are severally championed among them. Together they form a digest, a colloquium, on the question of what the human being is and ought to be—of what it should mean to be alive and human.

What gives these novelists a looming prominence with regard to these questions, and makes the interrelations among their work so dense and active, is that they constitute the three ruling idealists in English fiction in a period when human character underwent a revolution in goals and sanctions. They are the red and the white of this revolution, necessary to each other, and joined as only lovers and enemies can be joined. Apart from the Victorians, Lawrence and Forster are not quite complete, not quite intelligible: their fervor lacks occasion, their advocacy of the body seems *de trop*, rather as if one were to encourage the clouds to bloom, or to recommend drinking water. Full of response and contest, Forster and Lawrence form the antistrophe to George Eliot's strophe, the Nay to her Yea, the Yea to her Nay.

In these three writers lie the campfires of the conflicting ideals of human character consequent upon the decay of Christianity among English makers of culture. The struggle has lain essentially between the mind and the flesh, and between the desire to be whole against the extravagances of each. Even within the Victorian age, there was, of course, something of a skirmish; but the main battle has been almost a matter of succession to the field, one army appearing only as the strength of the other was giving way. Let us review this post-Christian struggle to devise a significant idea of the self, in order to grasp the great importance of George Eliot, Lawrence, and Forster within it.

"On or about December 1910 human character changed": Virginia Woolf's famous assertion, flourished like a red cape before the jaundiced gaze of historians, remains intact—a free, maddening, and deftly elusive pass. True, we might quarrel with her date—push it back to 1905, the year of Forster's *Where Angels Fear to Tread*, or ahead to 1915, the year of Lawrence's *Rainbow*. Yet 1910 is as sound as any other date: the essence of the change is fully concentrated there.

For Virginia Woolf, the revelation of change lay in the first London exhibition of Post-Impressionist paintings, which opened on November 8, 1910. Here, in the Cézannes and Manets, the Gauguins and Picassos, the Rouaults, Van Goghs and Signacs, was announced a new art—hence necessarily a new human character. The art, for the most part, was restless, subjective, erotic, *colored*. Clearly reality was not enough for it. It changed the lines of things, the light, the mass; it infused, as Virginia Woolf herself was to do, an aesthetic ebullience into the particles of the world. It was an art not of selfless mimesis but of immediate and carnal intuition. It brought to nature the prerogatives, the brilliance, the arrogance, of human desire.

And the human character it expressed—could this be any less instinctual? Reason, social conscience, selflessness, the worship of the nonego: the new art was far toward the antipodes of these. From singular caverns in the artist it emerged and, strange, unheard-of, took its place in the public world. Saturated in both biology and biography, it bespoke, not spirit objectified and universalized by social or rational forms, but spirit living, immanent, individual, concrete. In short, it was an art rooted in style, in idiosyncratic vision. No wonder, then, that letters protesting the exhibition saw Post-Impressionism—in Samuel Hynes's summary in *The Edwardian Turn of Mind*—as a menace not only to "native English art" but to "essential English morality" as well.

Of the new art, Virginia Woolf herself was to become the aesthetic—as Colette was the sensual—priestess. And of its pursuit of the luminousness of earthly life she is a perfect example—just as she exemplifies also, in *To the Lighthouse* especially, its metaphysical ferment and dazzle. *Of course* Virginia Woolf would recognize instantly, and welcome, the revolution in human character. All the same, she does not quite give us its pulse; in her its blood is anemic. Toward energy and rude Eros—both at the center of the new—she was, at best, on uneasy terms, a butterfly apprehensive near a waterfall. Almost entirely given over to intuition as Virginia Woolf was, her footing in instinct was yet insecure. An almost unworldly fragility is her note. The ruling impulse of her work is not an assent to life but a desperate defense against it. Life seems to hit her, always, with the force of a wind that, even as she runs to meet it, takes away her breath.

The special quality of the new human character is the alliance it forms between the soft stuff of fleshly desire and the steel of conscience: it is Eros in mail, with both the strength and the discipline that this suggests. Such is the combination, for instance, that confronts us in D. H. Lawrence, in whose fiction the new character is not only full blown but aggressively vindicated, messianic in its assertiveness. "I expect some people will want to annihilate me for it," Lawrence wrote of *Lady Chatterley's Lover*, "but I believe in it, its got to be done. One's got to get back to the live, really lovely phallic self. . . ." Here is the new tone, the new conscience in all its fervor. And it was true, of course, that some people wanted to annihilate Lawrence. Unlike the Post-Impressionists' exhibits, Lawrence's more obviously "phallic" paintings were suppressed, put away like criminals; and there were attempts, as is well known, to annihilate Lawrence's books. Whether or not the still-Victorian public and its police were conscious that what challenged them in Lawrence was more than an unruly member, they certainly acted as if they knew that the real danger was something formidable indeed: an attitude toward the flesh antithetical to their own, but equally righteous and relentless.

Some time between 1900 and 1930 human character did indeed change in British culture, changed completely and thoroughly, changed shape, components, values, changed advocates, magistrates, guards. Character as seized and shredded by psychologists and philosophers changed, and changed as biographers, novelists, and poets portrayed it, and as other artists expressed it. With respect to what is possible in the self, the period is the most fruitful and instructive in English history. It is true that the period 1800 to 1830 is similar; but it is a dry run by comparison. It is a sketch in pencil of what had later to be gone over more fully. What makes each age coherent and fascinating is the strength and brilliance of its opposition to a preceding age, with which it is unified in repulsion. In each period the self thaws from the cold of rational and social strictures and runs south into climates at once metaphysical and instinctual.

Of course, as we have already noted, this latest of revolutions in the name of human wholeness was not confined to England alone. The English revolution was in fact largely derivative and laggard—owing in part to the unparalleled height and weight of the Victorian cultural tablets that the English had laboriously to overthrow. It was Nietzsche, then (ambiguously) Freud, then Bergson, who had led and prepared the fight; and of these of course the great general and zealot was Nietzsche. No one so fanatical for change as he, no one so much that dangerous thing, a convulsed idealist, no one else so keen to ask, "What harm has come to mankind . . . through its morality?" Nietzsche is the arsenal, the fuse, of the modern revolution of values.

Nietzsche's "Critique of the Highest Values Hitherto" (1883–1888) and *Genealogy of Morals* (1887) are perhaps the two most deadly stones ever hurled at the great giant Morality. To be sure, it was Nietzsche who fell, or fell first, defeated by a disease contracted in one of those brothels that, as Blake suggests, are built with the giant's own bricks. Still, Nietzsche's aim, his critique, was true. Taken freely as an analysis of the Victorian ethos, it has tremendous force; it is a scourge. Even if Nietzsche had not written partly with George Eliot and Herbert Spencer in mind, who was more likely than the Victorians to seem the prime object of his attack? Victorian England had not only enshrined the "highest values hitherto"; it had pushed them as high as they could humanly go.

What makes Nietzsche so chemically active and instructive in association with the Victorians is that none of the latter could have ventured, or even conceived, that radical word "hitherto." The break and daring it implies, the antimorality and sense of a new dawn, lay beyond their reach. Their horizons were, precisely, "Victorian"; they were not in a position to look beyond. Restive and revisionary as some of the high Victorians were, none of them chose *not* to be Victorian (as, say, Blake had chosen not to be a late Augustan). None walked out of the present into the future, or back into the Romantic past. And the reason for this was that, with the exception of John Stuart Mill, none could bring himself to believe that he had a choice.

The Victorian ethos ruled with a totalitarian grip and force; and in consequence the Victorians, for all their self-criticism, almost entirely escaped the sting and surprise of a radical critique. Nietzsche's interest in relation to them is that he stands completely outside their moral world, looking back in as no Victorian would have thought it possible to do: not mockingly, which they could have dismissed, but indignantly. To the Victorian "sincerity" of the heart, Nietzsche opposed a total and remorseless psychological sincerity, an aggressive honesty of the depths. Scorning what Jacques Rivière calls morality's "perspicacious ignorance" of the mind it superintends, Nietzsche stripped away from the soul the yards of covering with which, for decency's sake, the Victorians had dressed it. It is "morality itself, in the form of honesty," Nietzsche said, that "compels us to deny morality."

What is more, Nietzsche went on to exalt the nudity he had bared. Of what shamed the Victorians, he made an idol. "We are the heirs of the conscience-vivisection and self-crucifixion of two millennia," he wrote; ". . . we have conjoined the natural inclinations and a bad conscience." He then adds: "A reverse attempt would be possible: to conjoin the unnatural inclinations . . . all previous ideals, which were all world-slandering ideals, with a bad conscience." And this, of course, is what Nietzsche did.

Nietzsche discovered in all intoxicated states of the soul not irresponsibility, which is what the Victorians perceived, but precisely responsibility to the soul itself. He laughed at the possibility of carrying a " 'beautiful soul' about in a cadaverous abortion." "One must be firmly rooted in oneself," he said—that is, in one's flesh; one must seek the enhancement, not the denial, of life; one must even tend toward "the innocence of becoming," "a total liberation from ends." Of morality he complained that it is itself "a special case of immorality," and of the ideal that it "has hitherto been the actual force for disparaging the world and man." So it was that Nietzsche himself became idealistic about the pit of horrors that underlies all high Victorian aspiration. Looking down, he found himself looking up: the moral universe, he concluded, had been set on its head. "My final proposition is: that the *actual* man represents a much higher value than the " 'desirable' man of any ideal hitherto. . . ."

From the Victorian point of view, Nietzsche thus accomplished two miraculous feats—or tricks. He collapsed the either/

or that made Duty appear to the Victorians (in George Eliot's famous words) "peremptory and absolute"; and he took a principled stand on what seemed to be quicksand or, worse, nothing at all. Morally, he performed the impossible—he leaped altogether beyond the Victorian horizon, yet without falling out of the world either of conscience or of a distinctively human nobility.

What explains the rigidity, the abruptness, the apparent insurmountability, of the Victorian moral horizon? Why was there no Victorian Nietzsche? The reason is at once conspicuous and hard to explain: a rampant and almost hysterical lack of trust in natural life. The age not only had little to no honest liking for the flesh; in some instances it even failed to recognize it. Let Lord Acton's words stand as an unwitting indictment of the good sense of the respectable (as against "the other") Victorians: "As a general rule, a modest woman seldom desires any sexual gratification for herself. She submits to her husband, but only to please him; and, but for the desire of maternity, would far rather be relieved from his attentions." Lord Acton was a brilliant man; but, like most educated Victorians, he knew next to nothing about the inescapable carnality of life.

For many Victorians, then, instinct did not even amount to an "or": it was rather a memory, the skeleton in the closet. But of course they caught glimpses of it, had their struggles with it, too: their innocence, after all, was a willed delusion, not an invulnerable condition of mind.

When the flesh did confront them, the Victorians were likely to recoil in terror. There were two reasons for this. On the one hand, the body struck them as "nothing," since only the spirit was something, had value. They experienced a metaphysical nausea at the thought of flesh. Except for morality, the human self appeared empty—so very empty that, as Alexander Smith said in his poem "Horton," a man looking into it would "die of fright at utter nothingness." To the Victorians, to be merely concrete and natural was thus to be a phantom. Never mind that, under morality's despotic rule, the "individual withers," as Tennyson put it, or that "society is training men and women for hell," as George Eliot once uncharacteristically admitted. Without morality, a man was "utter nothingness"; and so morality there must be.

On the other hand, the flesh appeared to the Victorians as "something" indeed: as a monstrosity of rude and threatening chaos. And if they then hastened to make a void of it, it was lest it make a void of them. For instance, George Eliot's Maggie Tulliver is brought to see—in agony, awe, and histrionic intensity—that to let go of the "clue" of Duty is but to "wander vaguely, driven by uncertain impulse." For Maggie and her author, passion is "wayward" in two senses: it is a wandering from the public path, and it is, precisely, not a Way, not "viable," not ontologically or psychologically stable and sound. The spirit is identified with duration, the flesh with the ephemeral. "We can only choose whether we will indulge ourselves in the present moment," Maggie explains to the young man she is dutifully rejecting, "or whether we will renounce that, for the sake of obeying the divine voice within us—for the sake of being true to all the motives that sanctify our lives." Either/or. And only an illusionary one at that. For if self-indulgence here seems possible, ultimately the terms leave no choice: on the one hand there is the "light" of sacrifice; on the other, all "the darkness of this life." Faced with such unequal alternatives, who could hesitate? Vagueness, uncertainty, darkness—gazing into the body, George Eliot saw only a sort of infinite and devious nullity, a dynamic void.

As Maggie's appeal to "divine" motives suggests, the Victorians considered the flesh, if not exactly diabolical, then at least an unforgivable affront to the dignity of the human spirit. "We should mortify the flesh—the terrible flesh," cries one of the last of the Victorian heroines, Hardy's Sue Bridehead. The body is to Sue but an animal that has the spirit in its jaws. "Arise and fly / The reeling Faun, the sensual feast," exhorts Tennyson;

Emily Brontë cp. mainstream of Victorian ideas [handwritten annotation]

"Move upward, working out the beast. . . ." So runs the anxious refrain.

Not to be self-created in the spirit is thus, for the Victorians, to fail to be anything significant. "But I was *born* to other things," exclaims Tennyson, almost petulantly. Underlying Victorian morality is an enormous spiritual pride. If the Victorians had a head for heights, it was not so much for love of the air as because they spurned a debasing identity with the depths. "A brute I might have been," says Browning's Rabbi Ben Ezra, "but would not / sink i' the scale." *Would* not sink: the boast is honest.

The same wave of spiritual hauteur washes up and spends itself on the natural world. Unless the soul itself is immortal, Tennyson reasoned, "earth is darkness at the core, / And dust and ashes all that is. . . ." If the spirit itself lacks inviolable being, then the entire universe is a cipher. The spirit first, the Creation after.

Of course some loving attention to life there inevitably was— torrents of it in Dickens, sporadic bursts in Meredith, quiet runnels in *Adam Bede,* and, not to extend the list further, lovely azure draughts in Tennyson himself. But even in the most sensuous writers the world is only consented to on the condition that its final meaning will be moral. In the absence of the latter, the rest, in Tennyson's phrase, is "a hollow form with empty hands." Of the great Victorians, only Emily Brontë seems to have essayed an aesthetic justification of life. Her isolation, her early commitment to the Romantic imagination, as perhaps also the fact that she wrote when the Victorian age was still young, help to explain her striking idiosyncrasy—the originality that shocked and bewildered her Victorian readers.

The Victorians, observes Walter Houghton in *The Victorian Frame of Mind,* felt that they had broken "irrevocably" from "the medieval tradition." In certain ways, however, the Victorians may be regarded as the last pool and remnant of the medieval surge. We find in them not so much a break as a melancholy diminishment. Such at any rate was the opinion of William Morris, who was probably the most balanced and appealingly natural of the late Victorians. In a book that had sadly to be called *News from Nowhere,* Morris portrayed an England different from his own exactly in being akin to "the Middle Ages, to whom heaven and the life of the next world was such a reality, that it became to them a part of the life upon the earth; which accordingly they loved and adorned, in spite of the ascetic doctrines of their formal creed, which bade them condemn it." The Englishmen of his own commercial age Morris judged unsparingly: "men who hate life though they fear death."

Moreover, it is just the perpetuation of the medieval habit of faith—its persistence where there was no oxygen for faith—that explains the sterile atmosphere of Victorian morality. The illusion of the necessity of faith to life seems to have been almost a fatality in the nineteenth century, the last of the smoke from the medieval fire; even agnostics genuflected to its form, however woefully uncertain they might be as to its contents. We must have "faith in something," wrote Charles Kingsley, "something that we can live for, and would die for." "Faith," Tolstoy elaborates, "is the sense of life, that sense by virtue of which man does not destroy himself, but continues to live on"; and even so collected and empirical a thinker as William James agreed. No, the Middle Ages had not yet come to an end.

The characteristic of medieval faith was, of course, that it looked above life. But with the toppling of Christian doctrine, what were the Victorians to *see* above life? Something, they felt, *had* to be seen. Here were—for the picture is complex—here were the Swarmeries of the collective natural man: the lower classes clamoring for the pie, not in the sky, but on the table. Here was the "preemptory" need for "faith," whatever that faith might be. And, finally, here was a menacing vacuum in the self, a threat of "utter nothingness." Down below, "nothing." Yet—terrible dilemma!—nothing discernible above.

No wonder that Leslie Stephen, in declaring his faith, could only contradict himself: "I now believe in nothing," he said, "but I do not the less believe in morality." And yet, as Stephen saw, there seemed to remain something "above" after all—something amid the nothing: a sort of cloud of morality, hanging and floating and brooding. And however secular it was, however unstreaked by light from beyond, at least it was there, an object to look up to. As a form of the "Invisible"—a word that even the agnostic George Eliot could not resist—morality might be all unsatisfactory. But invisible, in its way, it undeniably was. And so it happened that Duty became the Victorian deity, the substance of things hoped for, the evidence of things not seen. The face of faith, though blushing, had been saved.

The chief result was the translation into upper case ethical terms of the ancient and powerful religious ideal of selflessness. The Romantic self, with its self-absorption and enormous and glowing self-expansion, its strenuous and sensuous pride in life, paled and gave way to a human character whose pride lay precisely in its own self-abdication. Carlyle initiates the change, yet is Janus-faced, forcing upon Duty, as he does, the embrace of a vehement metaphysic of vitality—Duty, of course, scarcely knowing how to react to so fiery a lover. "Annihilation of Self . . . is yet the highest Wisdom that Heaven has revealed to our Earth," Carlyle proclaims in 1830, trumpeting in the Victorian age. Yet in boldly reaching out for a cosmic displacement of the self, Carlyle was, after all, typically Romantic. He was perhaps blessed in his middle position between two contrary generations. The true Victorians, a noble but bedraggled lot, could look neither so far nor so high as he. Carlyle is amphibian, they are stranded, even forlorn.

The peculiarity and poignancy of the Victorian ideal of selflessness lie in its metaphysical bankruptcy—its trembling status as an orphaned member of a great religious family. Duty had caught the setting sun of Christian faith and grown refulgent, even fiery; but precisely because its gold was derived and fading, the Victorians were anxious in their morality. Though moral "faith" might glow almost steadily, as in Dorothea Brooke, it yet shone against a profound and swallowing darkness. Even at its best, it knew that it was an unenlightened faith, its only fuel a noble wish. "I cannot help believing in glorious things in a blind sort of way," Dorothea says, almost as if confessing to an inability to shake a dubious habit. Her "belief," she adds, is "that by desiring what is perfectly good, even when we don't quite know what it is and cannot do what we would, we are part of the divine power against evil. . . ." Yet, pressed to explain exactly what she means by "divine," she could, one supposes, only falter, become troubled, lose heart. The basis of moral faith at this time is the hanging on of a scracely conscious spiritual addiction—a covert appeal to that dark place in the heavens where the comet of revelation had lately been seen to pass.

The sadness in Victorian moral faith is the forlornness that comes from offering oneself up to what is "infinite" only in the sense that no one can seize hold of it. Where Christianity establishes and expands the soul, the abstraction "the good" merely dissipates it. It affords no metaphysical elixir, only, at most, an agreeably painful feeling of being somehow in the right. "I have been bent and broken," observes Estella at the end of *Great Expectations* (1861), "but—I hope—into a better shape." "I hope"! If there is modesty in this, there is also, I think, a lurking melancholy uncertainty.

Not that Victorian selflessness remained utterly orphaned; there were foster parents aplenty, if all members of one tribe: Humanity, the General Good, the State. Some such motto as Auguste Comte's *Vivre pour autres* is the crutch of Victorian faith. And yet what sort of parents were these "others," after all? Was it possible to serve and love "humanity" as one could serve and love God? Or did not "humanity" amount to just another phantom? Regarded as natural men, the "others," of course, were forms of "nothingness." Yet as moral entities, could they be said to be "other" at all? How could one serve the "selves" of others when these had been annihilated? To stand outside oneself and look back upon one's life, as Maggie Tulliver does, "as an insignificant part of a divinely-guided whole" is to stand in a "whole" of insignificant parts. No wonder the goal of morality in this period seems so often to come down to morality for morality's sake. There was nothing else for its ardor to adhere to.

The radical failure of Victorian morality as a "faith" was that it canceled rather than nourished "the sense of life." If Tolstoy is right, if the felicity of faith is its gift of the sense of life, then the Victorian form of faith was self-defeating: it enhanced nothing, and if it saved pride, it wasted life to the same degree. It emptied the self out into a vacuum of existence. Though the Victorians won the moral right to hold their heads high, it was at the cost of finding anything to see there.

On the other hand, to substitute the human species for God is doubtless to serve *something*. Comte called it the *Étre Suprême*, George Eliot the "divinely-guided whole," but it was Nietzsche, I think, who hit upon the truest term: the "herd." It is, after all, a herd mentality that holds that a man's value increases in proportion to his self-denial. George Eliot, whom G. M. Young justly calls *the* moralist of the Victorian ethos, was to discover this herself, movingly, in *Middlemarch*, her great unintentional self-critique. For the most part, however, she succumbed, with her age, to the fiction of a species somehow greater than the sum of its members. The general acceptation of this illusion in Victorian literature gives it its strong affinities with the socialist realism of today.

Even so simplified and summary an account of Victorian idealism would be incomplete without taking note of a counterideal. This was the neo-Greek ideal of a complete and harmonious human character: the ideal for which John Stuart Mill and Matthew Arnold formed, as it were, a small opposition party. And yet, all told, what a feeble party this was. For one thing, only Mill was a bona fide member. In *Culture and Anarchy* (1868), Arnold, after appearing to take a stand on "a human nature perfect on all its sides," proceeded to address himself to reason and duty alone, as if these exhausted the sides of human nature. More, he then bent reason itself to the same "aim and end" as duty, construing it as a tool for "the basis of right practice." Thus, in the end, Arnold seemed to have been lobbying for Duty and Country all along.

Of the two, only Mill truly valued individuality. Where in Arnold man is referred away to the state, in Mill he is referred to his own greatest fulfillment. Mill's importance and originality as an English moralist is that, like Nietzsche, he discovered —or rediscovered after Blake—the natural as itself the ideal. In *On Liberty* (1859), Mill speaks of the ideal that is "embodied" in our complete human nature. "Human nature," he writes, "is not a machine to be built after a model, and set to do exactly the work prescribed for it, but a tree, which requires to grow and develop itself on all sides, according to the tendency of the inward forces which make it a living thing." "It is not by wearing down into uniformity all that is individual in themselves," Mill concludes, "but by cultivating it and calling it forth, within the limits imposed by the rights and interests of others, that human beings become a noble and beautiful object of contemplation."

This is not to say, of course, that Mill amounted to an English Nietzsche. In one sense, it is true, Mill was even greater than Nietzsche, and certainly a better Greek: for, while granting due respect to "all that is individual," Mill had also the generosity (call it the consistency) to honor the individual when manifested as "the other." If Mill encouraged the free exfoliation of the "inward forces" of the self, it was because he credited these forces—reason, will, and compassion as well as animal energy and Eros—with a system of mutual check and balance.

In another sense, however, Mill is smaller than Nietzsche, an all-too-Victorian Nietzsche. For though he attacked the repressive Victorian atmosphere, it yet wilted him. To gauge the extent of the damage, we need, perhaps, look no further than Mill's style, which, however "noble," is scarcely "beautiful." In its rational dryness, its inflexibility, its lack of individual fragrance, it is to Nietzsche's writing what a wintered tree is to a tree in blossom. Then, too, we might recall Mill's evidently chaste affair of twenty years with Mrs. Harriet Taylor, the Victorian sword of repressed impulse rusting between them. Or the way that Mill, after being converted to the view that "those only are happy . . . who have their minds fixed on some object other than their own happiness," instantly recurred, for an object, to "the happiness of others," the "improvement of mankind." When tested, Mill showed the Victorian reflex.

So it was that the Victorian ideal of "Annihilation of Self" sat securely enthroned, unshaken by either true or false pretenders. It imposed itself—one cannot say flourished—for over half a century. Of course, it is far from dead even today. But in English-speaking countries, at any rate, it was to lose its luster, its magic, its mystique. Well before the Victorian age was over, it had become politicized—given, as it were, an office and a union number by Marxists, Fabians, the English Positivist Committee, and other groups. Its imperious hold on the life of the spirit relaxed into disquisition and debate; an ideal that had once seemed almost otherworldly grew dim in the meeting-hall atmosphere of the historical dialectic and the Positivist polity of the future. Near the end of the century, the Positivist Frederic Harrison wrote: "To live for others, not for self, is . . . our plain and simple duty." It had come, then, to be as flat as that. With Dorothea Brooke and her blind belief in "glorious things," we had been in church—in a hushed if post-Christian sanctuary of moral feeling. With Harrison and "A Positivist Prayer," by contrast, we are in a committee room.

One writer there was, however, who almost gave back to Victorian selflessness its mature attraction and force—namely, George Bernard Shaw. ". . . the true joy in life," Shaw said in the Epistle Dedicatory to *Man and Superman* (1903), is "the being used for a purpose recognized by yourself as a mighty one. . . ." This has some of the old ring in it, the high note of belief and enthusiasm.

"*Unity* . . . divided by *Zero* will give *Infinity*," Carlyle had said. For the Victorians, this formula did not work, because their only Unity—"the others"—was itself actually a zero. Shavian selflessness, however, is a happy exchange of the merely personal for the universal. For Shaw there exists the wonderful reality of evolution—and not an evolution that simply manipulates man, such as Swinburne's, George Eliot's, Spencer's, but an evolution, like the doubting Tennyson's, of which man is himself the rising sun. Carlyle and Shaw—two cupidons, one rhapsodic, the other mischievous—thus bracket the Victorian age between them, each joined to it through a zeal for selflessness, the one, however, looking back and the other forward to a different, because metaphysical, age.

And yet, by distinction from the Victorians, Shaw is by no means some sort of rude vitalist. Shaw's worship of life is only an apparent one. It is in fact the future that Shaw loves: the hope, precisely, of a redemption from instinct. Jauntily tipping over the Victorian altar of the Others, Shaw moved on not to Vitality but to Mind, happily anticipating the time when "there will be no people, only thought."

Shavian selflessness is, then, essentially the fleshless Victorian ideal given a new object of sacrifice. And yet the old charisma is gone. Shaw's metaphysical buoyancy, together with what was evidently a light natural cargo, allowed him to venture into selflessness with joy. Selflessness in Shaw is light and bubbly, a kind of spiritual champagne. But, alas, how little deep appeal there is in joy. Shavian selflessness forfeits almost all of the grateful burden of suffering, the quality of self-punishment, and the invitation to self-congratulation, that gave the Victorian ideal its astonishing power.

The same marked loss of charisma characterizes a second variant on the Victorian ideal: the purely aesthetic selflessness of Pater. In *Marius the Epicurean* (1885), the self is, as it were, a prism intent upon distinguishing the rainbow colors of the "restless stream" of reality.[1] A river bed ready to receive every fresh-water flood, a pure "medium of reception," the Paterian self is, like the moral self, consecrated to externality. Indeed, to Pater it *is* a moral self, and precisely for the reason that it has been freed from the turmoil of active instinct. "That the end of life is not action but contemplation—*being* as distinct from *doing*," Pater writes in his essay on Wordsworth, ". . . is, in some shape or other, the principle of all the higher morality."

Despite its sensuous mode, the Paterian self is thus an *askesis*. However surprising it may seem, here the strings are as taut, the playing as strenuous, as in George Eliot. To perceive always "the aesthetic or imaginative side of things" is—no less than to live for others—to strain continually toward a beatitude of self-forgetting. In consequence, of course, Paterian selflessness is every bit as extreme, as impossible of complete realization, as the charitable Victorian and the cerebral Shavian ideals. It, too, represents an attempt to abdicate the instinctual basis, the actual and necessary impurities, of our lives.

With Shaw and Pater we exhaust the list of eminent English authors who stoked the ideal of selflessness in the Victorian twilight. The list is brief, and the reason, I believe, lies not in a diversion of energy into a contrary ideal but in a drought of idealism itself.

As an article of faith, the self fell, in the period 1890 to 1910, on evil days. In part, this was due, at least on the level of conception, to a kind of Humean backslide from a single identity into scattered multiplicity. Hume argued that because human consciousness is "but a bundle or collection of different percep-

[1] At the end of *Marius the Epicurean*, Pater shows himself willing to erase "aesthetic" from his ideal and write in "the power of sympathy." Such was the lingering despotism of the orthodox Victorian ideal. But when Pater is really in church, his subject is the beatific vision of reality.

ing, it is intact and still, fixed in an ecstatic stare. In Pater's essence," Wilde writes of Dorian in *The Picture of Dorian Gray*

gration. Only in the sphere of art—that is, of admitted, graceful,

tions, which . . . are in a perpetual flux and movement," there
is "no such idea" as the self. Of "perpetual flux and movement"
Pater himself, of course, had had a full, indeed a breathless,
knowledge, both of the "whirlpool" within and the "many
currents" without. Yet by turning to the principle of "eager
observation," Pater managed, nonetheless, to make of the self
an "idea." The Paterian self is an intensely mirroring lake
under a wild rapidity of cloud; though everything else is changing, it is intact and still, fixed in an ecstatic stare. In Pater's
"disciple" Oscar Wilde, by contrast, the bundle of the self falls
apart, tumbling away in a naughty thrill.

This notorious "aesthete" disdained the will to self-integrity
on the moralistic grounds that identity is merely an artifice.
With something of the explosive sincerity of Nietzsche, Wilde
conscientiously gave himself to "perpetual flux and movement,"
as one launches a boat into an unexplored sea. "He used to
wonder at the shallow psychology of those who conceive the
ego in man as a thing simple, permanent, reliable, and of one
essence," Wilde writes of Dorian in *The Picture of Dorian Gray*
(1890). "To him, man was a being with myriad lives and myriad
sensations, a complex multiform creature that bore within itself
strange legacies of thought and passion, and whose very flesh
was tainted with the monstrous maladies of the dead." A single
and simple human "form" could only be an "insincerity." Dorian holds in suspicion "the mask of goodness"; if he himself had
once worn it, he concludes, it was "in hypocrisy. . . . For curiosity's sake he had tried the denial of self."

Thus in Wilde the will is nullified both by the seductions of
"strange legacies" and by an "honest" submission to innate
multiformity. For Wilde, life is suicide. If he entered the "myriad" waters of human nature, it was, he believed, not only to
sport "monstrously" but to drown. "Pleasure," Gide reports him
as saying: "one must always set one's heart upon the most
tragic." The only legitimate will is the one that ratifies disintegration. Only in the sphere of art—that is, of admitted, graceful,

and frivolous "insincerity"—did Wilde find it in his conscience
to validate form (art thus becoming, for Wilde, life's comple-
ment, where for Pater it had been life's mode).

"People sometimes say that fiction is getting too morbid,"
remarks Gilbert in Wilde's dialogue "The Critic as Artist." "As
far as psychology is concerned," he adds, "it has never been morbid enough. We have merely touched the surface of the soul,
that is all." It was, of course, Conrad who became the supreme
novelist of this new morbidity. This must be said despite the
fact that, if one chooses one's texts carefully, or perhaps merely
gullibly, it is possible to speak of Conrad as a late, if almost too
late, Victorian idealist of selflessness—as one who, notwithstand-
ing his Wildean fascination with "monstrous maladies," or indeed because of it, still struggled to believe in "the idea of
Fidelity." Nonetheless, in Conrad this ideal is as withered, as
shaken with illness, as dreadfully disabused and prone to a
radical irony, as the Marlow who, in *The Heart of Darkness*
(1899), wearily speaks of its necessity.

How appropriate it is that Marlow should sit apart, in the
yawl of the Thames, "in the pose of a meditating Buddha"—not
only because, disillusioned with desire, he has renounced it but
because its secret life, its treacherous subversion of virtue, has
cast over the whole of life, for him, a dreamlike insincerity.
"Mankind does not know what it wants," says Heyst in *Victory*
(1915), and the words apply radically to Conrad himself; they
explain the heaviness and hopelessness in his prose. Guilt, with
its thin, heartsick ideal of a joyless "power of devotion, not to
yourself, but to an obscure, back-breaking business," namely
"civilization"—this and desire, with its ancient prerogative to
seek its dark and destructive ends, meet and neutralize each
other in Conrad, creating a pall in which effort seems "vain"
and appearances "illusory." "*Que désirez-vous être?*" Conrad
was once asked in a game of questions and answers: "Should
like not to be," he replied.

A morale-crushing fatalism shows up again at the end of this period in Conrad's one-time collaborator, Ford Madox Ford. In *The Good Soldier* (begun in 1913), idealism gasps for air and fails to find it. The very title sweats irony. One is reminded throughout of the confession of Conrad's Heyst: "Moralists and I haven't been friends for many years." "Shuttlecocks!"—the word that bursts so tragically from the insane Nancy, as so inevitable an inference—epitomizes Ford's impression (it is Conrad's also) that human beings are the playthings of two indifferent Players: "cruel Providence" and the "predatory beast" within. "Here were two noble people," states the narrator, Dowell, "—for I am convinced that both Edward and Leonora had noble natures—here, then, were two noble natures, drifting down life, like fireships afloat on a lagoon and causing miseries, heartaches, agony of the mind, and death. And they themselves steadily deteriorated? And why? For what purpose? To point what lesson? It is all a darkness." At the intersection of "destiny" and human nature, human character becomes an impossibility, like trying to take a stand on the tracks of a railway station.

In Hardy, too, the human being is a shuttlecock, but here the principal Players are mostly ironies of circumstance—"circumstantial will."[2] For Hardy, morbidity lies almost all without, as for Wilde it lies almost all within: it is the universe that is sick. Human will and human nature are comparatively innocent. Hence Hardy's unembarrassed use, in the subtitle of *Tess of the D'Urbervilles* (1891), of a phrase that might have made Wilde laugh and Conrad both wonder and cringe: "A Pure Woman." Hence, too, Hardy's sense of Tess, at the book's close, as the "sport," not of the sensual Alec and the spiritual Angel, but of the "President of the Immortals." Hardy, like Wilde, thus halves, as it were, the compound Fate of Conrad and Ford.

What distinguishes Hardy from these others is his frank liking

---

[2] This, however, must be taken as inclusive of impersonal social morbidities—the Christianity that warps Sue Bridehead, the social "justice" that punishes Tess, and every other social phenomenon that has "no foundation in Nature."

for natural man. There is in Hardy a large appreciation of the wholesomeness of desire that links him with Forster, Lawrence, and Joyce. Tess is "pure," Hardy explains, because Nature itself is pure. And when he writes that "the 'appetite for joy' which pervades all creation, that tremendous force which sways humanity to its purpose . . . was not to be controlled by vague lucubrations over the social rubric," we sense how glad he is that this is so. But in Hardy there is more than Nature, there is the Universe to contend with; and, alas, an "unsympathetic First Cause" has Nature squirming under its boot. Though Hardy's conscience sides with Nature, it is an anguished and feeble conscience—a conscience with a broken back. Hardy, accordingly, is elegiac, not idealistic. In him the modern revolution of human character is stillborn.

"The person in man," writes Simone Weil, "is a thing in distress; it feels cold and is always looking for a warm shelter." For the Victorians, as we saw, the body itself was the cold and the darkness, the lion prowling around the unreliable ring of the fire. As for the universe, though all reliable law, it was nonetheless a machine that gave off the fetor of mortality. Scientific positivism and a lingering Christian dualism thus combined to produce a bastard self whose legitimacy could be sought neither above nor below. The only refuge lay outward, in the community. There, however, the one slight appearance of warmth was the moral nimbus that shone above it, like the night glow over a city. And this was not enough to relieve the "thing in distress."

In any case, even this shelter had to be abandoned—made uninhabitable, as it was, by disillusionment with capitalism, by the doldrums of socialism, by suspicions of the "lie" of virtue, and by a damp and hanging mood of defeat.

Thus snowed in by the seeming foreclosure of possibility, the self could either freeze and harden to its distress or revolt into, precisely, self-assertion. Between 1890 and 1910 or 1915, it froze, and perhaps miserably enjoyed its own pathos. Between 1915 and 1930, it rebelled, at times innocently making so much of itself that it even colonized vast remotenesses of reality. Stepping out from its gray enclosure, it rediscovered the colors of the natural world, heights opened above it, depths opened below—its own heights and depths repossessed.

Before the self could be revived as an ideal, the forces of life had, above all, to break through the impacted crust of a defeatist determinism. The universe had to seem more friendly than it does in Conrad, Ford, and Hardy, and the unconscious more creative, or more subduable, than in Conrad, Ford, and Wilde. And so it was to be in the best novelists of the succeeding period. Taking another look into the underworld of the self, Joyce, Lawrence, and Forster espied not perfidy, terror, and violence—what Conrad had seen—but, on the contrary, the most radiant of the gods, Eros and his expansive positivity. There was, they concluded, nothing in the depths to mistrust: as Hardy and William Morris had glimpsed, the only theme of the depths was fertility. "Life knows us not and we do not know life," Conrad had lamented, speaking as always out of the disintegrating center of a dream. Lawrence, Forster, and Joyce, by contrast, as if just awakening from the same bad dream, come upon life, and life comes upon them, in the generative principle of the flesh and the soul. Their writing is a great Yes to the adventure and the body of being.

So Stephen Dedalus, in Joyce's *Portrait of the Artist as a Young Man* (1916), frees himself (in a reversal of the typical Victorian conversion) from "the pale service of the altar," the pervasive antilife of Catholicism, the contempt of the flesh, and, turning to the sea, to "the wonder of mortal beauty," even to those "foul and shameful words" and deeds in which (so Joyce seems to have felt) the soul first finds its articulation, greets excitedly "the fair courts of life." So Lucy Honeychurch, in Forster's *Room with a View* (1908), breaks away from the "armies of the benighted"—the sinners against Eros, the hypocrites in the face of life—and, discovering "the holiness of direct desire," stands in the sun for all she is worth. So, also, Ursula Brangwen, in Lawrence's *Rainbow* (1915), repudiates Anton Skrebensky—that Victorian hero, that "brick in the . . . social fabric"—and finds in her own vital "kernel" the "only reality": the "I" that answers to the call of eternity.

In these writers, then, the flesh itself becomes a shelter, a source of warmth to "the person," whose "distress," after all, had lain in nothing so much as its isolation from its own carnal home. Thus authenticated and vivified by the flesh, established with a residence in the world, the self now looks out upon life and finds it good. Not only does it acquiesce to life, but, essentially erotic, it is in itself an affirmative principle—for the flesh never waits to be asked to say yes. "Life is will to power," Nietzsche had asserted; but what Forster, Lawrence, and Joyce were to say—together with Sorel, Unamuno, Ortega, and other sojourners of this period—is that life is rather the thirst for more life, the ardor not to triumph over but to *be* everything, and to be, what is more, forever.

The ambitious scope, the effort to grasp life in its totality, the metaphysical and aesthetic upheaval characteristic of the fiction of this time, constitute, especially in Lawrence and Joyce, a direct and brilliant response to what Stephen Dedalus speaks of, simply, as "the call of life." They are the signs of a wholeness answering to a wholeness. They indicate the great hunger aroused by a multitude of sensuous and spiritual sparks and enticements—the desire to see everything, absorb everything, feel everything, and to eternalize the self by intuiting it as one with the traveling world. Accordingly, the greatest book of the period, *Ulysses* (1922), is inclusive—so nearly as is possible without the sacrifice of shape—of all time, all things, all moods, all ecstasies of the flesh, and all flights and applications of the mind.

This is not to say, however, that the thirst for life at this time was dependent for expression upon amplitude of form or even magnitude of scope. In the stories of Katherine Mansfield, for

instance, it was wonderfully compressed into a detonative style
of piercing impressions, into what are themselves short studies
of thirst. ". . . warm, eager, living life—to be rooted in life,"
Mansfield wrote. "That is what I want. And nothing else." And
the same sort of hunger is concentrated, too, as by a magnifying
glass, in the short poems of Yeats, who tried on first this mask
and then that, who climbed the tower of the spirit only to leap
off into "the frog-spawn of a blind man's ditch," and then as-
cended and descended again, and sang of faery and sang of foul,
unable to relinquish, in his great boyish greed for all imaginable
experience, any of the molds of a multiform being.

The warm invitation of life is thus the theme of this age (as,
in the thirties, it will continue to be a theme not only in the
last of Yeats but in the first of Dylan Thomas). Here speaks, for
a time, the voice not of the "twice-born," as in the mid-Victorian
age, nor of the aborted or unborn, as in Housman and Hardy,
Conrad and Ford, but, precisely, of the "born," the living, the
warm and eager for life.

Among these writers, a new ideal is cast and shared: a whole
self in relation to the whole of the world. Conscience forsakes,
in them, the haunted house of Victorian morality and sets its
standards freely flying where, in Bergson's phrase, the life of the
body becomes the road to the spirit. A new vision of wholeness
and integration—the vital counterpart of Stephen Dedalus's
aesthetic of "wholeness, harmony, and radiance"—overthrows
a morality of suppression, exclusion, and denial. And this it ac-
complishes in the name not merely of honesty but of what
William Morris had called greater "abundance of life."

The ideal of wholeness, however, proves quite as variable as
the Victorian ideal of selflessness. Selflessness, though fixed in
form, can vary in content; wholeness, though fixed in content,
can vary in form. Joyce and Lawrence, Forster and Yeats, Katherine Mansfield, Lytton Strachey, Virginia Woolf and still other
writers could say with Unamuno: "They tell me I am here to

realize I know not what social end; but I feel that I, like each of my fellows, am here to realize myself, to live." But what it means to realize oneself is, as it were, tossed and disputed among them.[3]

Of the four great creative writers of this period—Lawrence, Joyce, Forster, and Yeats—it is Joyce, of course, who is least an idealist. The enormous aesthetic presumption of *Ulysses* is inversely proportional to a kind of metaphysical modesty. If it was the "complete" man that Joyce took as the type of the desirable man, it was rather as one indicates a preference, not as one receives a faith. Leopold Bloom certainly testifies not only to the interest Joyce took in human completeness but also to his sense of its natural goodness. To its fertility—at once humane and instinctive—he gave an instinctive and humane assent. On the other hand, in the squirrel-cage historical world of *Ulysses*, all swagger of seriousness, all heroism, falls under a detracting comic light; and in consequence idealism, though everywhere molten in the novel, never forms into a cutting edge. Where *Portrait* lyrically registers revolt, *Ulysses* comically registers acceptance of things as they are. It is a work not of conscience but

[3] Perhaps nothing indexes better the almost inevitable disagreement on this matter among writers than the disparity between the ideal as the Lawrence figure of Huxley's *Point Counter Point* (1928) exemplifies it and the ideal as expounded by Lawrence himself. Lawrence is scarcely recognizable in Mark Rampion's achievement of "harmonious all-round living." "A man's a creature on a tightrope, walking delicately, equilibrated," Rampion says, "with a mind and consciousness and spirit at one end of his balancing pole and body and instinct and all that's unconscious and earthy and mysterious at the other. Balanced. Which is damnably difficult. And the only absolute he can ever really know is the absolute of perfect balance." Balance, however, is not quite Lawrence's note, as we shall see; and the "absolute" that *Lawrence* knows is universal and metaphysical. The "consummations" and the "universal reference" of Lawrence's ideal have been missed out altogether—or, rather, rejected as foreign matter by Huxley's own temperament as it assimilated Lawrence's ideal. Huxley's ideal is "Greek" and in the line of Mill and Arnold; Lawrence's predominant ideal is erotically mystical and in the line of Blake.

of the human fullness that a change in conscience has made available.

"This race and this country and this life produced me," says Joyce's Stephen; "I shall express myself as I am." And, indeed, in Joyce's fiction everything in Joyce himself is unashamedly affirmed. By contrast, in Forster man exists in halves until he struggles to be whole (at least if he is an Englishman). "Only connect . . ."—the famous epigraph to *Howards End* (1910)—is, then, a rallying cry. In Forster, the will is once again reborn in idealism, and in a world where it is required to make acrobatic leaps—to elaborate, in the difficult space between the hands that release and the hands that receive, the loops that connect the opposites of being.

It is not only the self that is thus stitched and made one in Forster but, so it seems, the whole universe, which thence becomes a universe of desire. In Joyce, Eros justifies (if it does no more) the world and its "heaventree" of stars. Though all may be based on an uncertain void, at least the vast "nothing" is "lovely."[4] In *Howards End,* by contrast, Eros grows heady in a higher atmosphere: it becomes a metaphysical hunger for connection, its tendrils of desire reaching out indefinitely into the world. Here life seems to stream out eternally in opposite directions—toward the flesh and the spirit, the seen and the unseen, energy and imagination, the past and the future (for in this novel, as in Shaw, "we are evolving . . . to ends that Theology dares not contemplate"). Margaret Schlegel, the heroic Person at the center, holds and weaves these fluttering banners together. Helen, her sister, observes of her: "You mean to keep proportion, and that's heroic, it's Greek. . . ." So it is that, exigently, the metaphysical comes to Mill and Arnold and their "Greek" ideal of a complete and harmonious human character. And the

---

[4] In 1935, Joyce wrote of his eyes: "For over half a century they have gazed into nullity, where they found a lovely nothing." For a superb appraisal of erotic affirmation in Joyce, see Lionel Trilling's essay "James Joyce in his Letters" (*Commentary,* February, 1968).

ideal swells with hope, bursts into faith, becomes heroic, in consequence.

In his sense both of the difficulty and of the glory of "Unity of Being," Yeats stands with the Forster of *Howards End.* For Yeats, however, the difficulty proves insuperable. Like Joyce, Yeats is unable to offer his ideal of human wholeness a supportive metaphysic, the concept of a consenting world. Convinced as he was that "ultimate reality . . . falls in human consciousness . . . into a series of antinomies," he managed to gain only desperate and moving Pisgah sights of human harmony and completeness, as in "A Prayer for My Daughter" (1921) and "Among School Children" (1928). Perhaps in *youth* "The body is not bruised to pleasure soul"; perhaps there, for a time, labor blossoms. But that state where "All thought becomes an image and the soul / Becomes a body"—for Yeats this, alas, is "too perfect . . . to lie in a cradle."

Yeats thus brings to mind Hardy and that form of tragedy in which the love of unity turns to anguish at the heart of a disfiguring world. And yet Yeats, of course, is not so consistently despairing as Hardy: the modern pulse of hopeful desire was sometimes strong in his veins. There are also in his work intervals of acceptance, moments when he seemed to find wholeness precisely by relaxing his will—moments that remind us of Joyce. And if Yeats can be said to dismount anywhere, perhaps it is near Bloom and 7 Eccles Street, where fair and foul are near of kin, and where one expresses oneself as one is. Like Joyce, Yeats was able, as he says in "Dialogue of Self and Soul," to "Measure the lot; forgive myself the lot!"

The erotic fusion that Yeats so often despairs of—the melting blend of mind and senses, the coincidence of self-delighting will and destiny— is precisely what Lawrence, never doubting after *Sons and Lovers,* takes to be the clue, the crown, the justification, of his world. In *Sons and Lovers* (1931) he is in tatters and halves; it is the Victorian novel in extremity—a turn of the screw, even, beyond *Jude the Obscure.* Then, of a sudden, in

The Rainbow (1915), Lawrence is whole and formidable. In the interim,[5] he has opened the sealed chambers of the world and found the forgotten treasures of "integral being." What the Victorians had sundered, he can now put together; and he is prepared to do battle with all who oppose.

In Lawrence the iron-fast Victorian either/or is seized and wrenched and turned upside down: be paradisally "integral," Lawrence inveighs, or burn in the flames of disintegration. Here is an idealism, a fervor, a sense of mission, as tremendous as George Eliot's, though exactly opposite in its message and morality. Lawrence simply turns inside out the Victorian drab-coat of values, showing its elaborate aesthetic, erotic, and religious lining. From adhering to the doctrine of living for others, conscience and faith pivot, in him, to the doctrine of living out all the "promptings" of the self. George Eliot had climbed up from the pit of impulse in the name of everything sacred and right. Lawrence, in the name of everything sacred and whole, very deliberately lets himself down into it, though not so far down that he is unable to make his ceaseless articulations about it heard.

Lawrence found his clue, as everyone knows, in sex—in the "Eros of the sacred mysteries," the god that seduces the mind into the body and thence into the ineffable. Lawrence was a mystic who turned downward, drawn like a divining rod, to the merciful streams of the flesh, there to find regeneration in the "inconceivable"—down to the blood that, unlike any idea, is undeniably from the "beyond," untainted by the "human." And opening his eyes he then saw, or believed he saw, a "new" and "living" universe, a world known "in togetherness"; he heard for the first time "the purring of the great gold lion of the sun, who licks us like the lioness her cubs." The gift of individual unity is thus in Lawrence, as in Forster, a germinating intimacy with the world.

[5] Or earlier, unwittingly, within *Sons and Lovers* itself, as we shall see.

Because of the surprising literalness of Lawrence's notion of "integral being," the modern revolution of character clicks, in his work, to an ultimate conclusion. And thanks to his tremendous physical and emotional needs and the vitality that held him firmly to the organic—to his own flesh and to "the rhythmic cosmos"—Lawrence was not only a richer novelist or "poet" than Forster, far more fertile and forthcoming with, among other things, what Arnold well named "natural magic"; he was also less liable to overshoot, as Forster did in *A Passage to India* (1924), the "joys of the flesh" in pursuit of the "inconceivable." After a diet of Victorian literature, nothing could be more salutary than a feast of Lawrence (except, perhaps, a feast of Colette). Lawrence's insistence on the flesh and the world, his great celebrations of both (though how much better he is on the world than on the flesh!), can help us, as he said of the novel in general, "not to be dead man in life."

Yet no doubt Lawrence's is at once too difficult and facile an ideal for most of us today—that is, if we are to take Lawrence, as he wanted to be taken, not only as an artist but as a teacher. The truth is that, far more than any of the great Victorians, Lawrence is humanly eccentric—eccentric, to begin with, because he is so much a mystic, and all the more eccentric because he is an erotic mystic. Lawrence took the dreamy, connecting, restorative consciousness of his own peculiar sexual experience as the measure of all sanity and reality. And he wrote and preached as if he believed that life could be lived entirely within the vital reverberations of sexual passion. Nothing seemed more natural to him, indeed fated, than a "phallic consciousness" in which "knowing and being" are "one and undivided." But what our common experience tells us—what Lawrence's own characters in fact make all too clear—is that, on the contrary, nothing is more natural, more inevitable, in human beings than a degree of independence of the mind from the body.

It is for this reason that we are lucky to have Forster, with his general balance and sense, his more "human" (if less striking)

"Greek" ideal of self-development, and his own considerable artistry and genius, standing with Lawrence on the near side of the revolutionary arc. Without him, this arc would not be quite the full, the finished, the richly exploratory and highly instructive cultural and moral episode that it is.

To take the full measure of the issues grouped and at stake in these post-Christian disputes over the best blueprint of human character, we can do no better, it should now be apparent, than to concentrate on three writers in particular: George Eliot, the chief moralist of the Victorian ethos; Lawrence, her zealous opposite; and Forster, who, though nearer to Lawrence in belief, represents, all the same, something of a median position. The major ideals of human character—Christian and ascetic, pagan and mystical, Greek and individualistic—are all clustered and tempered in these three writers and all in the burning centers, the crucial fevers, of their books. These are the three supreme creative consciences, the three major architects of the self in English fiction, in their adjoining and complementary eras. In them stands most of the story of what British writers since 1830 have held it humanly desirable to be.

PART ONE

George Eliot

I.   *The Social Self*

George Eliot is not primarily a realist, and insofar as she is, *Middlemarch* aside, she cannot be said to be a great one. It is thus with justice that Georg Lukács—perhaps the best recent analyst of nineteenth-century realism—excludes her from his list of realists. The great realists were militant social critics, propagandists for a manner of being that society had forsaken or never attained. What oppressed them was, above all, the concrete, total form of their own society, the inexorable circle it made for those who had to struggle within it. To them, present society was first and last a particular, inclusive, unhappy reality, to which they opposed, angrily, compassionately, a remembered experience or an imagined abstraction: the brotherhood of man, the sweetness and light of an aristocratic culture, spiritual intensity, the heart. And at its extreme this opposition took on a radical cast—a tone of objection, such as Walter Bagehot found in Dickens, to the necessary constitution of society itself.

By contrast, in George Eliot there is, for the most part, no objection whatever to the forces, the makeup, of her own society, much less to the idea of society itself. On the contrary, the chief burden of her novels is that human beings are not social, not "Victorian," enough—society having as yet failed to redeem them from what Freud called "the crude life of the instincts."

George Eliot's characteristic subject is the necessary submission of individuals to their own society, be it Renaissance Florence or nineteenth-century St. Ogg; and this submission is to be made not so much in the interest of this or that society as in the general interest of the socialization of the self. For her, any society is preferable to the explosive egoism of the individual. Society's function is to contain man, and it is not for the prisoner to complain.

Because of her devotion not to a unique or particular society but to the idea of society itself, George Eliot's documentary realism tends to function as merely the illustration of a moral. Of course no one will deny that George Eliot loved a long-vanished rural England or that she commemorated it warmly. Yet how significant it is that it was a vanished England: the England of her father's youth rather than of her own. Even this England, moreover, mirroring her own wishes as it did, failed to make an autonomous demand on her imagination. It was not to her what the South was to Faulkner, Russia to Dostoyevsky, or even England to Shakespeare: it was not the home of a peculiar soul. The essence of George Eliot's fiction is a mixture of moral caution and a strong sentiment of sociality—this rather than aesthetic intuition, or a sense of *being* as inseparable from a known and loved body of life as sight is from the eye.

There are, to be sure, partial exceptions. The chief one is *Silas Marner*, which is easily the most poetic of George Eliot's books. But then, of all her works of fiction, *Silas Marner* pretends least to be "realistic" or a novel, and it is the characteristic quality of George Eliot's reputed "realism" that I am trying here to trace down. The other exception that springs to mind is, of course, *Adam Bede*—the first and the most nostalgically vibrant of her novels. This glowing celebration of a former England, the overflow of a countrywoman's intimate knowledge, is deservedly a classic. Here we may delight in, because the novelist herself enjoyed, the virtual re-creation of an entire community. The Bede home by the creek where Adam's father drowns, the Poyser kitchen and dairy, the green where Dinah Morris preaches, the wood on the Donnithorne estate where Arthur and Hetty meet for their assignations—these and a dozen other scenes and as many characters are established forever, worked out with a close and patient love. The tang of country speech, "that moment in summer when the sound of the scythe being whetted makes us cast more lingering looks at the flower-sprinkled tresses of the meadows," the butter "turned off the mould with such a beautiful firm surface, like marble in a pale yellow light," are ours for the simple reason that George Eliot included them for their own sake. This novel pays homage to the world:

Grand masses of cloud were hurried across the blue, and the great round hills behind the Chase seemed alive with their flying shadows; the sun was hidden for a moment, and then shone out warm again like a recovered joy; the leaves, still green, were tossed off the hedge-row trees by the wind; around the farmhouses there was a sound of clapping doors; the apples fell in the orchards; and the stray horses on the green sides of the lanes and on the common had their manes blown about their faces. . . .

This is exquisite. Yet such a passage, with its remarkable sensuous specification and clarity, marks the exception in *Adam Bede*, not the rule. Moreover, even where such passages occur their effect is usually silenced, like the sudden placing of a hand on a cymbal, by a turn to moral reflection. "We are children of a large family, and must learn, as such children do, not to expect that our hurts will be made much of—to be content with little nurture and caressing, and help each other the more": so concludes the piece of limpid representation just extracted. For even on such a glorious day (we are to perceive) "a blighting sorrow may fall upon a man." So it is that, though admired, blessed, and blessing, the world is subdued in *Adam Bede* to disquisitions on right conduct. It comes to us, in the main, like music through a closed door.

What is more, *Adam Bede* is static. George Eliot's moral mind rules the book, and this mind itself is fixed and self-referring. For all its presentation of persons and events, of the sights and sounds of country life, the novel thus takes on, especially in memory, the character of comment. *Adam Bede* may charm us, it may even shake out of us a tear or two; but it does not begin to give us a sense of being introduced to the actual complexity of life. Picturesque, it passes almost always before us rather than in us. Its "realism" is such as can be reduced to a moral formula or two. The author never attempts, in this book, to discover more than she already knows.

As for the psychological realism in George Eliot, it is of course considerable: clearly it forms her best claim to be regarded as a realist; as Lord Acton remarked, she was an expert pathologist of conscience. Yet neither in this application nor in any other is "psychological realism" a precise or definitive term; it can be said of fantastic as well as of realistic fiction that it constitutes a true picture of the mind. Moreover, in George Eliot it was precisely this sort of realism that was most subject to vitiation. To fulfill her actual intent, which was not psychological realism, George Eliot was prepared to sacrifice it, and often did, though no doubt in complete ignorance of the sacrifice.

Moral realism? How much realism is there in a moral scheme so pat and puritanical as George Eliot's? And how can one define this term with any precision?

It would appear, then, that despite the frequent use of the term in George Eliot criticism, "realism" is at best an inexact and at worst a misleading description of George Eliot's work. It remains to be seen just how that work should be described.

– 2 –

At the same time that she thought of herself as a realist, George Eliot prided herself on being a tragedian. It was her "way," she believed, "rather too much so, perhaps," to "urge the human sanctities through tragedy—through pity and terror, as well as admiration and delight." In her view, the Greeks "had the same essential elements of life presented to them as we have": the individual clashing "irreparably" with "the general," Nemesis policing the law, "the Right" being somehow awesome, terrible, and inescapable. And as in ancient Athens, so in Victorian England, it is "the individual with whom we sympathize, and the general of which we recognize the irresistible power." There will always be tragedy until the individual learns to live at perfect oneness with the "law," whose shrine is society. And since the individual is still very far from a state of total socialization, the artist today, as in the past, must of necessity be a tragedian.

In actuality, however, George Eliot fell considerably short of writing tragedy. The reasons for this are complex, and perhaps this is not the place to enter into them; but a few obvious causes should be mentioned. To begin with, the "grand schematic forms" in which (as George Eliot saw it) the Greeks "symbolized" the essential elements of life have, necessarily, fallen away in her fiction, leaving exposed the essential elements themselves in all their scientific—or, as we shall see, pseudoscientific—nakedness. "Law," in George Eliot, purified of the gods, is reduced to the clanking Positivist machinery of cause and consequence. Thus is destroyed, in one stroke, the resources of wonder and terror that were available to the Greeks. Positivist tragedy, a tragedy of broad daylight, is a contradiction of terms.

Further, the logic of George Eliot's moral philosophy rigorously ruled against "sympathy" with the individual. "There is," she believed, "no kind of conscious obedience that is not an advance on lawlessness." If collisions arise between individuals and the general, the fault must lie entirely with the individuals and their impious egoism, their selfish appetites—as is indeed the case with Arthur Donnithorne and Hetty Sorrel in *Adam Bede*, with Tito Melema in *Romola*, with Bulstrode in *Middlemarch*, with Mrs. Transome in *Felix Holt*, and with Gwendolen

George Eliot

Harleth in *Daniel Deronda*. Certainly, George Eliot pities these
and other antisocial characters—pities them deeply. But sympathy, an unqualified feeling with, still less a siding with—this, for
the most part, she does not display. After all, these characters
have none of the excuse of an Oedipus or an Antigone; they
are the casualties of their own crass "narrowness." They deserve
their suffering—as Adam notably insists on making clear to
Arthur Donnithorne. Were they trying to live for themselves
and not for the community? Well, they were caught out, and a
good thing. Pity them we must, George Eliot seems to have felt,
insofar as they feel lost or guilty; but this will be the patronizing
pity of one sitting in the light for those wandering in the dark.
It will bear little relation to the anguished pathos of Greek
tragedy. The fate of an Antigone makes us fear for the principle
of justice in the world; it makes us fear for ourselves. The fate
of a Hetty Sorrel, by contrast, makes us feel that, yes, Hetty
certainly made a mistake in thinking only of herself.

As for the "irresistible power" of the "general," George Eliot
was only too eager to demonstrate and affirm it. She never ques-
tioned it; she could not afford to. She wrote not only out of a
pious memory but out of guilt, out of unexamined guilt, paying
in her fiction a debt that she had incurred by her own independent life—the life, first, of an agnostic in a pious family and,
later, of an unmarried Victorian "wife." What her own brave
life showed, of course, was that a "grand submission" was not
at all "inevitable." Submit, though, she does in her fiction; and
everything in her fiction she submits to the triumph of the general over the individual. We cannot stand in awe before a submission so longed for, so needed, so willed by the author herself.

So it was that, having made pity illogical, a mere indulgence,
having reduced mystery to science, and having exchanged the
metaphysical inevitability of the Greeks for the round of her
own psychological needs, George Eliot failed, failed utterly, to

write the tragedy that she held to be implicit in the enduring conditions of social life.

— 3 —

Neither a decided type of realism nor formalized tragedy, what George Eliot actually wrote is, if not difficult to describe, difficult to name. "Novel"—that blanket term—of course covers it, but conceals rather than reveals its character.

It is impossible to define the novel without raising hackles or leaving holes through which some of the greatest "examples" of the form plummet through. Nonetheless, I should say that, when most fulfilling its potential, the novel takes as its special subject the full complexity of life. Its illimitable particularity as to time, place, and character equips it to display, to make us *see*, not simply the full moment of subjective experience, which poetry may also do, or the tense line of objective experience, which drama does equally as well, but the whole of life, both inner and outer, in all its multiform unfolding. By this measure, *Middlemarch* and the first eight or nine episodes of *Ulysses* constitute perhaps the acme of the novel in English. Here is life, in fiction, full in its moment and full in its unfolding; here is life in its honest complexity.

"The birthplace of the novel," writes Walter Benjamin in *Illuminations*, "is the solitary individual, who is no longer able to express himself by giving examples of his most important concerns, is himself uncounseled, and cannot counsel others. . . . In the midst of life's fullness, and through the representation of this fullness, the novel gives evidence of the profound perplexity of the living. . . . If now and then, in the course of the centuries, efforts have been made . . . to implant instruction in the novel, these attempts have always amounted to a modification of the novel form." However, it is probably "life's fullness," and not "the profound perplexity of the living," that gives the best report of the novel—of its special magic and potency. For of course the novel also gives evidence, profound evidence, of the human need, and of the active human will, to move beyond perplexity to assurance. It is a curious reading of *War and Peace* and *The Brothers Karamazov*, of *Don Quixote* and *Emma*, that could call their authors "uncounseled." Yet, precisely because of the novel's great openness to life, complexity will certainly seem, where the form is most fully itself, either to threaten or to overwhelm the counsel. Though the best novels may not leave us in the midst of perplexity, at least they will lead us through it, and the shock of it will still be upon us. So it is, for example, in *Vanity Fair, Great Expectations, Wuthering Heights, Tess of the D'Urbervilles, A Passage to India, Sons and Lovers, Women in Love,* and even *Ulysses* (much as this last is comically assured in its modes).

Now, except in *Middlemarch*, where the attempt to "implant instruction" *instructively* meets with the resistance of a hard soil, it is just George Eliot's characteristic, as a "novelist," to implant instruction in her plot and characters; indeed, the characters and plot are primarily there as a field for the sowing of counsel. And what ought to be noted about the typical George Eliot critic is that he seems to welcome the counsel, and not to notice or else not to lament the dearth of that sort of vigorous complexity, probing and helpless rather than token or picturesque, that characterizes the novel at the peak of its special competency. The resurrection of George Eliot's reputation in recent times—the reputation of her entire canon, not simply of *Middlemarch* or *Adam Bede*—has been accomplished, in the main, not by aesthetic critics as such but by moralists, and by moralists, to all appearances, of George Eliot's own persuasion. This novelist is seldom regarded today from any but a neo-Victorian point of view.[1] One meets, in conversation if not in

---

[1] Recently, however, there has developed a trend—equally sterile—to regard her from a purely academic or formal point of view. With considerable strain, her novels are being treated as if they were highly

print, with Victorian specialists who cannot abide George Eliot
—who, alas, will not even admit the merits of *Middlemarch*; but
these people do not write about her, and it is left to Edmund
Wilson and Cyril Connolly (neither, significantly, an academic
critic) to make passing and disparaging remarks about her work.
The truth is that, as a novelist of the first water, as an artist with
more than one or two decidedly successful, entire, and still living
novels, George Eliot is a far more dubious and controversial
figure than current criticism would lead one to suppose. She is
a novelist who, at her most typical, was not at all supreme,
judged by the highest standards of the art: a novelist who, in
thinning out the form to instruction, sacrificed much of its
potential force and complexity.

As Benjamin notes, the narrative form truly fitted to give
counsel is the tale; and one way to view George Eliot's novels
is as highly particularized tales. To be sure, this interpretation
lacks exactitude, and it is even too flattering, since at its greatest,
as in Isak Dinesen, the tale has a mystery and natural magic
that are either faint or altogether lacking in George Eliot. Nonetheless, it illuminates the place of *Silas Marner* in her canon as
not a curious exception, in its simple quality of the tale, but the
quintessential expression of her leading artistic impulse: the
novelist exposed, or freed, as the counselor.

Silas Marner, as F. R. Leavis has judged, is a minor masterpiece [2] (though not a masterpiece of the novel). And it is so, in
part, because it is at perfect oneness with itself. Released from
the burden of a novel's complexity, it is light of step and light of
touch, a book feelingly and carefully wrought, a craftsman's
product in every sentence—this last being a characteristic, as

---

(and not merely moderately) self-conscious and aesthetically intricate
words of art. See, for example, *Middlemarch: Critical Approaches to
the Novel*, edited by Barbara Hardy (New York: Oxford University
Press, 1967).

  [2] See *The Great Tradition* (London: Chatto and Windus, 1948).
Leavis later remarked that he thought his stress on "minor" had been
"infelicitous" (Penguin: Peregrine Books, p. 60n); I think it was not,
the substance of *Silas Marner* being too slight to warrant "major."

Benjamin notes, of the tale. Considered as counsel, *Silas Marner*
is, I think, simple-minded at best. It inculcates the message, dear
to peasant superstition, that, though all may seem dark here
below, the world is in beneficent hands. And yet because it was
conceived and shaped in feeling, and because it is true to itself,
the book succeeds as art. Unlike *Romola*, or *Felix Holt*, or
Daniel Deronda, it does not present itself, unwarrantedly, as a
"faithful" picture of life; it is, effectively, but a tale.

"I think aesthetic teaching is the highest of all teaching,"
George Eliot said, famously, "because it deals with life in its
highest complexity. But if it ceases to be purely aesthetic—if it
lapses anywhere from the picture to the diagram—it becomes
the most offensive of all teaching." This statement is usually
cited as an earnest of George Eliot's aesthetic integrity. Yet it
defines, I should say, precisely what is weak in all her novels
except *Middlemarch*. Indeed, these books, as a rule, do not even
so much as lapse from the picture to the diagram: though they
are always something more than a mere diagram, they are usually less than a picture or—what George Eliot appears to mean by
this term—an independently living and breathing representation of life. We should not be misled by the fact that they are
prosy with detail. Detail by itself is a sign neither of openness
nor of a complexity extending beyond counsel. Rather, where
a profound intuition is not grappling with fact, it is merely
stuffing for the goose.

– 4 –

The master pattern of George Eliot's fiction was first established in the apprentice novella *Janet's Repentance* (1857).
Janet Dempster, a provincial woman miserably married to an
egoistic and brutal man, drinks in private, feels rebellious
against everything, and selfishly burdens her mother with her

troubles. Janet, however, is not unredeemable: she is habitually kind and, more important, she feels a need to "do right." (No doubt it is also in her favor that her beauty is "majestic.") Cast out one night by her drunken husband, Janet undergoes a crisis of moral faith: she has suddenly "left off minding about plea-sure" (as if, indeed, she had ever really had a mind for it), but how will she now find the strength for self-sacrifice? Why "do right" when that means continuing to live with a bestial hus-band? Perhaps what she needs in order to make her sacrifice is simply someone else's approval: ". . . if I felt that God cared for me. . . ." If there is any strength in Janet's nature, it is "the strength of the vine, which must have its broad leaves and rich clusters borne up by a firm stay"; and Janet can find no stay. At this point, however, she appeals to a Mr. Tryan, an Evangelical clergyman. There follows a heartfelt exchange of confessions— he, too, it seems, has sinned; but, having repented long since, he is now the very "image of self-renouncing faith." ". . . you have been choosing pain, and working, and denying yourself," Janet says, after listening to his story, "and I have been thinking only of myself. I was only angry and discontented because I had pain to bear." Chastened by Tryan's example but, even more, warmed by his tender concern, Janet renounces her "spirit of rebellion." "Blessed influence," George Eliot observes, "of one true loving human soul on another."

Persuaded now in her inmost being that "there is nothing that becomes us but entire submission, perfect resignation," the heroine hastens to beg her mother's forgiveness ("I have not been a good tender child to you, but I *will* be . . .") and returns to her husband. The latter, however, is soon dispatched by "Nemesis"—serially, in the form of a fall from a horse, menin-gitis, delirium tremens, and death. We are then teased for a while with a growing intimacy between Janet and the clergy-man; but Tryan, who has all along been ill, soon dies of con-sumption. (The faces were not hard at *his* funeral, we are assured—in contrast, of course, to those at Dempster's.) The repentant Janet then continues on "in the presence of unseen witnesses—of the Divine love that had rescued her, of the human love that waited for its eternal repose until it had seen her endure to the end."

Here in bald and hence revealing form is the outline, the central plot, the obsessive pattern, of George Eliot's fiction.

The typical characters. The Repentant Egoist: like Janet, the individual who, having rebelled against his lot, burns in the fire of his rebellion until he learns, anew, the meaning of love, reverence, and submission. Hetty Sorrel, Arthur Donnithorne, Maggie Tulliver, Godfrey Cass, Silas Marner, Romola, Bulstrode, Esther Lyon, and Gwendolen Harleth are later examples of the type. Then the Unrepentant Egoist: the hardened, irretrievable sinner who "deservedly" meets with misery or death. In the novels, Dunsey Cass, Tito Melema, Lawyer Jermyn, Raffles, Grandcourt, and Mirah Lapidoth's father are among those who follow Depmster to a dark end. Others, such as Casaubon, Rosamond Vincy, and Mrs. Transome, are near relations to the type. Then the Confessor: the moral physician who, like Tryan, often serves also as a model of the altruistic uses of suffering. Other examples are Dinah Morris, Dr. Kenn, Dolly Winthrop, Savonarola, Felix Holt, Dorothea Brooke, and Daniel Deronda. Finally we must notice the minor characters who, like Janet's mother, represent average, "lovable" human nature—those numerous stable, unchanging people who exemplify unquestioning submission and commonplace goodness, and who frequently suffer from the selfishness of the egoists.

The typical action. From rebellion against Duty through suffering and crisis to repentance and submission.

The typical climax. The cathartic scene of conversion.

The major themes. The "dreadful vitality" of selfish deeds and their Nemesis; the injuries to others resulting from the spirit of rebellion; the "all-sufficiency" of human love as a substitute for God's care; the transmutation of suffering into sympathy; and the moral absoluteness of self-renunciation ("All sacrifice is good").

The typical embarrassments. The subliminal bartering of the conversion (as if to say, "Care for me and I will cease to care for myself"); the suspect *numen*, the idealization, of the Confessor; the half-revealed sexual attraction between the Penitent and the Confessor; the sobbing and hysterical scene of conversion; the protagonist's anxiety to become a little child again; the patness of the avenging destiny that rids the regenerate of obligation to the unregenerate, leaving the new soul free for effusive love and sympathy;[3] the intellectual vacuity of the entire scheme; and finally the readiness with which the author assumes that all sacrifice is for the best.

Pre-established, rigid, closed, this pattern constitutes an autonomous structure, a portable outline, in George Eliot's fictional world. Though her artistry was to increase phenomenally in subtlety and range, her plot, the vehicle and paradigm of her moral "philosophy," remained frozen, fixed in its own half-examined assurances. It was a plot always *applied* to particular times and places, a parable merely illustrated by the trappings of history.

– 5 –

The fundamental theme of George Eliot's fiction is the necessity of dying unto the self: "For whosoever will save his life,

---

[3] ". . . the real Janet," wrote George Eliot to her publisher John Blackwood, "alas! had a far sadder end than mine, who will melt away from the reader's sight in purity, happiness and beauty." There is irony in her words—for Blackwood had advised her to *"soften* your picture as much as you can." All the same, she has shown herself willing, and without prompting, to give something less (in the well-known words of Chapter XVII of *Adam Bede*) than a "faithful account of men and things as they have mirrored themselves in my mind."

shall lose it. . . ." The characteristic process is that of un-selving; the invariable goal, the socialization of the ego. ". . . it is the community that is the protagonist of this novel," Dorothy Van Ghent shrewdly writes of *Adam Bede*, "the community as the repository of certain shared and knowledgeable values that have been developed out of ages of work and care and common kindness." And the same holds for all George Eliot's other novels, except, significantly, the greatest, *Middlemarch*. In each novel, the antagonist is the individual ego, viewed as lawless, selfish, narrow if not blind—a cancerous cell in the social organism. And the drama of the books consists in the gradual revelation of the inexorability of "the general." The ego awakens to three "facts" at once: its own insignificance, its desecration of the community, and its inadmissibility as a principle of being. It then empties itself out, filling the vacuum with the collective.

The result, as also the cause, is an ideal of human character that, following the sociologist Charles Horton Cooley, we might designate the "social self"—a term Cooley defines as a "spiritual identification of the member with the whole." F. H. Bradley also provides a definition: "I am morally realized," he writes in *Ethical Studies* (1876), "not until my personal self has utterly ceased to be my exclusive self, is no more a will which is outside others' wills, but finds in the world of others nothing but self." The social self is, then, the whole in the part, a spiritual "we." It is a shared collective self where individual lives are, in George Eliot's simile, as "thoroughly blended with each other as the air."

The characteristics of the social self, as shaped by George Eliot, are, first, its absolute necessity according to psychological and social law; its nonetheless local and circumstantial determination; its aspect of an existence lived solely out of charity to others; its psychological openness and transparency; its grateful sacrificial nimbus; and, finally, the compensation it affords of an infinitely expanded existence. It might be well to look at each of these features in turn.

Though George Eliot's novels have at their center and as their form a moral pattern independent of history, the justification for this pattern (insofar as the novelist offers one) nonetheless proves to be "the historical life of man." With few exceptions, Duty, to George Eliot, means what is widely known to be right, what the community expects of the individual. And this "knowledge" is construed as being the accumulated wisdom of the past —as the discovery, by history, of inescapable moral law. *Middlemarch* once more excepted, the past, in George Eliot, is always wiser than the present, tradition more knowing than the individual. "That cannot be duty," the novelist wrote, "which is not already judged to be for human good. To say the contrary is to say that mankind have reached no inductions as to what is for their good or evil."

History and moral tradition thus take the place, in George Eliot, of revelation and the infallibility lost by Scripture. History becomes a form of science. It is Positivism, as it were, spread out, awkward and inefficient in its investigation of causes and effects, but just as incontrovertible in the end. And so, having already found a form of it in history itself, George Eliot turns to nineteenth-century Positivism as the ultimate sanction for morality. Opening its volumes she discovered, not abstract analysis, but the grinding wheels of Nemesis, the vengeful screams of the Furies. Here, in "that invariability of sequence which," as she observed in her review of Mackay's *Progress of the Intellect,* "is acknowledged to be the basis of physical science, but which is still perversely ignored in our social organization, our ethics and our religion"—here she found, however unexpectedly, the authority for the ethical life that the "disappearance of God" had left void. Accordingly, her work became an attempt to rescue the doctrine of self-abnegation from the sinking ship of Christianity and remove it to the mainland of science, or to that "belief in invariable laws" which, as Mill said, "constitutes the Positive mode of thought." Virtually, all she had done was to anchor in the Biblical saw that whatsoever a man sows, that shall he also reap. Wrapped up in the language of science, however, this old chestnut appeared to be a nugget. And George Eliot was never to relax her grip on it long enough to perceive that it had not quite the rigor of inevitability that she needed to find.

To submit to what is "already judged to be for human good" is, then, a universal necessity. It is as futile, or damning, to resist it as it is to resist the will of God. Indeed, "the will of God is the same thing as the will of other men, compelling us to work and avoid what they have ascertained of the facts of existence which compel obedience at our peril." To try to live for oneself is, in George Eliot, not only to attempt to murder the community but almost certainly to murder oneself; it often leads literally to death. "Surely terror is provided for sufficiently in this life of ours," the novelist wrote, "—if only the dread could be directed towards the really dreadful." And it was this task that, all too deliberately, she set herself in her novels: "It is my way (rather too much so, perhaps) to urge the human sanctities through tragedy—through pity and terror, as well as admiration and delight."

Yet universal as the necessity for self-abnegation is, the "world of others" that one takes as one's very "self" is not mankind, but the local community into which one has been born. After all, on a wide view the "inductions" of mankind become confused in the crash and foam of myriad creeds; they appear to be not inductions at all, only guesses, conventions, or superstitions. Is "mankind" Christ or Nietzsche, Comte or Buddha, Blake or Edmund Burke? Is polygamy or monogamy its "induction"? Class system or egalitarianism? It is only in the most provincial of views and places that "mankind" appears to have reached "inductions" that have the simplicity and solidity of a local outcrop of rock.

It is this provincialism that, for the sake of keeping the individual restrained, George Eliot endorses. With her, Duty not only begins but also ends at home, in the little world in which one has been raised. "Affection, intelligence, duty," George Eliot writes in her essay "The Modern Hep! Hep! Hep!" "radiate from a centre, and nature has decided that for us English folk that centre can be neither China nor Peru." Indeed, for a resident of Hayslope or St. Ogg, neither can it be London or Cambridge. The "inductions" of mankind, which one disobeys at one's peril, are the customs of the local village, however lost it may be in the downs.

"Nature has decided . . .": the arbitrary and the inevitable thus combine peculiarly in George Eliot. Nature is, on the one hand, "invariability of sequence"; on the other, the accident of being born in this or that place. The chance of birth in a particular region condemns one to it, a life imprisonment. "Our lives are determined for us," instructs Maggie Tulliver. ". . . man cannot choose his duties," seconds Savonarola in *Romola*; ". . . every bond of your life is a debt." Life is preordained service, as among bees and ants. Each individual does his part; and his part is waiting for him at birth. The task of the individual is to take up the burden of the community without becoming a burden to it. "Duty" means to stay put and stay quiet—to make oneself invisible while standing in one spot. After all, the ground one stands on belongs to the community. The many come and go, the community endures.

In George Eliot, each community thus takes on the characteristics usually attributed to God. The community, for one thing, is a "centre" sacred to feeling; limited as it is, it is a "divinely-guided whole." Because of its indefinitely extending past, moreover, an effluence rises from its every stone and corner that makes the head light with the fragrance of eternity. Like God, the community is the same through all its changes; there is a stillness at the core. Like God, too, it expects the individual to submit the hard stuff of his ego to its crucible. The community can pardon; it can punish; it can honor; it can condemn. If it can be jealous and wrathful, it can also be a reservoir of blessings. And no matter how wrong it may seem, it is always right: its will (so we are to perceive) is to be trusted and obeyed.

In George Eliot's world, submission can be made sweet by

affection, and easy by dullness. But the intelligent and the passionate—those who have selves to lose—are put upon the cross. Their misfortune is that they know and feel that their life has become (in words from *The Mill on the Floss*) "a long suicide." George Eliot bore no brief for the extraordinary nature—for individuals like herself. On the contrary, it was her purpose to bring herself, as it were, to heel in her fiction, having failed to do so in her life. And for such natures, "resignation to individual nothingness"—the common fate—is tantamount to self-murder. George Eliot knew it, she deplored it, she wrote of it acutely in *The Mill on the Floss,* if less so in *Romola* and *Daniel Deronda.* Yet she felt compelled, all the same, to exact self-extirpations in her fiction. Nor, having married late and carrying a great repressive weight of consciousness and responsibility as she did, was she free of the melancholy of resignation outside her fiction—at her desk, during her Sundays "at home," or in her ties with George Henry Lewes's wife and children. "To me," she said—and at the crest of her fame, not in her painful early years—"early death takes the aspect of salvation. . . ."

However, she immediately added: ". . . though I feel, too, that those who live and suffer may sometimes have the greater blessedness of *being* a salvation." Her fiction was intended to serve just this purpose—to save others, and so afford the author a blessedness greater than that of an early death! And "being a salvation" is, of course, the subject as well as the aim of George Eliot's fiction. Dinah Morris, Romola, Dorothea Brooke, Felix Holt, Daniel Deronda—all attempt to save others. Unfortunately there is, as a result, a touch of the ghoul about them. They flock to suffering as the dead in *The Odyssey* flock to blood; for it is in the suffering of others that they find their own justification, their principle of vivacity.

"There was, even from the first," as Saintsbury said of George Eliot, "a taint of the morbid and the unnatural upon her." It was the suffering in life that gave George Eliot the little zest for it that she possessed. The suffering of others was, she knew, her opportunity. It is with a sense of something gone wrong in

the priority of wishes that one comes upon, in the letters, George
Eliot's regret that Lewes's son Thornton, just dead, was no
longer there, where, as she said, she could make him feel her
love! The same need to be a spiritual *host*, to be the rallying
point for others and to thrive in their gratitude, consumes the
fiction. "If you had a table spread for a feast," Dinah Morris
says to Lisbeth, "and was making merry with your friends, you
would think it was kind to let me come and sit down and rejoice
with you, because you'd think I should like to share those good
things; but I should like better to share in your trouble and
your labour, and it would seem harder to me if you denied me
that. You won't send me away?" And later Dinah says: "It's very
blessed on a bleak cold day, when the sky is hanging dark over
the hill, to feel the love of God in one's soul, and carry it to the
lone, bare, stone houses, where there's nothing else to give comfort." To such egotism of altruism did the justification of life
by charity lead both the author and her characters.

A fourth characteristic of the social self, its necessary openness to others, we can perhaps pass over, as too obvious to need
discussion in view of what has already been said, noting only
that George Eliot's novels are, in large part, arraignments of
falsity and secrecy—of the sin of being private rather than public. The ideal is again set forth in Dinah, whose "open glance
. . . told that her heart lived in no cherished secrets of its own,
but in feelings which it longed to share with all the world."
More in need of emphasis is what might be called the teleology
of this open and public self, the eschatology of the resignation
to individual nothingness.

It is hard to sacrifice without an altar, and for George Eliot,
as for Comte, the altar elected was "the development of Humanity." She conceived the ages of mankind—in words with
which Savonarola entices Romola to virtue—as "the history of
a great redemption"—a "great work by which sin and sorrow
are being made to cease." If there is "great hope for the future,"
George Eliot wrote, it lies "in the improvement of human nature by the gradual development of the affections and the sym-

pathetic emotions, and by the slow, stupendous teachings of the world's events." Comte, too, spoke of "the progress of our humanity towards an ascendancy over our animality." And Herbert Spencer—at one time George Eliot's intellectual companion —argued that the "conflict between egoism and altruism, which now constitutes the crux in all ethical speculation, is transitional, and is in process of gradual disappearance," since evolution is working toward their "ultimate conciliation."

For Comte, Spencer, and George Eliot alike, it is thus (in Spencer's words) "complete adaptation to the social state," the biological "moralization of the human being," that constitutes the "great hope for the future." "The obligation of seconding this movement," as Mill noted in his little book on Comte, became "the nearest approach . . . to a general standard of morality." Still more important, it put a little of the blood of life into the ghostly spirit of resignation. George Eliot found it "cheering to think . . . that the higher moral tendencies of human nature are yet only in their germ." And yet the future, somehow, seemed a long way off, and in consequence it is the melancholy of the present, not the ebullience of hope, that dominates George Eliot's books.

Even despite its melancholy, however—despite its necessity, too—the social self remained, for George Eliot, something to strive for. Never mind that its nimbus could pale in the cruel light of present sacrifice. The social self was yet the only "existence" that could give the individual a sense of value—not of his own value, to be sure, but the value of the "whole" of which he was a "part." The concept of the significant life had not been lost; it had merely been transferred to the community. In the superindividual of Hayslope or St. Ogg or the Jewish race—in this, for George Eliot, lay all the glory of *being*. And to partake of and diffuse its light was, she felt, no mean fate, even though it meant converting one's ego into the glass that received it. There was, in any case, no light elsewhere.

Moreover, the larger existence of the community offered a haven from "troublesome self." "The refuge you are needing from personal trouble," says Deronda to Gwendolen Harleth, "is the higher, the religious life, which holds an enthusiasm for something more than our own appetites and vanities." The ego is a Pandora's box of "perturbations," the community the great cabinet where personal troubles are laid away. After stating that our lives are determined for us, Maggie Tulliver adds: "and it makes the mind very free when we give up wishing, and only think of bearing what is laid upon us. . . ." And thus a good face is put upon a painful necessity, a consolation not unlike the "blessedness" of an early death.

– 6 –

So it was that morality—which, as Thomas Mann reminds us, is the correction of life by mind—became in George Eliot, within a secular and social world, actively opposed to the very condition that makes life possible: namely egoism, the force that, in Unamuno's words, is "the principle of psychic gravity, the necessary postulate." Should we not be suspicious of a doctrine so antinatural? Of course it was not an individual invention: it was the aberration of an age. George Eliot's distinction lay not so much in devising it as in coloring and shaping it against the contours of everyday life—in demonstrating its glory through the medium of narrative.[4] And yet how does it happen that, where her friend Herbert Spencer, for instance, merely urged

[4] Of all the gifted Victorian writers, George Eliot most fully matches Sartre's description of the typical bourgeois writer. "The bourgeois," Sartre writes in *What is Literature?* "saw only *psychological* relations among the individuals whom his analytical propaganda circumvented. . . . If he started reflecting on the social order, he annoyed and frightened [the bourgeoisie]. All it asked of him was to share his practical experience of the human heart." And since "man had to be governable as a matter of course, . . . the laws of the heart had to be rigorous and without exceptions. . . . For the writer it was no longer a matter of addressing his work as an appeal to absolute freedoms, but of exhibiting the psychological laws which determined him to readers who were likewise determined."

self-sacrifice "within reason," George Eliot could never rest content, in her fiction, until she had torn the ego out amid tears and cries of repentance, and as if once and for all? Without doubt there is more in her persecution of the self than a simple mirroring of the Victorian ethos. It is only, after all, the relatively superficial artist, like Trollope, who constitutes a placid social mirror. George Eliot was more than a mirror; she was a burning glass. In her the Victorian ethos came to an inflammatory focus. One has but to hear the exigency of her appeals, the solemnity of her accents, to comprehend that she wrote from deep and compelling necessities of her own.

At least four psychological goads appear to have driven George Eliot to enshrine the social self in the pages of her fiction. One was her conviction of her own physical unattractiveness. She was, wrote Henry James, "magnificently ugly—deliciously hideous." As her letters show, the sense of being "a hideous hag" weighed her down throughout her life and led her to feel, in her youth especially, that no one could love her. Oppressed by the notion of being physically exceptional, she could not help feeling drawn to "the social point of view," from which the only measure of worth is moral, or the degree to which the individual has ceased to think of himself as physical and separate from others.

George Eliot perhaps suffered even more, however, from the "evil perturbations" of a passionate and imaginative nature. Had she not had the makings of a great sinner, she would not have struggled so earnestly to become a saint. There were, she said when young, demons "mopping and mowing and gibbering" within her, inciting her into forbidden regions. And once astride the stallion of imaginative impulse, would she ever return to the dull pathways of England—that "land of gloom, of ennui, of platitude"? "What shall I be without my Father?" she wrote shortly before the latter's death in 1849. "It will seem as if a part of my moral nature were gone. I had a horrid vision of myself last night becoming earthly sensual and devilish for want of that purifying restraining influence." Phrenology told her that her "moral and animal regions are unfortunately balanced"—a judgment "too true," she said, "to be heard with calmness." Gordon Haight's recent biography shows her affections repeatedly acting, in her own phrase, as "disturbing forces" in relationships with men who, at first merely intellectual friends, invariably became more. Cursed both with "passions and senses" that, she said, "decompose" and rush with "fury . . . to their own destruction" and with an imagination that was "an enemy that must be cast down ere I can enjoy peace or exhibit uniformity of character," no wonder George Eliot sought, in words inspired by Thomas à Kempis, an "outside-standing ground," a domicile in the social self. The Victorian sibyl who held in thrall in her Sundays "at home" some of the most sober and brilliant intellects of her day was at heart, it seems, Maggie Tulliver with her "illimitable wants," the same Maggie who was "quite wicked with roses," liking to "smell them till they have no scent left"—only standing now as far from herself as it was possible to retreat.

And yet did not the social idea itself satisfy an imaginative hunger? Not, to be sure, a sensuous hunger (at least as such), but the imaginative and, indeed, egoistic hunger for a significant existence? The land of gloom, ennui, and platitude was also the land of "duty and affection"; and where was the imagination to focus *legitimately* in England if not on Duty itself? More, how could the "dead level of provincial existence" be made tolerable if not by finding "infinite issues" in everyday duties?[5] For all her reverent defense of "commonplace things," of "the low phase of life," as a fit subject for both art and sympathy, George Eliot was yet prone to think (and in speaking of German peasant life, at least, felt free to indicate) that human life, take it in the

---

[5] "To live with her," George Eliot wrote in 1852 of her provincially situated sister, "in that hideous neigbourhood amongst ignorant bigots is impossible to me. It would be moral asphyxia and I had better take the other kind—charcoal myself and leave my money. . . ."

raw, is a "narrow, ugly, grovelling existence." However, attach
infinite issues to it, redeem it by the idea of Humanity, give individual sacrifice an epic size, transfigure provincial daughters
into Madonnas and provincial sons into "social captains," and
then both conscience and imagination, both humility and an
enormous egoism, could be satisfied.

Nor, finally, can it be doubted that George Eliot's liaison with
George Henry Lewes compelled her to seek, in her novels, a
reconciliation with both public opinion and her own smarting
conscience. That she lived with Lewes (in Gordon Haight's
words) in "open defiance of convention" can have affected her
fiction only for the worse. Mrs. Gaskell, when apprised of the
real identity of the author of *Adam Bede*, "refused at first to
believe," as Haight reports, "that the 'noble grand book' could
have been written by one whose life did 'so jar against' it." But
doubtless it was George Eliot's apprehension of just this sort of
response that spurred her to make her books the "noble" and
"grand," the all too noble and grand, works that they are. "My
own books scourge me," George Eliot said when acknowledging
to a friend that she had painted in Romola "a goddess, and not
a woman." As a novelist, George Eliot had set out, she said, "to
exhibit nothing as it should be," only "things as they have been
or are, seen through such a medium as my own nature gives me."
But as to that "medium"—weren't people prepared to find it
bespattered with mire? How tempting, then, to make a display
of its purity! No one more noble, more sympathetic to all wrong
and suffering, more *charitable*, than the disreputable author of
Adam Bede: that was how it would be.

To Jane Carlyle, whom *Adam Bede* thus appropriately left
feeling "in charity with the whole human race," George Eliot
wrote that "gentle thoughts and happy remembrances" were
what, as a novelist, she desired to produce. And somewhere,
surely, in the great bath of charity that her novels amount to,
she found the forgiveness and atonement that, for years, neither
her family nor several of her friends nor society in general had
been willing to tender. Doubtless the fiction of Marian Evans,

whatever her social position, would have been much the same as the fiction we know—as the fiction, that is, of the "wife" of George Henry Lewes, whose personal example (so it was rumored) was "pernicious." It might, however, have been a little freer and more faithful to life. It might have been less constricted by a compulsion to demonstrate the inexorability of self-renunciation—an inexorability that the novelist herself, in sensibly and courageously pursuing her own self-fulfillment, had successfully defied. It might have been less heavily saturated, too, in a maternal and overbearing and patronizing pity for all those who, like the author herself, had "wandered" and been condemned too harshly.

– 7 –

George Eliot's compulsion to make the social self regnant in her fiction is nowhere at once so conspicuous and so much to be regretted as in her final novel, *Daniel Deronda* (1876). Here it is the ruin of what promises at first to be a remarkable book. The special interest of this novel lies in the extremes of its strengths and weaknesses. It shows George Eliot both at her most self-forgetting and at her most reprehensibly self-indulgent.

Unlike most of George Eliot's books, *Daniel Deronda* begins not as a dogmatic paradigm but as a novel; it is directed to actuality, not to a moralistic idea about it. Or if the paradigm can indeed be said to be there, it is as yet merely waiting; it has not yet closed its hand on the bird. How psychologically subtle, fertile in observation, lively in procedure, and vivid with sensuous detail this opening is. Here is an illustration selected at random:

"Well, dear, what do you think of the place?" said Mrs. Davilow at last, in a gentle deprecatory tone.
"I think it is charming," said Gwendolen, quickly. "A romantic place; anything delightful may happen in it; it would be a good background for anything. No one need be ashamed of living here."
"There is certainly nothing common about it."

"Oh, it would do for fallen royalty or any sort of grand poverty. We ought properly to have been living in splendour, and have come down to this. It would have been as romantic as could be. But I thought my uncle and aunt Gascoigne would be here to meet us, and my cousin Anna," added Gwendolen, her tone changed to sharp surprise.

There follows an explanation that "satisfied Gwendolen, who was not prepared to have their arrival treated with indifference;

and after tripping a little way up the matted stone staircase to take a survey there, she tripped down again, and followed by all the girls looked into each of the rooms opening from the hall—the dining-room all dark oak and worn red satin damask, with a copy of snarling, worrying dogs from Snyders over the sideboard, and a Christ breaking bread over the mantel-piece; the library with a general aspect and smell of old brown leather; and lastly, the drawing-room, which was entered through a small antechamber crowded with venerable knick-knacks.

"Mamma, mamma, pray come here!" said Gwendolen, Mrs. Davilow having followed slowly in talk with the housekeeper. "Here is an organ. I will be Saint Cecilia: some one shall paint me as Saint Cecilia. Jocosa (this was her name for Miss Merry [the governess]), let down my hair. See, mamma!"

Mrs. Davilow smiled and said, "A charming picture, my dear!" not indifferent to the display of her pet, even in the presence of a housekeeper. Gwendolen rose and laughed with delight. All this seemed quite to the purpose on entering a new house which was so excellent a background.

There are blemishes here—for example, the slipshod conclusion, "All this seemed quite to the purpose," the clause itself meaning nothing but merely pointing up vaguely (what scarcely needed pointing up) that Gwendolen's happy egoism is a ripe subject for irony. Yet Gwendolen and the entire scene survive George Eliot's obligatory condescending attitude. For, miraculously, Gwendolen has come out of George Eliot free, intact, alive.

In creating Gwendolen, George Eliot's imagination gave birth to a character who both exceeds and resists her novel's predetermined moral content, who stands out against it as a bonfire stands out against moonlight. What is astonishing, considering that it was George Eliot who authored her, is not only that Gwendolen eludes the judgment prepared against her (for, as we shall see, she proves far less injurious to others than the novelist assumes); it is that she is fully there to be judged—that judgment must be applied to her, in some uncertainty, from outside. Ordinarily the characters of this novelist exist primarily as judgments—as traits of moral good or evil animated and made exemplary. Their minds are ruled by the lines of the author's intentions, and for the most part they take their place docilely in the acting out of preestablished lessons. Gwendolen, however, is first of all herself. Though she very much belongs to the first part of *Daniel Deronda,* she yet appears to have wandered into the world of George Eliot's novels by mistake. Clearly tagged for the role of the egoist who repents, how harmless she seems compared, say, to a Rosamond Vincy or a Mrs. Transome. She is essentially independent of her predestined role, and she comes to us as absorbing, delightful, amusing, rather than ripe for evil.

Gwendolen gets around George Eliot not only in circumventing the latter's moral purposes but also simply by charming her —or else how could the novelist have made her so charming? If we are amused by Gwendolen, it is because George Eliot was amused by her. Amused and stimulated: for through Gwendolen George Eliot herself is, for a time, roused to unusual life. She thrives in her, enjoying a far more buoyant and confident youth than she had had on her own. In consequence, her art here betrays, not its customary sympathy with all that suffers, but, on the contrary, an immediate and strong sympathy with the instincts of life. Characteristically George Eliot used fiction largely as a mode in which to realize two interlocking conceptions—that of "invariability of sequence" in the moral life and that of the need for "tolerant judgment, pity, and sympathy." In the early pages of *Daniel Deronda,* however, she used fiction (at least such is the effect) simply to look upon life and to delight in it: above all to delight in what may be its essential quality, *play.*

In Gwendolen, life is a free occurrence, a prodigality of playful invention and "vital beauty"—the beauty defined by Ruskin as "the felicitous fulfilment of function in living things." When Gwendolen strikes the pose of Saint Cecilia at the organ, she is, admits the author, "admirable." Heady with "the intoxication of youthful egoism"—but heady, also, with sheer health—Gwendolen enjoys nothing more, she says, "than taking aim—and hitting." She is "determined to be happy—at least not to go on muddling away . . . life as other people do, being and doing nothing remarkable." But it is play, not will, that gives the note of her character—her only plan, as she says, is to do what pleases her.

"The first and original activity of life," writes Ortega in "The Sportive Origin of the State," "is always spontaneous, effusive, overflowing, a liberal expansion of pre-existing energies." And it is this "first and original activity" that Gwendolen happily exemplifies. "Free and exuberant energy" characterizes not only her physical activity—her horseback riding, her dancing, her archery—but also, as we have witnessed, her mental life. Of all George Eliot's characters, Gwendolen has the keenest, most joyful sense of "role," of "effect," of the dramatic possibilities of *being someone*; and she sparkles in her vital possession of this sense. In all she does, she embodies the element of life that, as Huizinga says in *Homo Ludens,* is "at play," that "transcends the immediate needs of life"; she exemplifies vital freedom. And though George Eliot attempts to circumscribe Gwendolen's appetite for life within the judged circle of "egoism," her novel knows better and reveals it also as health and youth.

"Play only becomes possible, thinkable and understandable," writes Huizinga, "when an influx of mind breaks down the absolute determinism of the cosmos." Moreover, he notes, when an action "has an ethical value," "it ceases to be play." No wonder, then, that the nineteenth century, with its deterministic and ethical modes of thought, and its ethos of work and production, stifled and distrusted the ludic impulse. "An innate blindness seems to have closed the eyes of this epoch," Ortega observes, "to all but those facts which show life as a phenomenon of utility, an adaptation."

Yet of George Eliot, at least, it must be said that she was not at all blind to the "exuberant inner energies" of life. On the contrary, it was just her large-eyed anxious glimpse of them that tightened her art into its habitual seriousness. The "absolute determinism" of Duty, the transfer of the effusive, the overflowing, from the biological to the evangelical—these were both her response to, and her refuge from, her perception of the fearful freedom of play.

In exemplifying play and what Huizinga calls "its profoundly aesthetic quality," Gwendolen thus stands opposed not only to her age (of all George Eliot's novels, *Daniel Deronda* is the only one that is set well into the Victorian period), but to George Eliot's art—an art in which the playful aesthetic spirit is conscientiously "adapted" to the utility of moral dogma and all but numbed by a cold atmosphere of ethical determinism. In George Eliot, as we have seen, the moral life is strongly conditioned. Indeed, the "inexorable" and the "peremptory" are its chief characteristics; and Nemesis and the Furies attend it. All the more wonderful, then, that George Eliot was able—and willing—to give Gwendolen free rein. Gwendolen is her contrary and negation: the heroine is to the novelist what play is to seriousness, freedom to necessity. And yet, in what is truly charity, George Eliot not only gave birth to her opposite but, for a time, let the creature bloom and live in its own alien terms. In Gwendolen, she so forgot herself as a moralist that she became a novelist. The two functions, of course, are not necessarily incompatible; but in George Eliot they often were.

Sooner or later Gwendolen, and hence the novel itself, would have to suffer for this early tolerance, this allowance of freedom. George Eliot, to keep her own equanimity, would have to intrude on her creation; she would have to turn Gwendolen into herself. Everything within her book would have to be brought into the gravitational field of the "necessity" of submission. Having given release to Gwendolen as to her own repressed vitality, George Eliot must then repress her again; having lit the bonfire, she must put it out. Gwendolen's delight in life must be turned to sorrow ("The one deep strong love I have ever known," George Eliot wrote as her father lay dying, "has now its highest exercise and fullest reward—the worship of sorrow is *the* worship for mortals"). Where there is freedom in Gwendolen, there must be a conscious necessity; where there is egocentricity, charity. Gwendolen must be allowed only one "instinct": what Nietzsche called "the social instinct resting on the valuation that the single individual is of little account, but all individuals together are of very great account provided they constitute a community with a common feeling and a common conscience." George Eliot's novels represent this community, and Gwendolen must be brought into the fold.

But how transform Gwendolen, whose only loves are of play and of herself, into a social saint, whose only loves are for others and for an "ideal whole"? Only, alas, by shrinking her from a character into an example. This the novelist initiates, first, by planting within Gwendolen—as one might graft a pine to a rose bush—an improbable susceptibility to sudden terror. (George Eliot herself, Gordon Haight remarks, had "something like" Gwendolen's liability to fits of spiritual dread.) The novelist thus means to equip her character with the matrix of a conscience: Gwendolen is to be one of those who, as Daniel Deronda observes, "could never lead an injurious life . . . without feeling remorse." With the design of exploiting this susceptibility to terror and guilt, George Eliot then tempts Gwendolen into injuring someone else; and this of course sets rolling, as by the push of a button, that great machine of Nemesis that, so the novelist believed, waits to crush all those who indulge in capricious and selfish behavior.

The injury and the Nemesis are both comprised by Gwendolen's marriage to Sir Charles Grandcourt, a wonderfully sinister and repellent example of the Unrepentant Egoist. By accepting Grandcourt, Gwendolen knowingly interferes with the "wishes" of Lydia Glasher, who, long separated from her own husband, has had four children by Grandcourt and wants to marry him. ". . . you have chosen to injure me and my children," Lydia writes to Gwendolen, making the matter explicit for all. As Gwendolen reads the letter, terror and remorse strike into her heart, and, with the author's "sympathy," she begins at last to learn the several inevitable lessons of George Eliot's fiction: that consequences are unpitying, that the word "Duty" is sacred, that "inexorable sorrow" can take the form of fellowship and make the imagination tender, and the rest:

It seemed at first as if Gwendolen's eyes were spell-bound in reading the horrible words of the letter over and over again as a doom of penance; but suddenly a new spasm of terror made her lean forward and stretch out the paper towards the fire, lest accusation and proof at once should meet all eyes. . . .

After that long while, there was a tap at the door and Grandcourt entered, dressed for dinner. The sight of him brought a new nervous shock, and Gwendolen screamed again and again with hysterical violence. He had expected to see her dressed and smiling, ready to be led down. He saw her pallid, shrieking as it seemed with terror. . . . Was it a fit of madness?

In some form or other the Furies had crossed his threshold.

It is at this point that, with a forceful wrench, George Eliot wins her character back from an inadmissible freedom. The rest of the book, insofar as it concerns Gwendolen, is merely the playing out of George Eliot's usual and autonomous moral scheme: *Janet's Repentance* with a change of cast. And what is offensive in this is not only the destruction of a remarkable characterization—indeed, of a virtual living creature—but the inadequacy of the paradigm to the circumstances it comes in to order.

It has not enough been observed of George Eliot that her moral preoccupations blinkered as well as directed her insight, or that the moral glare in her work is sometimes stronger than the moral detail, not to mention the moral justice. "The casuists have become a by-word of reproach," the novelist writes in *The Mill on the Floss*; "but their perverted spirit of minute discrimination was the shadow of a truth to which eyes and ears are too often fatally sealed: the truth, that moral judgments must remain false and hollow, unless they are checked and enlightened by a perpetual reference to the special circumstances that mark the individual lot." It is, however, just a failure to refer to "special circumstances" that marks the novelist's presentation of Gwendolen's supposed injuriousness; and the consequent moral judgment is indeed "false and hollow." "I have been a cruel woman!" Gwendolen cries at the climax of her moral crisis. But what exactly has she done? True, she has broken a promise extracted from Lydia Glasher. But what of the special circumstance that this promise was extracted under conditions cruel and surprising? And would Lydia's own situation really have been any different if Gwendolen had not married Grandcourt? "He had meant to marry me," protests Lydia. "He would have married me at last." After nine years of putting her off? After nine years of ever-increasing coldness to her? After all, Grandcourt first meets up with Gwendolen while in the course of searching for a wife; and Grandcourt is obviously not the sort to pursue a course lightly.

The truth is that the only certain injury resulting from Gwendolen's marriage is to herself. But this George Eliot ignores; it is of no moral interest to her. The self, for her, is not a locus of moral concern: "the others" alone occupy the moral sphere. And so it is that she attempts to implicate someone besides Gwendolen in the consequences of the latter's "recklessness." Lydia is brought in solely to serve as Gwendolen's victim. She is introduced as a token of the inescapable complexity, the crowdedness, as it were, of the moral life. She is meant to remind us that it is impossible to gratify oneself capriciously without harming others. This is indeed very often the case. But the point to note is that George Eliot treats the matter rigidly and hence unreasonably—treats it as a dogma. She is writing by compulsive formula, not by intelligence, observation, or a "spirit of minute discrimination." And thus, having included Lydia for the sake of pointing a moral, she does not attend to what she herself has wrought. She has created not a clear-cut but a problematical situation. It is not, however, any part of her purpose to step into clouds; she is, rather, in haste to dispel them, to reduce everything to the "absolute" clarity of "inexorable" sorrow and submission. Accordingly, that it is ironically presumptuous of Lydia to claim a right to Grandcourt after having abandoned her husband and child does not seem to have occurred to the novelist. And that Gwendolen has virtually sold herself into a loveless marriage—this, too, she scarcely troubles to take in. Her overriding aim is to set in motion the Furies of conscience. Her moral "vision" is largely limited to this.

There is another aspect to the author's compulsive treatment of her heroine. Gwendolen is radically free from George Eliot up until her marriage; yet even before that she is dressed in a derogating demonic imagery. "In positing one thing," as Kierkegaard notes, "we also indirectly posit the other which we exclude." So Christianity posits sensuousness. And so the sanctification of Duty posits the demonism of play. In George Eliot, where Duty is called "sacred," play becomes indistinguishable from recklessness, and recklessness the same thing as evil. Between the saintly and the sinful, between necessity and nemesis, there is, then, no neutral space: it is, as we have earlier seen, a world of either/or.

In *Daniel Deronda,* accordingly, gaming and wickedness dovetail, wickedness here being labeled the "devil's game." And since Gwendolen's "favourite key of life" is "doing as she liked," or dicing for what she wants at the table of life, she is, of course, automatically numbered among the devil's party. When we first see her, she is before a gaming table at a German bath. What is more, she is in a green and silver "ensemble du serpent," her neck winds about, her eyes are long and narrow, and whether the "genius" in her glance is "good" or "evil" is said to be difficult to tell—though in view of the other details included, we can scarcely be left in any doubt.

And so it goes throughout the novel, glints of evil nuance flashing out like a code. And yet this serpentine Gwendolen is never more than a fiction; she imposes on no one, not even on the novelist. Is this "empress of luck" with her ominous trace of "demon ancestry," her "resemblance to the serpent," this girl who is associated through her gaming with all the "wicked" characters of the book—with Lassman who games away Gwendolen's mother's fortune in the "wicked recklessness" of speculation; with Grandcourt, that "chancy personage"; and with the senior Lapidoth, a habitual gambler and a man who tries to toss away his daughter's Jewish heritage—is this girl one and the same as the charming, callow girl who cries, "See, mamma!" as she strikes the pose of Saint Cecilia, or who says: "I never like my life so well as when I am on horseback, having a great gallop. I think of nothing. I only feel myself strong and happy"? She is not, and George Eliot as much as confesses it. Throughout the novel, Gwendolen is presented as a well-meaning girl, utterly untainted by either malice or cynicism. And George Eliot speaks of her toward the end simply as having followed "a lure through a long satanic masquerade, which she had entered on with an intoxicated belief in its disguises"—as not herself satanic, in other words, merely deceived. And so if Gwendolen cries absurdly, "I was always wicked . . . ," and if George Eliot seems ready to grant the claim, we need not. We may discount it as a symptom of this novelist's excessive fear of all impulse at play outside the law.

The only justice in all this is unfortunately a poetic one. For to the degree that *Daniel Deronda* suppresses impulse, it also suppresses itself as a work of art. It only lives so long as Gwendolen lives—but, foolishly, it is in a rage to undo her. About midway the novel "lapses," in George Eliot's own terms of disapprobation, quoted earlier, from a "picture" to something nearer a "diagram." However, it still pretends to be dealing with "life in its highest complexity" and it thus "becomes the most offensive of all teaching."

Since the second half of the book constitutes only an awful extension of the weaknesses already noted, let us consider it but briefly. Here in the "Deronda" portion of the book, there is nothing whatever to resist the dogma of the social self; it triumphs in all its abstractness from actual men and women. The reason this half of the novel marks the nadir of George Eliot's fiction (even her most uncritical admirers concede a major failure of creativity) is that the author here makes her ritual journey to the shrine of the social self not, as usual, from the near but from the far side of the ideal. This is to say that Daniel Deronda, with his impotent and overwhelming altruism, his "vague social passion," his devouring sacrificial impulse, is the form of the social self in search of a content. He is a transparency waiting to be tinted, a "world of others," in Bradley's phrase, longing to find the others who will make up his world.

As we have already noted, the content of the social self is determined for each individual by the community into which he is born. Deronda, however, raises in this connection a problem: for, of Jewish parentage, he has been reared by others as a gentile. George Eliot resolves the problem by taking her notion of the determinism of inheritance literally into the veins; there is talk of Deronda's Jewish "blood." Accordingly, once Deronda discovers that his parents were Jews, he *ipso facto* has his "charter" for action: "our duty is faithful tradition where we can attain it . . . ," he says. This is pale stuff for fiction, and a ghastly bloodlessness is the price the novel pays for patiently seeing Deronda through his search for the communal identity of his blood.

To make matters worse, George Eliot annexes to Deronda, in the prophet Mordecai and his sister Mirah, two characters equally waxen and improbable in their approximation to the social self. And as if to add a final obstacle, George Eliot, warming to her subject, indulges here unrestrainedly in what is elsewhere held in some check in her fiction: her practice of "precious seeing," of "bathing . . . all objects in a solemnity as of sunset-glow, which is begotten of a loving reverential emotion." In consequence, the prose is sodden with sentiment. "I speak not as an ignorant dreamer," says Mordecai, "—as one bred up in the inland valleys, thinking ancient thoughts anew and not knowing them ancient, never having stood by the great waters where the world's knowledge passes to and fro." By such "precious" words as these, however, we shall not be persuaded that either Mordecai or the novelist who makes him speak them has ever stood by the great actual waters of the world.

– 8 –

The failure of the latter half of *Daniel Deronda* is identical in cause and essence with the failures in all of George Eliot's books; it is only more unrelieved and more extreme, more self-exposed, more self-betraying. George Eliot's main weakness as a novelist took its rise in her idealism. Idealism in itself is not necessarily a weakness for a novelist, merely a countercurrent to what must always be the flow and direction of the novel itself if the form is to fulfill its rich potential: the flow toward the undefined areas, the wide curving shore, of reality. And, as *Middlemarch* perhaps proves beyond all other novels, idealism, when deeply disappointed, may even enhance the innate poetry of reality. What compounded the problem for George Eliot as a novelist was the particular nature of her ruling ideal. For reasons already noted, the social self spells the end of the vital coloring, the spontaneous and individual impulse, of human beings. It is an abstraction from human nature: a transformation of the "whole man alive," in Lawrence's phrase, into the fiction of a self composed solely of charity. It is an ideal impossible of complete or lasting realization, given human nature as we know it.

As a result, George Eliot's only truly admirable novels are those in which the ideal of the social self is soft-pedaled, still-born, or aborted. Chief among these is *Middlemarch,* which is not merely a fine novel but a great one, indeed possibly the greatest in the language—*Middlemarch,* in which the ideal, struggling to come to life, fails to find breathing space in reality. There is also *The Mill on the Floss,* which, though it enshrines the social ideal, yet lacks the heart to worship it—a book that almost disintegrates under the counterpressures it tries to contain. Finally, there is *Adam Bede,* more even textured and less prosy than *The Mill on the Floss* and charming with remembered and imagined pastoral, as warm with it as the ground after a hot day: the least of the three, as a novel, because the one most penetrated and placid with the social ideal, but pleasantly successful nonetheless, because the ideal is here very gently diffused through the stuff of reality, diluting but not decomposing it.

II.   *The Radicalism of Virtue*

What becomes of politics when the ideal of the social self, in all its unworldly innocence, is set down as a shrine in its midst?

In *Felix Holt, the Radical* (1866), George Eliot addresses herself to the most pressing political phenomenon of her century: the unrest and rising of the working classes. The time is the early 1830s, the place, Treby Magna, a market town newly complicated by mines and manufactures. Felix Holt—a shaggy-headed, large-eyed, strong-limbed "Radical"—having recently returned to Treby from Glasgow, where he had quit his studies and been converted to righteousness "by six weeks' debauchery," has made himself a journeyman to a watchmaker. His father, now dead, had been first a weaver, then a maker of quack medicines. Felix, afire with virtue, publishes a notice that the medicines are worthless and takes his mother's support upon himself. He means, he says, to be an honest worker and "stick to the class" he belongs to—to "people who don't follow the fashions." Yet, in his way, Felix is ambitious: he aspires to become a "demagogue of a new sort; an honest one, if possible, who will tell the people they are blind and foolish." He teaches a few boys in his home and sets up an informal "academy" in "the beerhouse," where he educates "the non-electors." When election day arrives in Treby Magna, Felix takes it upon himself to quell rioting workers whom a shady election agent has loaded with drink. To the eyes of the authorities, however, Felix appears to be leading the mob, and, having unintentionally killed a man who attacked him, Felix is tried for manslaughter, and convicted. His sentence: four years in prison.

Much of the rest of the novel concerns the dilemma of Esther Lyon, the apparent daughter of Treby's Nonconformist minister. She is apprised that she is the heir of the estate of Harold Transome—the local "Radical" candidate (in reality, as his uncle says, a Tory who believes that "if the mob can't be turned back, a man of family must try and head the mob, and save a few homes and hearths") whose agent was responsible for the riot. Rufus Lyon, she now learns, is not her actual father; she is the daughter of a certain Bycliffe, a "gentleman." Esther must decide between, on the one hand, a life of luxury and "moral mediocrity" as Harold's wife or simply as the single mistress of Transome Court and, on the other, a life of comparative poverty with Rufus or (even better) with Felix Holt, should he ever ask her to marry him—a life passed in the moral altitudes that Felix has recently opened to her view. At length, Esther renounces the greater part of the Transome estate and, upon his release from prison, marries Felix. The two young lovers then depart, Rufus to follow later, to another town, where there are other workers to educate and improve and where the life of Felix and Esther will be cushioned by the part of the estate that Esther did not renounce.

As even this rough summary should indicate, *Felix Holt* has little to do with either the working classes or politics. If the book is almost unread today, the reason is that it has the dismaying badness of a project that was false from the start.[1] To write well about misery or injustice, it is not enough, after all, that the imagination should warm to abstractions; it must take

[1] The book, however, has its champions. See, especially, F. R. Leavis, *The Great Tradition*.

fire from realities and burn. To write well about political movements, moreover, one must regard them as something larger than an attack on one's own cherished beliefs: one must appreciate their Laocoön dynamics—enter their depths, measure their meaning. Of all novelists, however, George Eliot was one of the least qualified to write about politics. Politics is, after all, a contest for power. Yet as a thinker George Eliot's entire bent was toward the obliteration of the self. She could not but view political activity as a manifestation of illegitimate egoism—unless, indeed, it were activity directed toward keeping intact an order already achieved. Moreover, politics implies that, at least for some, the better days are yet to be. And though George Eliot was certainly a millenarian, it is also true that for her the millenium was already implicit in the past and the present—in all the days of "mankind." It was already, that is to say, under way, an automatic result of effort after effort of self-renunciation. It needed no push or shove from noisy radicals. George Eliot's ideal of the social self is in fact posited on the immediate ideality of the social whole.[2] Were self-abnegation to wait on the improvement of society, we can imagine her to reason, it would never be made. The time for renunciation is now.

So it was that George Eliot approached politics from a point of view that annihilated them. In writing *Felix Holt*, however, she was not quite aware of this. On the contrary, she affected an interest in the Radical movement—even permitting her hero to say that he scorns those who fail to take "a strong interest in the great political movements of these times." The result is false and offensive: a book well meant, no doubt, but which merely feigns concern for an oppressed and miserable class—a book pathetically complacent in its limited and inapplicable wisdom.

In *Culture and Society 1780–1950,* Raymond Williams classes *Felix Holt* with *Sybil, Mary Barton, North and South, Hard Times,* and *Alton Locke* as an "industrial novel" and sees it as having "a quite different status" from the other works, *Hard*

---

[2] See her essay "The Modern Hep! Hep! Hep!"

Times excepted, because of the "intelligence," the "quality," of
George Eliot's "witness." However, by the time Williams has
properly pointed out that "the discriminations one would expect from a great novelist are certainly not drawn in *Felix
Holt*," we can only infer that the superior quality of George
Eliot's witness here is something very abstract indeed. In my
view, *Felix Holt* is superior to the other novels (*Hard Times*
again excepted) only in its aesthetic deployments and pro-
cedures; and these are far from being so remarkable that they
offset the political and moral defects of the book. For the rest,
Felix Holt is actually inferior to these other works—inferior as
a moral and political act. It displays, not more moral *insight*
than they do, merely more moral *tone*. In penetration, charity,
and compassion, it is comparatively deficient.

Unlike *Felix Holt*, the other novels are all works of democratic sympathy. And even today they cannot be read in dispas-
sion, without jolts. Embedded in their Victorian pieties are
jagged pieces of social reality—vignettes of the desperations and
miseries, the humor and hopes, of England's poor. "Here I was
to work—perhaps for life!" says Alton Locke: "A low lean-to
room, stifling me with the combined odours of human breath
and perspiration, stale beer, the sweet sickly smell of gin. . . .
On the floor, thick with dust and dirt, scraps of stuff and ends of
thread, sat some dozen haggard, untidy, shoeless men, with a
mingled look of care and recklessness that made me shudder."
Admittedly, this is a far cry from, say, Dostoyevsky, and there is
in it, as in *Alton Locke* as a whole, little of the art that conceals
art; but it is humanly engaged; it says, "Look! Grasp! Act!"; it
is radical with compassion. By contrast, we are not subjected in
Felix Holt to any radical experience of seeing. When Felix says,
"This world is not a very fine place for a good many of the
people it it," we concur, but from the basis of our own experience, not from anything brought to view within the novel. And
when a trade unionist says, "The greatest question in the world
is, how to give every man a man's share in what goes on in life
. . . ," we may feel momentarily stirred, but finally we cannot

assent: the empty expression "what goes on in life" amounts to an evasion of the real issues involved. It costs George Eliot too little to utter these platitudes. Her passion, as was observed, lies elsewhere: not in a "man's share" but in his sacrifice. To her the "greatest question" is always that of the "ideal whole," and what she really has to say to the poor, and about them, is addressed not to their "rights" but to their "duties."

Because George Eliot felt a strong attraction to suffering, it might have been expected that, faced by the poor, her pity, if not her politics, would have proved wonderfully radical. But in truth only two sorts of suffering really touched her imagination: the suffering entailed in a difficult renunciation and the suffering resulting from a failure to make one. In *Felix Holt* the working classes exemplify neither. And their actual misery—of dirt, disease, and despair—fails altogether to pierce the sealed and self-referring world of this novelist's moral preoccupations.

Indeed, Williams's term "industrial novel" is quite misleading when applied to *Felix Holt*. For here the poor can scarcely be said to constitute a presence at all. Somewhere off the page, so to speak, there is a coalpit and individuals who work it. But except as a "mass of wild chaotic desires and impulses"—except, that is, as a mob—these last are never made real to us. They are kept at a defensive distance; or, simply, George Eliot knows and cares too little about them to touch them to life in her book.

It is in this regard that *Felix Holt* radically fails as an act of moral recognition and intelligence. It conveys not compassion for but disapproval of the masses; not understanding of their needs but fear of their actions. To George Eliot the poor present themselves merely as an effort—blind, anarchic, and brutish—to throw off the "inexorable" yoke of renunciation and make exorbitant claims for self; they but batter at the glass palace of the Ideal Whole. And in consequence of this shrinking reaction, she fails to fulfill in *Felix Holt* one of the avowed purposes of her art: that of encouraging "that vision of others' needs which is the source of justice, tenderness, sympathy in the fullest sense."

". . . there comes a season," George Eliot once observed, "when we cease to look round and say, 'How shall I enjoy?' but . . . think only how we shall help the wounded." And helping the wounded is, in part, what Felix returns to Treby Magna to do. Significantly, however, George Eliot's emphasis falls not on the precise state or even the existence of the wounded but on Felix's generosity in wanting to help them. The doctrine of renunciation called out from George Eliot a compensatory romance of self-sacrifice. And it is this that *Felix Holt* is "about," not the suffering of the socially wounded.

". . . the finest fellow of all," observes Felix, "would be the one who could be glad to have lived because the world was chiefly miserable, and his life had come to help some one who needed it." But surely the finest fellow would be the one who wished there were no misery to alleviate. Felix's words betray the self-seeking in his "sacrifice." The truth is that without a purportedly miserable world, George Eliot's protagonists would be at a loss to justify their lives. Renunciation would still be "inevitable"—but how could the imagination bear its dullness, the ego its deprivations? The more wounded there are or seem to be, the more reasonable sacrifice appears and the more needed the attending physician. Thus Romola is almost delighted to come upon a village stricken by the plague: ". . . this suffering that I can help is certain," she says, as if relieved and a little surprised. And Felix Holt, it must be said, is more grateful for the existence of the poor than pierced by their particular needs. What he sees when he looks at them is chiefly a pretext for his own self-sacrifice. And this is typical of the moral introversion celebrated in George Eliot's novels.

If Felix has another use for the poor, it is as an occasion for preaching submission to the general will. "I . . . mean to work all my life long against privilege, monopoly, and oppression," he says. But in fact he works against none of these things; by exhorting the workers to renounce their "small selfish ends," he tends rather to uphold them. From the first publication of the book, readers have been given to remark that Felix has nothing in him of a Radical—nothing of a Cobbett or an Owen. And there is, indeed, only one Radical in the book: an anonymous trade unionist who says, in part, ". . . if we working men are ever to get a man's share, we must have universal suffrage, and annual Parliaments, and the vote by ballot, and electoral districts." Even this, of course, is tame stuff for radicalism. Nonetheless, it proves too radical for Felix Holt. Felix dismisses all these proposals, claiming that a still more basic reform must precede them. If they sound like the simplest of appeals for justice, he will answer that justice is not the critical issue. The critical issue is the conduct of the working classes. The critical issue is their lack of respect for what has been "called Right in the world." Until they learn virtue, Felix says, "extension of the suffrage can never mean anything for them but extension of boozing." In short, before they are granted their rights they must show that they deserve them.

We must therefore accept Felix's claim that he glories "in the name of Radical, or Root-and-branch man," but wants "to go to some roots a good deal lower down than the franchise." For what Felix preaches is indeed radical in nature: it is the radicalism of virtue. "There's a power to do mischief—to undo what has been done with great expense and labor, to waste and destroy," he says, alluding to "all the results of civilization"; but "it's another sort of power that I want us working men to have." This is "public opinion—the ruling belief in society about what is wrong, what is honorable and what is shameful. That's the steam that is to work the engines." So the workers should make their employers and exploiters comply by thinking ill of them! More, they should root out any particular regard for themselves; they should desire only "the right thing for all." This is radicalism indeed: a radicalism to end all Radicalism.

Not that Felix thinks it likely that the workers will ever number among the finest fellows in the world. There is, however, a lower sphere of virtue—a valley level, as it were, of the social self; and this, he seems to feel, the workers could come to occupy. Though here we find no heroic pitch of sacrifice, no eager self-immolation on the pyre of the law, neither is there any gratification of "small selfish ends." If there is no earnestness, at least there is soberness; if no self-annihilation, then at least self-modesty; if not the glory of the Physician, then the esteem of the Aide. Independence, honor, self-control, courtesy —surely these, the novel implies, are not too much to ask of the workers. So Felix believes that they ought to wash their faces, save their money, play less at pitch-and-toss, have done with quarreling, set up a school—in a word, take hold of themselves. And all in virtuous acknowledgement of "what is honorable."

What Felix expects of the workers is thus, in effect, that they should conduct themselves like gentlemen—singular as this may seem.[3] It is true that the word is never once addressed to the miners, and we can imagine the disbelief and derision with which it would have been received. All the same, the term is there, so to speak, waiting for them to walk up to it. And this explains why the ideal of the gentleman, which elsewhere lies rather low in George Eliot, enjoys in *Felix Holt* a high, indeed a normative, place.

Though Harold Transome is an Unrepentant Egoist, he is yet, in his measure, a gentleman. And it is the ungentlemanly lawyer Jermyn—a mob, as it were, disguised in singular form— who gives us the measure. Where Jermyn is but an "amateur gentleman," "one of your middle-class upstarts who want to rank with gentlemen," Harold, we are assured, has a "sense of honor and dignity" and "all the susceptibilties of a gentleman." Without the author's irony, he is able to congratulate himself that he has "acted so that he could defy any one to say he was

___

[3] See Ortega's essay "Man the Technician," *History as a System* (New York: W. W. Norton, 1941). "The principal element, the atmosphere, as it were, of the gentlemanly existence," Ortega writes, "is a basic feeling of leisure derived from an ample control over the world." Felix, of course, is far from anticipating a life of leisure for the workers; but he does anticipate their ample control of circumstance.

not a gentleman." While to Jermyn George Eliot offers no sympathy whatever, to Harold she thus gives a gentleman his due. After all, with the gentleman type the "human sanctities" are secure. And nothing makes her consequent approval of the gentleman so clear as the scene in which Jermyn discloses to Harold, with a "grating" voice in a public gathering, that he is in fact Harold's father. Harold is not without support at this crisis: a baronet steps up and says magnificently, addressing Jermyn: "Leave the room, sir. This is a meeting of gentlemen." It is morally the smallest moment in George Eliot's fiction.

What the scene just described suggests, in part, is that a gentleman is made, not born. And *Felix Holt* may be seen as reflecting the mid-nineteenth-century moralization and democratization of this ideal. "What is it to be a gentleman?" asks Thackeray in *The Four Georges* (1860). "Is it to have lofty aims, to lead a pure life, to keep your honour virgin; to have the esteem of your fellow-citizens and the love of your fireside; to bear good fortune meekly; to suffer evil with constancy; and through evil or good to maintain truth always? Show me the happy man whose life exhibits these qualities, and him we will salute as gentleman, whatever his rank may be." And Mrs. Craik, in *John Halifax, Gentleman* (1857)—a crude book that nonetheless possesses power—tells the story of a tanner apprentice who rises by "honest manhood" and other honorable qualities to both wealth and respectability. It was this sort of contemporary liberalization of the gentleman ideal that made it not absurd, on the face of it, for George Eliot to apply it as a measuring tape to the behavior of working men.[4]

The application is not quite direct. But Felix himself provides a meeting point. He may boast that he has "the blood of a

[4] What makes it in fact absurd is George Eliot's characterization (in Felix's "Address to Working Men," published separately) of those who are to get a grip on themselves in the manner of gentlemen: "broods of creatures in human shape, whose enfeebled bodies and dull perverted minds are mere centers of uneasiness in whom even appetite is feeble and joy impossible."

line of handicraftsmen" in his veins. But Esther Lyon, the daughter of "a gentleman" and herself a "real fine-lady," is not fooled. For all his lack of chivalry, she discerns in Felix's behavior "the highest gentlemanliness."

Esther, however, then adds: "Only it seems in him to be something deeper." And we are thus reminded that the ideal of the gentleman is an ideal for the many, not the few. If Harold Transome is a gentleman, Felix Holt is something more: one of George Eliot's social saints. His life is not merely referred, it is consecrated, to the "will of all men." "Some are called," Felix says, "to subject themselves to a harder discipline, and renounce things voluntarily which are lawful for others." And this, we are to understand, is his own distinctive and glorious destiny. Fine as the gentleman is, he but breathes the "air of moral mediocrity." In Felix, by contrast, there is supposed to be something towering, something sublime. The social self is meant to assume in him that nimbus of sacrifice which constituted its ultimate attraction for George Eliot. (In point of fact, however, Felix renounces nothing that is of any value to him.)

Felix Holt is, then, ultimately concerned neither with politics nor with a "chiefly miserable" world but rather with varying degrees of virtue. And perhaps, given George Eliot's obsession with a social ideal of human character, we could not have expected it to be otherwise. She was to transcend herself in only one novel, *Middlemarch*, and then as if by a strange and fortunate accident. It is to this novel that we must now turn, to pay it some of the homage that is so richly its due.

III.   *Middlemarch:*
Touching Down

$\mathbf{L}$ike all examples of literary realism, *Middlemarch* belongs to the negative province of the mind, where greatness is attained through renunciation. Its imaginative asceticism, its discipline of seeing, are heroic. And in this renunciation lies its essential virtue. Having submitted herself to reality in this novel the way a pool submits to the sky, George Eliot achieved the bare beauty of veracity. *Middlemarch* is not merely the Everest of English realism; it is the epitome of literary realism itself.

In art the only renunciation that counts is contrived in anguish, or out of love. For asceticism is only creative, indeed it is only asceticism, when it attests to a damning of the floods. For this reason, the best realists are, precisely, idealists—artists who wrestle heroically with reality and suffer terribly when they are thrown. What T. H. Green called the characteristic outlook of the novel, "the circumstantial view of life," becomes literature only when it is taken up, weighed and felt, lamented and loved, by a full human mind.

In his "Short Treatise on the Novel," Ortega says of this genre that it consists "essentially" in the absorption of the mythic by the real—of what the mind invents by what it cannot avoid. No doubt this is too narrow a view: it leaves outside the pale, for instance, a novel like *Emma*, in which myth and reality, far from being mutually exclusive, work out a happy harmony. As a literary genre, the novel, of course, has never been welded to reality. Almost frantically restless, it has jerked about from fact to fantasy like an animal in a bag, and there is nothing to hold it down. And yet where the novelist aims, as George Eliot felt it was her "highest vocation" to do, to represent things as they are, not "as they never have been and never will be," then his theme is indeed likely to be, as Ortega says, "the collapse of the poetic," "the insufficiency . . . of culture, of all that is noble, clear, lofty"; and his realism will then be poetic to the degree that it stings and torments him.

Few writers have even been so idealistic as George Eliot; few, therefore, have been so ripe for a poetry of realism. And yet, "faithful" accounts though her novels aim to be, dealing with "life in its highest complexity," what a waste for both realism and poetry most of them are. "Reality," in them, becomes the medium of myth, not its hostile condition. All assert the high sufficiency of altruism, of society as some "divinely-guided whole," of aspiration to the "Right." And with the exceptions of those in which the heroine closely resembles the novelist— *Romola* and *The Mill on the Floss*—all "lay the axe to the root," namely the ego, with a good deal of righteous complacency. These novels exist primarily to salve the author's sense of her wrongful independence. Restagings of her traumatic separations from family and society, they are not so much novels as therapeutic parables of revolt and submission. In each George Eliot vicariously reenters, with sobs of gratitude, the narrow space of her childhood, of strict filial and social duty. As a consequence, they amount to little more than scriptures in a religion of home, community, and tradition; they float in an unexamined sentiment of social sanctity. Bent as they are to a predetermined end, they not only lack freedom as novels; they also portray repeatedly, and as a supposedly edifying spectacle, the surrender of personal freedom.

Of George Eliot's novels, only *Middlemarch* takes upon itself the full burden of things as they are. Indeed, that this novel was written at all is one of the miracles of art. Though no one but

George Eliot could have written it, how surprising it is, none-theless, that she was able to write it; what purging and temper-ing flames she must have endured. In *Middlemarch* George Eliot transcended herself, creating heroically. Nothing in her other novels prepares us for its strong achievement. Provincial society as a field of "spiritual falls"—this she examines with the rigor of a physicist. Her concentration is magnificent. The im-pulse to discover the truth establishes itself, steely and relent-less, from the first page and, execpt for a passage or two, is present in every prosaic and honest line. (The prose is prosaic, the novel not.) Reading *Middlemarch*, we need not discount the author and her noble, her compulsive illusions. Here, as it were, she stands off to the side of her work, having performed creatively that self-abdication that her novels themselves always urge upon the reader. With magnificent restraint, she lets her sanctities fare as they can—which is very poorly indeed. It is this unexpected detachment, this impersonality, this freedom and hardness of observation, that makes *Middlemarch*, all con-sidered, a creative miracle.

Middlemarch alone among George Eliot's novels was written out of her full intelligence. In it she tells us all that she knew; for the first and last time, she is a perfect naturalist of the self and of society, and not just for a chapter or two but for the entire length of a novel. Her concern, her alarm, release her into objectivity—or tie her at last to its stake. Here she hides nothing from herself; she is as large as the truth, even though the truth is dreadful and dispiriting. For the only time in a novel, she does not impose a scheme, she reveals a condition. She lays bare, unanswerably, the truth about the "embroiled" medium of social life and about the inherent illness and weedy persistence of the ego—essential truths about man and his social world. To be sure, her tendency to delude herself as to the potency of altruism and the sacredness of society—to read her wishes into reality—persists even here; but the important thing is that it falters, it cannot find its voice. Where in her other books her desire for community burns and consumes the realism, in *Middlemarch* it is her desire that burns, and reality is the fire. And, thus disabused, she now confronts, with great disquietude, the implications of her own strongest allegiances. Remarkably, she finds herself lamenting the very things she has hitherto enshrined: the tyranny of others," the inertia of the past, the insignificance of the self.

Middlemarch describes the fall of those myths that in the other novels float on undisturbed, spectral and silvery as clouds piled at twilight. The "poetry" that thus collapses is, in part, that myth and product of the nineteenth century, the deification of society. The ordinary George Eliot shared with Ruskin the belief that "the noblest word in the catalogue of social virtue is 'Loyalty,' and the sweetest which men have learned in the pastures of the wilderness is 'Fold.' " Indeed, to her, loyalty to the fold constituted that "binding belief or spiritual law, which is to lift us into willing obedience and save us from the slavery of unregulated passion." Her early religious faith, having broken, had been scraped together and erected into a "social faith," which, for all that, was nonetheless a genuine faith. To die to oneself and live for others; to be governed always by the "reliance others have in us"; to reverence every society as a kind of sacred organism: these were the essential practices of her faith— a faith of which her protagonists formed the priesthood, the saints. These last, finding themselves not only problematical but "insignificant," invariably live for others. And yet it never occurs to them that, if they are indeed insignificant, the "others" —so frankly presented as their inferiors—must be insignificant, too. But in *Middlemarch*—and here lies the key to its difference from the other novels—the insignificance of the "others" obtrudes itself. It dominates; it is dreadful.

In this "Study of Provincial Life," George Eliot steps into a trap formed by both her purpose and her subject. Inadvisably, she "studies" the fold—and, closely examined at last, how dismaying it is. How it bleats and shoves as—ah, can it be?—it tramples her hero, Lydgate, and suffocates her heroine, Dorothea. This Middlemarch with its "hampering threadlike pressure of small social conditions," where men are "shapen after the average and fit to be packed by the gross"—this Middlemarch is not a sacred cause but a menace. Impossible to exalt it. Impossible to speak of it in reverential tones. For what is the community of Middlemarch, after all, but the electric accumulation of the petty self-interest of its inhabitants? And let a window open on the "larger" world in this novel, and it discloses another Middlemarch.[1] So it is that, finally caught in a harsh light in George Eliot, the iridescent mist of the "We" evaporates. And what lies bared, in the form of the community itself, resembles nothing so much as that ego from which the author had always been fleeing.

The community of Middlemarch is characterized by precisely those qualities that, according to Ortega, mark brute actuality in *Don Quixote* (the novel that, as he says, every subsequent realistic novel bears "within it like an inner filigree"): stubborn presence, heaviness, inertia. The explanation for this is that, by epitomizing the plebian, Middlemarch represents the "real" element in society. As Georg Simmel observes, the center of gravity in society lies somewhere near the lowest common denominator of its members—it is our most primitive desires that drive us into association with others. Just where it begins to gain mass, then, the collective is irremediably plebeian. And, consequently, on all that is new and rare and individu-

---

[1] The young doctor Lydgate has come to the provinces—and of course there is hard irony in this—to avoid "London intrigues, jealousies, and social truckling." Nor does idealism fare better abroad. There is a lesson in Trawley, who shared Lydgate's apartment in Paris. At that time "he was hot on the French social systems, and talked of going to the Backwoods to found a sort of Pythagorean community." At the present time of the novel, however, "he is practising at a German bath, and has married a rich patient." In *Middlemarch,* no matter where you live, "you have," as Farebrother says, "not only got the old Adam in yourself against you, but . . . all those descendants of the original Adam who form the society around you."

al, society exerts a constant force of gravitation. Now, as a novelist, George Eliot was habitually opposed to the individual and the new, if not to the excellent and the rare. But in *Middlemarch* she is forced at last to acknowledge that "it seems as if the paltry fellows were always to turn the scale." As a result, she here becomes a champion of progress and excellence. It is the social, not the individual, that now wears the aspect of the primitive. Far from being a guide as before, it is society itself that now stands in need of guidance.

In *Middlemarch,* however, the superior few not only prove too light to deflect society's course; they themselves are sucked into the orbit of the plebeian. And in large part it is the sorrow of their fall that gives the novel its realistic poetry—its disillusioned poignancy and impact. For *Middlemarch* portrays the fall, not only of the myth of a "divinely-guided whole," but also of George Eliot's most intimately possessed and heartfelt theme: what in *The Mill on the Floss* is called "the poetry of ambition." Indeed, these two mirages were doomed to disappear together. For to George Eliot the only conceivable object of "poetic" ambition was a sacred collective. In consequence, having laid bare in *Middlemarch* the social as the unredeemed, she stands bewildered; and Duty, Sacrifice, Aspiration, Achievement—all that great fleet of the nineteenth century—lie becalmed. That heroic aspiration might fail, that a noble sacrifice might be resisted, that the crowd is not at all eager to welcome, to adore, to understand the hero—this seems to strike George Eliot with the force of a blow. Always before, in her novels, noble achievement had seemed so easy; and it was to seem so again in *Daniel Deronda.* But *Middlemarch* makes the discovery of the age—of Comte, Darwin, Marx—that the environment is the only protagonist. Here, dismally, the community seeps into the noble characters and gradually fills them with itself—though Lydgate, who slips from the heights of medical research to the depths of fashionable practice, is, it is true, the only thorough example of this process. The "blight of irony" cast over "all higher effort" is thus the conscious burden of the novel.

Yet, fundamental as it is, the irony of aspiration, the failure of higher effort, is not in itself the grievance that runs like a ground hum through the book. It is only the circumstance of a grievance still more profound. Contrary to George Eliot's own assumptions, aspiration is never a purely disinterested motive; it is always driven by, it always serves, the ego, which thereby seeks to overcome its suspicion of its own insignificance. But in *Middlemarch* this suspicion is not successfully overcome; on the contrary, everything increases it. And hence it is that, heard at its deepest, *Middlemarch* is a prolonged protest of the dissatisfied ego, a lamentation on the darkness of life without fame.

It is this egoistic dissatisfaction that accounts for the deep sadness of the book. No one knew so well the melancholy wastes of a sense of personal inconsequence as this famous, highly influential novelist. The isolation, the unhappiness, of her youth had taught her to believe that life without ambition, without fame, was unendurable. When, late in her life, she was urged to write an autobiography, she replied: "The only thing I should care much to dwell on would be the absolute despair I suffered from of ever being able to achieve anything. No one could ever have felt greater despair. . . ." Her loneliness, her ugliness, her liaison with Lewes, were wounds that no amount of fame could ever heal; and yet only fame could ever heal them. And thus her yearning for glory was sharp and insatiable; she was helplessly and almost mindlessly in its spell. This Comtean apostle of selflessness, this emissary of "the others," was in reality the most self-anxious of the great Victorians. If, after becoming famous, she still entered fictional provincial parlors and remembered the "unhistoric," she was, in part, engaged in a rescue mission, the object of which was herself. True, she liked to insist that "infinite issues" belong to humble, everyday duties; but what her heart told her, what her novels tell us, is that to be obsure is not to be. From Dinah Morris to Daniel Deronda, her heroes and heroines are impelled by one half-admitted desire:

to be famously good. They would shine in the glory of their selflessness. To them, an illustrious achievement is not only visibility, or compensation for sacrifice; it is also the reservoir and guarantee of "significance." For what is life without aspiration? In words from *The Mill on the Floss*: "A narrow, ugly, grovelling existence, which even calamity does not elevate, but rather tends to exhibit in all its bare vulgarity of conception."

To George Eliot, then, nothing could be more desolating than the collapse of aspiration. Not to aspire is to faint in obscurity—to pasture in the grass of a vulgar conception. As a consequence, of the many causes for complaint in *Middlemarch,* the great if inarticulate cause is the ego's insolvency. The gray weather of the novel blows in from the coast of "naked, shivering" selves, from egos experiencing acutely their compulsory need for attention and esteem. In this connection, the decay of Christian therapy makes itself felt on every page, and in Farebrother the minister as much as in Ladislaw the aesthete. Unamuno is right: self-affirmation is the modern hysteria. Alien from its own creations—a loving God, eternity—the ego inhabits a shadow, Death and neglect. If in our day it fidgets, broods, strikes out, turns sour, complains, in George Eliot's time it buckled on its sword and rode out to conquer the world. But whether it asserts itself or collapses in vexation, its problem is the same. Having been emptied of its faiths, it finds itself once again at the starting point: that of a famished need for recognition. Where can it turn for corroboration, for nourishment, for vivification? If not to a loving God, then to love; if not to immortality, then to fame.

This feverish yearning for fame makes George Eliot our contemporary. The substitution of the good opinion of posterity for Christian immortality had been made by the eighteenth-century Philosophers. But not until George Eliot did this post-Christian hunger force its way into the English novel. And then only to be all-consuming: it is the single, the almost secret source of whatever intensity her protagonists display.

Nowhere is this hunger so naked, so uncontrolled, so like being under a possession, as in the Prelude to *Middlemarch*. Here, indeed, like an addict suddenly confronted by what he needs, George Eliot cannot help but betray her weakness—she speaks beyond embarrassment. If ever she had looked into *The Life of Saint Teresa of Avila*, to which the Prelude appears to refer, she had closed it as if dazed by glory. Snow-blinded, envious of a feminine name three hundred years old, George Eliot falsifies everything that she here recalls, evoking Teresa out of her own fantasies of fame. Thus where the real Teresa loved only one country, the Kingdom of God, the Teresa of the Prelude had, as a child, a heart "already beating to a national idea." Where the Teresa of the *Life* is clutching, even terrible, with egoism, George Eliot's Teresa is an angel-minded inanity. In George Eliot's eyes, Teresa's life formed "a constant unfolding of far-resonant action." To the saint herself, however, life was a "disorderly farce," and this, it must be said, is what her conventual reform resembled. Moreover, nothing in this world seemed good to her except "its refusal to tolerate faults in good people, and its way of perfecting them by speaking ill of them." What was fame, what was the opinion of humanity, to her? She was not of this earth, her home was elsewhere, her exile bitter. Why think of this Christian heroine at all in connection with the humanist, Dorothea? Because, whether she had wanted it or not, she won fame.

The Prelude, with its falsifications, is a vestige of the ordinary George Eliot. In the novel itself, her fascination with fame is dry, objective, dramatic: the designation "Study" is honestly earned. Having denied herself for so long, however, she cannot forego sentimental reflection in her Finale; and though her portrait of Dorothea has been clear, her final comment about it is confused. Contemplating her heroine, she is overcome by pathos. Somehow—she cannot say just how—Dorothea has been wronged. And the proof is that she has not won the fame of a Teresa. Generously indignant, George Eliot casts about as if for devils. And yet she does not know where to find them. Though she throws out her net in the Finale of the manuscript, again in that of the first edition, and still again in that of the Cheap edition of 1874,[2] she fails, each time, to bring in a reality. To the charges of the manuscript version—of a "society which smiled on propositions of marriage from a sickly man to a girl less than half his own age" and, in general, self-interested behavior—she adds, in the first edition, the miseducation of women, and hypocrisy. But as reviewers of the novel observed, this indictment has no foundation in the novel itself. Helplessly and vaguely, George Eliot then reduced her criticism, in the second edition, to "the conditions of an imperfect social state." But even this, of course, is wide of the mark. Since Dorothea aspires above all to make the world a better place to live in, an imperfect social state is precisely her opportunity. And how, exactly, could a perfect social state have helped Dorothea? The answer seems to lie in the Prelude: ". . . these later-born Theresas were helped by no coherent social faith and order which could perform the function of knowledge for the ardently willing soul." But socially administered "knowledge," an "epic" life passed out like an assignment—this is not heroism but servitude. And, once again, Teresa, after all, is hardly a relevant comparison. Teresa acted not because faith and order were perfect but in order to give them a perfection they lacked.

The truth is that Dorothea has scarcely any of the courage of a Saint Teresa. Like all George Eliot's heroines, she is weak in self-trust. It is Dorothea's diffidence, combined with the vagueness of her ambition, that accounts for her failure to lead an epic life—she allows her foolish uncle Mr. Brooke, and her conventional brother-in-law Sir James Chettam, to dissuade her from even somewhat less than "epic" actions, such as setting up a model village. In any case, what is the precise reason for the regret that George Eliot expresses in the Finale? Not, it seems,

[2] See Jerome Beaty, "A Study of the Proof," *Middlemarch: Critical Approaches to the Novel,* edited by Barbara Hardy.

the waste of Dorothea's gifts; indeed, what far-reaching actions is Dorothea gifted to perform?. No, what George Eliot resents, what makes her strike out against phantoms, is Dorothea's lack of fame. Many who knew Dorothea, she remarks, "thought it a pity that so substantive and rare a creature should have been absorbed into the life of another, and be only known in a certain circle as wife and mother." To be only known in a certain circle! As wife and mother! The pangs, the emptiness, the comparative vulgarity of an inglorious life—it is this that George Eliot regrets on Dorothea's behalf. Her pity flows unchecked and is almost palpable; for in Dorothea she sees her own worst fears enacted. Never will Dorothea's acts be classed as "historic"; she will rest in an "unvisited" tomb: so the closing words of the novel remind us, as if pointing out some sad and impressive truth.

"There is no sorrow," Dorothea says, "I have thought about more than that—to love what is great, and try to reach it, and yet to fail." And whether or not we sympathize with her somewhat vacuous idealism, her disappointment is affecting. For we —like Dorothea, like the novelist herself—may also feel, indeed we are apt to feel, besieged by personal insignificance in an insignificant world, unconfirmed, unattended, yet anxious, withal, to prove ourselves equal to some unarticulated challenge. However that may be, egoistic disappointment is not restricted in *Middlemarch* to Dorothea alone. It is multiplied throughout the characters. And it is this that gives the novel its powerful identity. Despite the openness of its realism, the book has a marked uniformity of mood. Everywhere there is an impression of abortion, a sense of eggshells downed by wind, a feeling of limbs lopped off. The effort—and failure—of self-monumentalization embraces almost the entire cast. Nearly every important character tries to carve his name on the world—to become as permanent as history, as significant as all mankind.

Dorothea's asset in this attempt on immortality is simply (no doubt too simply) her moral feeling. Indeed, Dorothea, like the novelist herself, has a genius for sympathy, which possesses her and makes her something of a monster. People only exist to her as "objects of rescue"—hence, not until Ladislaw has been treated unfairly does she feel that "sudden strange yearning of the heart." What she seeks in the realm of feeling is a kind of infinity of sympathy, an omnipotent goodness. For this reason, her actual accomplishments—the starting of a village school, and instrumentality in the building of certain cottages—count to her as nothing. Her dreams are grandiose; she would be as absolute as Providence. "I should like," she says, "to make life beautiful—I mean everybody's life." It is, as Lydgate reflects, "as if she wanted nothing for herself but a chair to sit in from which she can look down with those clear eyes at the poor mortals who pray to her." But great feeling cannot be monumentalized without great deeds, and, lacking these, Dorothea fails.

Will Ladislaw also attempts to vault into greatness through feeling—in his case, artistic sensibility, which gives him, he thinks, a "high individual value in the universe." Indeed, Will's conviction of having been summoned to "peculiar work" leaves him with so great a sense of personal significance that it threatens to keep him from doing any work at all. (The novelist treats him, in this connection, with a sympathetic irony.) Circumstances, however, shake Will loose from his sense of his own high value—or perhaps we should say that George Eliot, rescuing him from the field of art, which is mined with immorality, converts him to the nobility of politics. But politics are also, after all, a field for glory, and once translated into them, Will not unexpectedly wonders why he should "not one day be lifted above the shoulders of the crowd, and feel that he had won that eminence well." In the end, however, the novelist, weathered and sober as a headstone, merely remarks that Will worked "well in those times when reforms were begun with a young hopefulness of immediate good which has been much checked in our days. . . ." How it falls, how it continues to fall, she seems to say, that rain of disappointment and insignificance.

By contrast to Ladislaw and Dorothea, Lydgate, the hopeful

young doctor, and Casaubon, the aging scholar, seek to transcend insignificance through the mind. Each is engaged in, as we say, an "ambitious" investigation, the first in the field of biochemistry, the second in the field of mythography. And the reason they are willing to undertake so much is that, where the risk is great, the reward for success must be proportionate: they are speculators in fame. It is "the prospect of living to future ages on earth," "final companionship with the immortals," that drives them on. Yet, in keeping with the temper of the book, neither succeeds in making himself "stupendous"—Lydgate because of the old Adam in himself and others, Casaubon both because of his intellectual provinciality and because he procrastinates, his ego cowering before its own audacity.

For feeling and mind, Bulstrode the banker substitutes power. At once an "eminent Christian" and "prime minister" of Middlemarch, he plays both heaven and earth, Christian immortality and public renown, as a man might play two gaming tables simultaneously. And thus his ego aspires to walk the tightrope of its life insured. Like the other major characters, Bulstrode deliberately pursues a sense of high individual value; and because he really is superior, at least at the game of power, plebeian Middlemarch hounds him out, as it hounds out Lydgate and Dorothea.[3] And as Bulstrode's ego, too, becomes abject, George Eliot extends even to him—to this man of criminally dishonest conscience—the powerful pathos she holds ready for

---

[3] "Locally and socially," writes J. M. S. Tompkins, "Dorothea does not belong to Middlemarch, and is not immersed in its atmosphere. Dorothea is county." (See "A Plea for Ancient Lights," *Middlemarch: Critical Approaches to the Novel*.) It is true that Dorothea is principally discouraged by Sir James Chettam and not by anyone in Middlemarch. But Sir James, in his entrenchment in tradition and in the prosaic, may be said to represent an extension of Middlemarch into the county. Indeed, "Middlemarch" is a ubiquitous element of provincial life, as Dorothea leads us to see when she complains of the social life of the county as "nothing but a labyrinth of petty courses, a walled-in maze of small paths that led nowhither."

those who fail to escape the conviction of personal nullity.
And then on through the list, to parodies and vulgarizations
and lesser outbreaks of personal ambition. As to parody, there
is Mr. Brooke, whose trivial "documents" are the comic counterparts of Casaubon's; like the scholar, Mr. Brooke only talks of
doing something with them. As for vulgar ambition, there is,
to begin with, Rosamond, Lydgate's wife, who strives for "that
middle-class heaven, rank," and thus helps to destroy her husband's higher aspirations; then her brother Fred, who affects
the life of a gentleman and banks on gaining Mr. Featherstone's
property (Fred even practices the flute with "irrepressible hopefulness"); and Featherstone himself, who attempts to perpetuate
his mean power beyond death, through his wills. And the hunger for prominence and permanence that we may see in these
characters crops up even in the more self-effacing characters, like
thistle through cement. Thus though mild Mr. Farebrother is
forced to admit, "The world has been too strong for *me* . . . I
shall never be a man of renown," he cannot resist publishing,
in the "Twadler's Magazine," "small items about a variety of
Aphis Brassicae, with," he ruefully adds, "the well-known sig-
nature of Philomicron." When plain and plain-living Mary
Garth writes a little book for her boys, she has it "printed and
published by Gripps & Co., Middlemarch." Nor does her
humbly situated father, Caleb, quite escape the infection—like
a slight fever, it may be felt in the words: "His early ambition
had been to have as effective a share as possible" in the practical
labor of the world.

To be sure, there are characters outside this charmed circle,
but they are very few indeed. Decisively, we may mention only
Sir James and his wife Celia, both of whom enjoy a kind of
vegetable peace, and Mrs. Garth, who exemplifies the peace of
self-abnegation. Now, without doubt, these two alternative
modes of being held much attraction for the novelist; but finally, I suggest, she is merely grateful that they exist, like places of

shelter in a storm. On the whole, she must agree with Dorothea: "Failure after long perseverance is much grander than never to have a striving good enough to be called a failure." And thus her heart is with her heroes, not with these comforting counterweights.

There is in *Middlemarch*, then, a collapse of both the poetry of social life and the poetry of ambition: a collapse of George Eliot's world of belief. And it is this devastation, so quietly recorded, so selflessly documented, that sets *Middlemarch* apart from and high above her novels of faith. Here, gathering her courage, she walks into the far side of her beliefs, where the community lies heavy as granite and the ego is a famine. She faces the negations of her own fond illusions. The book then would seem to constitute an awakening, and yet, oddly, George Eliot was next to write *Daniel Deronda* in a sleep of forgetting, as if she had never seen the sand behind her mirages. Perhaps this only confirms one impression *Middlemarch* makes: that of being a book that has written itself, a book that merely passed through the novelist. It may be that she never quite realized what escaped her pen. In any case, the isolated and remarkable achievement of this novel in the canon is that here, instead of floating up to the surface, George Eliot touched the bottom, or somewhere very near the bottom, of the nature of the ego and of social life.

There are a few great books that, in their powerful recognition of negations, have the effect of making life appear more precious, of making us feel that the fate of individuals matters more than we had known; and for all its painfulness, indeed because of it, *Middlemarch* is one of these books. No other novel has ever shown so much comprehension of the agonies of personal insignificance. True, it is with a wholly characteristic moralism that George Eliot writes in *Middlemarch*: "We are all of us born in moral stupidity, taking the world as an udder to feed our supreme selves." But in none of her other novels does

she appear so much to regret that the self is not, in fact, supreme, and that only the world may be said to be "stupendous."
And nothing reveals this new sympathy for the individual so
wonderfully as Dorothea's elopement with Ladislaw. Involving,
as it does, a defiance of public opinion, it breaks through the ice
of that social timidity which otherwise encases this novelist's
work. In *Daniel Deronda*, it is true, Catherine Arrowsmith will
defy Mammon in the persons of her parents; but Dorothea does
a braver thing—she throws off "the opinion of everyone connected with her."

So it is that *Middlemarch* counters—and excels because it
counters—George Eliot's other books. With the exception of
The Mill on the Floss (which, however, finally unravels into
self-indulgence), it is the only novel of George Eliot's that leads
us, in Benjamin's phrase, into "the profound perplexity of the
living." Only *Middlemarch* among her novels colonizes the
desert of actuality—where, paradoxically, the novel most thrives,
providing always that it had been looking for water. And in
ceasing thus to be ingrown and "emotive," George Eliot becomes, for the only time in her novels, a major poet, and a poet
of the most difficult kind: a realistic poet.[4] It is chiefly as her
"poetic" ideals suffer outrage and death that they partake in a
genuine poetry; it is then that they move feeling and command
imagination. *Middlemarch* is poetic because it renounces the
"poetic" in pain.

The "poetry of realism," observes Ortega, lies in "the force
of attraction which reality exercises over meteor-like ideals."
And certainly what stirs us in literary realism is, in part, its
night of falling stars. There would seem to be also, however, a
poetry in the night itself—a separate pleasure and interest. Just
as the night brings out the brightness of meteors, so meteors,
once they have vanished, bring out the power of the darkness,

[4] In *Silas Marner*, she is a minor poet of another kind, a fabulist.

which seems to increase and press the heavier upon us. So, too, the dynamism of the realistic novel appears to lie not only in the collapse of the poetic but in the emerging utterness of reality itself.

The beauty and power of *Middlemarch*, at any rate, resides as much in its commitment to the truth as in its devotion to a doomed idealism. Everywhere within it we feel the force of an absolute: we touch reality. And this absoluteness results not only from a truthful intention combined with an astonishing vigor of observation but also from a fundamental asceticism of method. As *Middlemarch* registers drop by drop the formation of an immense stalagmite of disillusionment, it calls no distracting attention to itself. Its patient documentary procedure amounts to both aesthetic courage and aesthetic humility. In effect the book is all vehicle, all medium, all transparency: dead to itself. And this must be said even in the face of the vast formal mining to which it has recently been subjected.[5] For what does it matter, after all, that *Middlemarch* contains sharp contrasts, summary metaphors, stitches of imagery—numerous devices? The significant thing is that, like chameleons, these are merged in the color of their subject. To the natural gaze the novel wears no aesthetic garment, only the hair shirt of the world.

There is an utterness, then, both in the findings and in the procedure of *Middlemarch*. And it is this that gives the book its pre-eminence among English novels. Beside it, the rest of English fiction appears—fictitious. And this is true even of novels that also bear *Quixote* with them: by comparison *Great Expectations*, for instance, is half fairy tale, and *Vanity Fair* a spree of humor and style. These and other works are rich in imagina-

[5] See, for example, *Middlemarch: Critical Approaches to the Novel*, where, in the essays by Derek Oldfield, Hilda M. Hulme, and Barbara Hardy, formal analysis moves into the smallest veins of the book. Mark Schorer's well-known emphasis on metaphor, continued here in an essay called "Method, Metaphor and Mind," is another case in point.

tion; *Middlemarch* is rich in reality. Or such is the impression it masterfully gives; for *Middlemarch* is in fact rich, of course, in the imagination of reality. Yet when we read about the problems of Lydgate's marriage or about Casaubon's "inward trouble" or about Bulstrode's public fall, it does not occur to us that these are imagined realities. For here the imagination seems as absolute as reality itself. And when the imagination has attained this bareness and directness, we can no longer think of it as simply aesthetic. Having arrived at the real through a kind of heroic submission, its quality is moral and philosophical as well. It is the mind in its negative fullness.

IV.   *George Eliot and D. H. Lawrence:*
Either / Or

In his book *D. H. Lawrence: Novelist*, F. R. Leavis asserts, as an "important truth," that "Lawrence belongs to the same ethical and religious tradition as George Eliot." Thus in the opening scenes of *The Rainbow*, Leavis explains, "George Eliot would have recognized the known and poignantly familiar. . . ." But what, exactly, is "important" in this? The common "tradition" it implicates is scarcely more than geographical. It tells us, not what these writers "belong" to, but what they had absorbed in their youth—what, in a sense, belongs to them. The truth is that George Eliot would have viewed the life at Marsh Farm through a lens entirely foreign to Lawrence's—a lens different, precisely, because it *was* ethical.

Here is a portion of the opening chapter of *The Rainbow*:

It was enough for the men, that the earth heaved and opened its furrow to them, that the wind blew to dry the wet wheat, and set the young ears of corn wheeling freshly round about; it was enough that they helped the cow in labour, or ferreted the rats from under the barn, or broke the back of a rabbit with a sharp knock of the hand. So much warmth and generating and pain and death did they know in their blood, earth and sky and beast and green plants, so much exchange and interchange they had with these, that they lived full and surcharged, their senses full fed, their faces always turned to the heat of the blood, staring into the sun, dazed with looking towards the source of generation, unable to turn round.

Here, if we cannot miss the final hint of limitation, neither can we miss the marvellous sympathy with the subject—evident from the pure and vigorous aesthetic immediacy of the passage, the "exchange and interchange" of the echoing phrases, their dazed rhythmic movement, so evidently unable to spring forward, "to turn round." Clearly the impulse in this writing is not "ethical" but aesthetic and religious. It is aesthetic in that it courts and loves and preserves appearances. And it is religious in the sense that it reveals familiarity—the sort of knowledge that cannot be faked—with a tremendous longing to merge into the world. Indeed, it is just the restriction that "surcharged" senses impose on mystical union that accounts for the note of judgment in the closing words.

Here, by contrast, is a portion of the opening chapter of *Adam Bede*, "The Workshop":

> *"Let all thy converse be sincere,*
> *Thy conscience as the noonday clear."*

Such a voice could only come from a broad chest, and the broad chest belonged to a large-boned muscular man nearly six feet high, with a back so flat and a head so well poised that when he drew himself up to take a more distant survey of his work, he had the air of a soldier standing at ease. The sleeve rolled up above the elbow showed an arm that was likely to win the prize for feats of strength; yet the long supple hand, with its broad finger-tips, looked ready for works of skill. . . . The face was large and roughly hewn, and when in repose had no other beauty than such as belongs to an expression of good-humoured honest intelligence.

Here the original and dominant thrust is obviously neither aesthetic nor religious, but ethical. Everything in the passage has a kind of ethical transparency. Each sense impression advances directly to its consummation in an ethical judgment. Adam's rolled-up sleeve displays, not the beauty of power, but its utility in the contest of life; his rough face has a moral radiance that by implication outshines beauty; even his repose bespeaks the discipline of "a soldier standing at ease"; and so on. Here appearances have been lifted out of the matrix of experience—have been cleansed, freed, and organized by an ethical principle of selection. In keeping, the sentences have the sort of purpose and composure attributed to Adam. The only aesthetic operative in this is, in Kant's phrase, an "aesthetic of morals."

What these laboratory tests indicate is that it is superficial, at best, to think of Lawrence and George Eliot as belonging to the same ethical and religious tradition—or, for that matter, to the same tradition of the novel.[1] The truth is that where George Eliot belongs to an ethical but not to a religious tradition, Lawrence belongs to a religious but not to an ethical tradition: George Eliot is with Paul and Kempis on their ethical side, Lawrence with Blake and a long line of mystical vitalists.[2] Leavis himself virtually acknowledges this difference when, alluding to a remark of Lord David Cecil's, he observes: "It has been said of George Eliot, by way of a limiting judgment, that the word for her is 'ethical' rather than 'religious.' This could not have been said of Lawrence, and a great difference lies there." A great difference indeed.

There is, to be sure, a sense in which George Eliot is "religious" and Lawrence "ethical." We find the measure of the first in a phrase from *Daniel Deronda*: "the sacred word duty." George Eliot gave to the ethical life the ultimate commitment of her fate, the kind of faith that a Savonarola or a Saint Teresa gives to God. Lawrence, on the other hand, displayed in his very scorn of morality the sort of concern that we naturally think of as ethical. More, Lawrence was as anxious as George Eliot that human conduct be "good" and not "evil." "This we know, now, for good and all," he writes in "Him with His Tail in His Mouth": "that which is good, and moral, is that which brings into us a stronger, deeper flow of life and life-energy: evil is that which impairs the life-flow."

And yet if George Eliot is "religious," it is about morality;

[1] See F. R. Leavis, *The Great Tradition*.
[2] For a summary account of mystical vitalism, see Chapter II in *Mysticism*, by Evelyn Underhill (Cleveland: Meridian Books, 1955).

and if Lawrence is "ethical," it is in the interest of the sacred. The two writers represent distinct categories of the human spirit. It was in morality that George Eliot believed; of life itself she was shudderingly skeptical. Conversely, Lawrence believed in life, and in its name contemned morality. The term "moral" or "ethical" denotes in both Lawrence and George Eliot, as in ethical discourse generally, the principled control of life by mind. And yet it is just the fashioning of life "from the mind, downwards" that Lawrence set himself to oppose, to correct. Lawrence could not help fearing the very concept of the ethical.

Lawrence's novella *The Virgin and the Gypsy* illustrates his frequently burning sense of the *sacrilege* of the ethical. The heroine, Yvette Saywell, having "borrowed" money that she had collected for a church window, is angrily censured by her father, the parson of the church involved: " 'You *would* do the large with somebody else's money, wouldn't you?' he said, with a cold, mongrel sort of sneer. . . ." This is, in essence, the kind of moral offense that we meet with everywhere in George Eliot— this "reckless" disregard of principle and others' rights. Of course George Eliot herself would respond, not with the cold ethical sneer of a Reverend Saywell, but with a quite overpowering and charismatic sympathy: George Eliot would deluge "poor" Yvette with pity. The point to grasp, however, is that Lawrence would find the pity only slightly less unacceptable than the sneer. To his mind, it would not exactly "defile" the "sanctity" of the "sensitive, clean flesh and blood," as Mr. Saywell's sneer is said to do; but, patronizing and "forgiving," it would deny it nonetheless. It would reveal that George Eliot, like Yvette's father, was "an utter unbeliever . . . at the heart."[3] "They were the life unbelievers," Yvette concludes of the Say-

---

[3] Thus Hetty Sorrel's "spring-tide beauty," "the beauty of young frisky things, round-limbed, gambolling, circumventing you by a false air of innocence," is not "sanctity," only trouble: ". . . people who love downy peaches are apt not to think of the stone, and sometimes jar their teeth terribly against it."

wells. And, shifting her allegiance to her sensual "pride in life," she herself becomes a "moral unbeliever."

"Life unbelievers" versus "moral unbelievers"—humanity falls into these groups in both George Eliot and Lawrence. But the sheep and the goats are just the opposite in each case. They are not, to be sure, quite the *same* sheep and goats. For George Eliot's "moral unbelievers" are usually mean and Lawrence's glorious, while her "life unbelievers" are usually saintly, and Lawrence's "mongrel." Even this difference, however, serves only to reveal the deep and contrary bias of their worlds.

George Eliot and Lawrence do indeed resemble each other, but with the abstract resemblance of opposites. They are alike as cold and heat are alike—ironically alike in their contrasting extremity. Each had a temperament evangelical and fervent; only they were evangelical about opposite things. Each demonstrated, over and over, that but one cast of being could find favor with Justice; yet where the one would deny all direct desire, the other would deny all sublimation. Both deplored the wormy complacency, the devastating folly, of the ego—but judged the ego, nonetheless, in mutually exclusive courts of law. And though each held aloft, in his fiction, the chalice of an ideal human character, the chalices were of contrary shapes and consecrated to antithetical communions.

The truth is that Lawrence simply turned upside down George Eliot's tablet of values. Where George Eliot flees from Being, Lawrence runs toward it. Be charitable, says the first; be fertile, inveighs the second. George Eliot's refrain is "Renounce and Worship Sorrow"; Lawrence's is "Have the Courage to Be." To George Eliot an early death was salvation; to Lawrence, on the other hand, "Nothing is important but life." Principle as against Impulse, Self-Annihilation as against Integral Being, Ethical Generosity as against Mystical Wonder: such are the Commandments that rule their opposite worlds.

George Eliot—one with her age, in fact its moral spokesman—accepted the view that we must lose the natural life before we can participate in the spiritual one. Lawrence, harmonious with his age if not quite its spokesman, rejects this view. To him the natural and the spiritual, in isolation from each other, spell death; the two of them together make up "the whole man alive." "The blood," writes Lawrence in "A Propos of 'Lady Chatterley's Lover,'" "is the substance of the soul, and of the deepest consciousness." Here "knowing and being, or feeling, are one and undivided: no serpent and no apple has caused a split." So we lose our very souls if we participate in the natural or the spiritual alone. When "the relation between the senses and the outspoken mind" falls to nothing, Birkin reflects in *Women in Love*, then "the soul in intense suffering breaks . . . ," and "we lapse from pure integral being, from creation and liberty. . . ." The "blood" soul is the estuary where the separate streams of the body and spirit merge into the divine. "If we look for God, let us look in the bush where he sings."

We must not, however, rest with the easy view that Lawrence is himself a novelist of "the whole man alive." "The Bible," he writes in "Why the Novel Matters," "—but *all* the Bible—and Homer, and Shakespeare: these are the supreme old novels. These are all things to all men." But is any novel of Lawrence's, are all of them together, "all things to all men"? Or are they not, rather, for all the beauty of the world that they haul alive into their pages, for all the heat of the blood that warms their style, peculiar and eccentric? There is in all Lawrence's writing a glint of strangeness. And, indeed, it is impossible even to speak of his concept of wholeness, as we have just done in connection with the "blood," without triggering a suspicion of anomaly— of a man who writes from outside our common human experience. Doubtless it is in *genius* that Lawrence is off-center; and there is nothing to boast of in common human experience. All the same, we cannot say of Lawrence, as of Shakespeare or Homer, that his books convey intact and untroubled an image of the whole man alive.

"In all this wild welter" of living, Lawrence says, "we need some sort of guide." And for this, he adds, nothing is so useful as the novel, "the one bright book of life"; nothing else portrays or involves so fully the whole man alive. If Lawrence's own novels are untrustworthy guides, the reason is his restlessness before the natural world—that world which he yet attended to more freshly and keenly than any English novelist before him. Lawrence liked to say that "life itself . . . is the reason for living," but he wrote, increasingly, as if going "beyond" were the only end of being. His spirit was always in a ripple, and its ripples extended, or fought to extend, indefinitely. And because Lawrence's novels are, in large part, Lawrence himself, saturated in his sensibility and seething with his needs, what we find in them is "whole man alive" refracted through the dazzling but distorting diamond of mysticism. Far from being free, as it is in Homer and Shakespeare, life, in them, is strangely bonded to the Absolute.

Listen not "to the didactic statements of the author," Lawrence advises in "The Novel and the Feelings," "but to the low, calling cries of the characters, as they wander in the dark woods of their destiny." And if we listen to the cries of Lawrence's characters, we must wonder at how peculiar they are, how anguished in their longing. The characters who matter most to Lawrence himself are all like the Ursula who, in *The Rainbow*, stands "at the edge of the solid, flashing body of the sea," crying in "a strong, dominant voice," "I want to go. I want to go." We read and prize Lawrence for such an effortlessly vital picture as "the solid, flashing body of the sea," and for the vibrant and glistening spectacle that his characters provide no matter how "inhuman" or unheard-of their actions. But we do not, I think, read him for the lifelikeness or representative quality of his cast (though it is true that the more one reads a novel like *Women in Love*, the more ordinary the characters come to seem). Lawrence is exotic, like Van Gogh, and his cypresses swirl equally in the stress of an invisible storm.

George Eliot's books were, she said, "carefully constructed" on her "conviction as to the relative goodness and nobleness of human dispositions and motives." ". . . the inspiring principle" that alone gave her "courage to write," she added, is "that of so presenting our human life as to help . . . readers in getting a clearer conception and a more active admiration of those vital elements which bind men together and give a higher worthiness to their existence." Yet is this not as much as to confess that her dice are loaded? In view of it, we can scarcely wonder that her novels fail to give us a sense of the whole man alive. They fall, in throw after throw, on the side of the "social right" and the "nobler emotions." They are teaching tools by intention, not primarily works of art.

The aim of Lawrence's novels, it happens, is also that of binding together, only in this case the elements are all the particles of the world. Each novelist ached to lose himself, to shake off his self-burden and isolation, in some glorious "divinely-guided whole." In Lawrence, however, the need for otherness or wholeness was mystical. And because Lawrence's mysticism was vital in kind, his books are more easily works of art than George Eliot's. Unlike the Victorian novelist's ethical "conviction," Lawrence's mysticism is not applied to life but rather works through it, as a fever works through the flesh. The didacticism in his books is secondary and, as it were, grabbed from out of the darkness—which is not to say, however, that it is never insistent. And yet Lawrence's mystical intuition was in its way as "peremptory" as any dogma, and it kept him from becoming the sort of writer whose great usefulness he rightly celebrated: a writer of sanely appealing balance and wholeness.

As George Eliot's defect as a novelist was her compulsive pursuit of the "social right," so Lawrence's was his pursuit of "the knowledge which is the death of knowledge"—a subject to the other extreme of the novel's range and competency. Lawrence's formula for "the whole consciousness in a man"—"bodily, mental, spiritual at once"—might at first blush seem perfect for the novel. In fact, however, it issues not in the wholeness we find in

Shakespeare and Homer and Tolstoy but in the wholeness of the infant or the mystic, the wholeness of an unlimited ego.

Lawrence complained, famously, that what ailed him was "the absolute frustration" of his "primitive societal instinct"; and he added, "I think societal instinct much deeper than the sex instinct." Yet Lawrence seems to have had in mind, not the social relations we normally think of as "societal," but that "infinite" knowing of "the world in togetherness with ourselves" that, thanks to Freud, we sometimes speak of as "oceanic." Lawrence continues: "There is no repression of the sexual individual comparable to the repression of the societal man in me, by the individual ego, my own and everybody else's. I am weary even of my own individuality, and simply nauseated by other people's." No wonder Lawrence's Birkin makes haste to pronounce the "I" a dead letter—amusingly, in view of its vigorous persistence in Birkin and, of course, in Lawrence himself. So strong was Lawrence's desire to escape what he called the "menace" of being separate, hence "over against" others, that he was as wishfully blind about the ego's strength and necessary part in "the whole man alive" as George Eliot was about its continuance in the social man.

With the intellect itself, as distinct from the ego, George Eliot had no quarrel, so long, at any rate, as it listened to the heart. "In proportion as I love every form of piety—which is venerating love," she wrote, "—I hate hard curiosity": yet she found it not inconsistent to be the best informed woman of her times. Indeed, it was in the rational philosophy of Positivism that she found, as it were, the ally and wrathful God of "venerating love": "that invariability of sequence," in words quoted before, "which is acknowledged to be the basis of physical science, but which is still perversely ignored in our social organization, our ethics and our religion." Of Lawrence, too, it may be said that he tolerated intellect so long as it shored up his venerating loves. But in Lawrence the intellect is merely a light to show the way; once the way has been glimpsed, the light becomes superfluous

—"the knowledge that is the death of knowledge" lies beyond the mind's poor tired beams.

Lawrence's ambivalence toward the mind often resolves into hostility. " 'Knowledge' has killed the sun," he writes, "making it a ball of gas, with spots; 'knowledge' has killed the moon. . . ." The "abstracted mind inhabits" a "dry and sterile little world," has knowledge only in a "pettifogging *apartness.*" Clearly it is time, Lawrence thinks, to have done with knowing "which is mental, rational, scientific" and turn to "knowing in terms of togetherness, which is religious and poetic." After all, "the Word is uttered, most of it; we have only to pay true attention." In fact, we have only to listen "inwards . . . to the lowing of the innermost beasts, the feelings, that roam in the forest of the blood." "The true self is not aware that it is a self"; it just *is.* And so it comes about that Lawrence would effectively take us back not only past the development of the ego to infancy, but past the development of human intelligence to instinct. The ego and the intellect: formidable blocks of stone to clear out before erecting an ideal human character!

For all that he writes in the name of self-fulfillment, Lawrence is thus no less extreme, no less a partisan of a mere portion of the self, than George Eliot. Indeed, it is precisely their fervor for what does not come naturally, for what must be forced out of "the whole man alive," that gives them their common evangelical tone.

To buttress their compulsive preference for an unnatural form of the self, Lawrence and Eliot each subscribed to an absolute either/or. Each became a novelist of Nemesis and inexorable law. The Bulstrodes, Melemas, and Grandcourts of George Eliot's pages have their counterparts in the Skrebenskys the Criches, the Ricos of Lawrence's. In each *oeuvre* egoists are impaled by the stake of Inevitability, and either left squirming or finished off. Severely, each world gives support to only one way of life. To attempt a different way is to step into quicksand.

In George Eliot, as we have seen, the Furies cry down and

harrow those who care for their own and not for others' gain. Should a man even inadvertently raise his fist at the "will of other men," which is "the same thing" as the will of God, the novelist's lightning, if not God's, will strike him. "Poor Hetty's vision of consequences," writes George Eliot two-thirds of the way through *Adam Bede*, "at no time more than a narrow fantastic calculation of her own probable pleasures and pains, was now quite shut out by reckless irritation under present suffering, and she was ready for one of those convulsive, motiveless actions by which wretched men and women leap from a temporary sorrow into a life-long misery." From this point on we know that Hetty is doomed—doomed by her author's set convictions, if not by life. Once we are on to George Eliot, we scarcely need to finish the novel to know that the "pretty thing" will die, obscurely, a "poor wanderer." Despite George Eliot's solemn, weighted, and often penetrating intellection, her basic mentality, as this instance suggests, was that of a prophet—simplified, overalarmed, inflexible.

And no less is this true of Lawrence, whose "vision of consequences" could be equally bullying. The great apocalyptic example of this, of course, is the "dark" half of the plot of *Women in Love*, in which the whole of Northern Europe, brought to a demonic focus in Gerald Crich and Gudrun Brangwen, is burning itself out, spectacularly, in a "black" ecstasy of destruction. Here, too, most men are recklessly "shut out," in George Eliot's words, from a "good strong terrible vision," because, in Lawrence's, they are "hideous with egoism." Where a Hetty Sorrel is piteously isolated from the "divinely-guided whole" of (no more and no less than) the community of Hayslope, a Gerald and a Gudrun, incestuously locked upon themselves, are adrift from the great vital current of Being. So even though Gudrun—high in the snow valley of the Alps, the symbolic cul-de-sac of the Egoistic Way—*knows* "how immortally beautiful" the peaks of snow are, "great pistils of rose-coloured, snow-fed fire in the blue twilight of the heaven," she is yet "not of it" but "divorced, debarred, a soul shut out." And so Gerald, seeing a "half-buried Crucifix" at the head of the same valley, feels that he is "murdered" by it, doomed by what in "A Propos of 'Lady Chatterley's Lover' " his author calls the "tragic" Christian epoch; and Gerald can but wander on "unconsciously" till something breaks "in his soul" and he falls "to sleep."

In both George Eliot and Lawrence, then, the penalty for missing the eye of the needle is that of falling away, in desolate disconnection, from the divine coherence of being. Both writers constitute a sort of Terror or police of the soul. Each himself in desperate need of being saved—George Eliot from guilt, Lawrence from the fear of being separated from his mother—each became a salvationist in his fiction, as if hoping, each time a new novel was begun, that *this* time he would himself be converted by his message.

As I have suggested, it is refuge in the "whole" that George Eliot and Lawrence were both seeking. Their fictional worlds, still more their views of the world, are contrary ways of escaping the same thing, the palpitating center of suffering in the human being. Whether through a social transcendence or a vital transcendence of the ego, the novelists seek a common end. And yet how troubled, in each, is the attempt at escape itself; for what they would forsake, they also require.

". . . it makes the mind very free," states Maggie Tulliver, "when we give up wishing and only think of bearing what is laid upon us, and doing what is given us to do." And so, innocent of the pain involved, Maggie grasps eagerly "the clue to life" that she finds in Thomas à Kempis: that of "taking her stand outside herself, safe from the boiling pit of her "illimitable wants" and "evil perturbations." And yet, significantly, Maggie does not find peace. Like George Eliot herself, she is too much alive to pretend to be dead. And rather than leave her in the coffin of St. Ogg, George Eliot (following her usual impulse to rejoin her own estranged family vicariously in her fiction) sends her to the bottom of the Floss locked in her brother's arms. The peculiar interest of *The Mill on the Floss* in George Eliot's canon is thus that it pits against the "divine" imperative to exclude the natural self the *impossibility* of such exclusion, at least in a full-blooded nature. The book confesses rather helplessly to the infeasibility of the either/or that it yet insists upon throughout—so that it appropriately ends with the heroine's death, as if only there would the gates of things give way to her. It is a flawed and perverse but deeply truthful work.

Lawrence's characters, also, desire peace above all. Deep carnal peace, a lovely sleep of the mind—such is their mastering wish. ". . . I hate ecstasy, Dionysic or any other," Birkin says to Ursula. "It's like going round in a squirrel cage. I want you not to care about yourself . . .—be glad and sure and indifferent." But of course it is as hard to be indifferently oneself as to take a stand outside of oneself, and when Lawrence's characters are believable they are anything but "glad and sure": they are Sisphysus shouldering the stone of their own mystical desire—as George Eliot's nobler characters, when believable, are shouldering the stone of what is supposed to make "the mind very free." Lawrence, too, was to confess that only death could give his characters the degree—though not the kind—of reprieve they want. Starting out ambivalently with a longing for a dead mother who yet represents "life," his work resigns itself increasingly to the seductions of the world "beyond." ". . . creative life," Lawrence wrote in "The Reality of Peace," "is the attaining a perfect consummation with death." And perhaps he meant as much, or almost as much, as he said.

The novels of George Eliot and Lawrence thus stand, in part, as their own refutations. They themselves reveal what is unreasonable in their excesses. There is, then, truth to the claim both writers make that the novel is the surest guide to life—in George Eliot's words because it represents "life in its highest complexity," in Lawrence's because it reveals "the changing rainbow of our living relationships." For all that, the bias these novelists give to "relationships," the lies they tell when they try to quash complexity, must be deplored, since these are of no help either to life or to art. Because of them, the books of George Eliot and Lawrence are not quite the "bright" things they might have been. They are expressions not only of their author's great strengths but also of their fatuities and weaknesses. They harbor special pleading; they bespeak failures of nerve.

It is true that the intensity we respond to in both novelists depends in part upon their weaknesses as human beings: without their suspect fervor, would they have become so great? It is also true that, despite themselves, so to speak, George Eliot gave us in *Middlemarch* and Lawrence in *Sons and Lovers* and *Women in Love* supreme examples of the art of the novel. Obviously any regret we feel cannot go far; the rock of their real achievement will shatter and survive it. What a pity it is, though, that the ideal of human character that sweeps through each of these writers' works should represent, as much in the one case as in the other, a reduction of our full humanity.

PART TWO

D. H. Lawrence

V. *The Vital Self*

Nineteenth-century English novelists submitted, on the whole, to the dry world shrinkage of positivism. Their Christianity, where it obtained, was likely to be the echo, not the genuine cry, of faith. Jane Austen, Thackeray, Dickens, George Eliot, Meredith, Hardy—all relinquished the eternal in an attempt to take hold of the temporal; all were empiricists of human life. By mid-century the metaphysical hunger and ferment of the Romantics had all but disappeared. No wonder G. K. Chesterton found it necessary to complain, in 1905, that "everything matters—except everything." "The modern idea," Chesterton wrote in *Heretics,* "is that cosmic truth is so unimportant that it cannot matter what anyone says." By 1905, however, Shaw's *Man and Superman* had already been written, and Forster's explorations into a "terrible" and "mysterious" reality were under way: the Romantic appetite for the infiniteness of the cosmos was at that very moment being reborn. In Lawrence, Forster, and Virginia Woolf, in Yeats and Shaw, British literature was once again to open itself to wonder, to let in the stars.

It was in Lawrence's work above all that the eternal made inroads into the temporal, tearing up nineteenth-century skepticism and nearly tearing up the novels as well. No one else could approach Lawrence, in those early, metaphysically anarchic decades of the century, in the vigor and drama and urgency of his belief. Here was a prophet, not out of the pages of history, but, of all things, in the Café Royal, in Taos, in Oaxaca—a prophet very much in the flesh. He did not belong, and he was not understood. Yet nothing could shake his certainty and his mission. Almost alone in this century, Lawrence enjoyed the forgotten luxury, and labored under the responsibility, of a metaphysical conviction.

It is curious how Lawrence's critics have held back from granting him his great fundamental certainty. Bewildered, perhaps, by the secondary inconsistencies so rife in his work, by the absolute tone of each partial statement—perhaps driven, too, by the notion that they are "saving" Lawrence's art from ideas—they tend to see him as lacking, in William Troy's words, "some cohesive view of the universe wholly absorbed in the personality" and to regard his works as "records of the successive steps taken by his mind in the effort to discover for himself some such view." The truth, however, is that there was nothing but coherence for Lawrence. When Lawrence said, for example, that everything lies in *being*," he spoke sincerely, religiously, categorically. It was intuition, however, not intellectual argument, that told him this was so. And, cohesive in itself, his intuition cast a philosophical shadow that was also to prove cohesive, for all the broken appearance it took on from the changing planes of Lawrence's mind. What sets Lawrence's work apart from that of his great contemporaries, what makes it so strange and yet so compelling, is precisely its anachronistic passion and certitude, the way Lawrence was immersed in it, breathing it like an atmosphere. If there is anything "successive" in his work, it is his effort to unfold an intuitive assurance already known, to lay it *finally* bare, and to capture the satisfactions that seemed to be inherent in it.

What has yet to be noted is how Lawrence's metaphysic

sprang from and, indeed, *was* his experience—and also how it answered to poignant psychological needs. Here was a man who believed—unaccountably, it seemed—that there is in the universe a "principle towards which man turns religiously—a *life* of the universe itself." And yet instead of appearing to be toying with metaphysics, he seemed, on the contrary, to be burning with faith. His world-uniting and world-revering belief glowed in everything he wrote, and constituted his mission. He spoke, not at a venture, but from the pulpit of a certitude. How does a man come upon so much conviction? Surely not at the behest of intellect. We must, I think, discount Troy's opinion that it was "undoubtedly" in reaction "against the scientific rationalism of the later nineteenth century" that Lawrence "plunged himself into the most abject nature-mysticism." The mind cannot do so much. Lawrence reacted, certainly, against scientific rationalism; but he reacted because of his mysticism, not into it. Lawrence's mysticism was a natural—or, as one prefers, an unnatural —involuntary growth. "It is not really helpful," Troy writes, "to be told by psychoanalysts that he suffered from one or another malady. . . ." On the contrary, Lawrence cannot be understood apart from his maladies. "Physical belief" of the kind that drove him can spring, like a geyser, only from subterranean pressures. And in Lawrence "physical belief" was, it would seem, the same as mystical belief. It is safe to guess—and, as we shall see, the records confirm—that something in Lawrence's notoriously strained filial experience, in combination with his exquisitely fluid sensibility, gave rise in him to a propensity to mysticism—to that whole world of "marvelous" feeling that would later crystallize into his rainbow-sensuous yet profoundly metaphysical world view. And thus it happens that to find the union of the man and his faith we would do well to look, not to his intellectual history, but to the point where his emotion finally bursts into the fire of his thought.

It is in *Sons and Lovers*, as I read it, that this conflagration first occurs. The book affords the rare opportunity of observing the genesis of an aesthetic metaphysical vision. And this genesis is not only of keen psychological interest in itself; it also provides a key to Lawrence's later development.

Alfred Kazin nearly puts his hand on this key when—in his fine introduction to the Modern Library edition of the novel—he notes that Lawrence's motive as a writer was his attempt to re-create "the mutual sympathy he had experienced with his mother." Kazin, however, goes awry when he adds that this "ecstasy . . . never congealed into a single . . . idol or belief." In fact, it congealed into a metaphysic that was to become the mainstay of Lawrence's fiction. After *Sons and Lovers,* especially, the universe Lawrence lived in, and wrote in so beautifully, was but the glowing flesh or, at worst, the eternally renewed promise of the mystical self-dispersal that Lawrence had known with his mother. Both belief and idol, it was a universe of apotheosized feeling.

This burgeoning of psychology into metaphysics is the hidden drama of *Sons and Lovers.* If it is easy to miss, the reason is that the oedipal drama, with its crackling tensions and dilemmas, is the foreground in a novel that is, after all, almost entirely foreground. Consisting, as it does, of a few scattered paragraphs, the metaphysic of *Sons and Lovers* might seem merely incidental—musings in the intervals of the oedipal conflict. Indeed, Lawrence presents it as scarcely more than incidental. In reality, however, it constitutes, not a digression from the psychological dilemma, but precisely its solution—insofar, that is, as it was to admit of one.

On the oedipal plane itself we find an impasse, a crippling relationship too powerful to overcome. Paul Morel cannot desire where he loves; and he cannot love where he desires. Body and soul will not conjoin. His soul is bonded to his mother's, irrevocably; his body, however, "mad with restlessness," urges him "towards something else." Yet with neither the refined and thoughtful Miriam nor the robust and sensual Clara does Paul manage to free himself from his mother. He only appears to travel from her, as a man in a snowstorm, wandering in a circle, only supposes he is leaving the scene of his despair.

Sensing Paul's misery, Mrs. Morel grows tired and takes ill; and both Paul and his mother hope, even as they fear, that her death will free him at last to "really love another woman." His life has been "like a circle where life turned back on itself"—his mother "bore him, loved him, kept him, and his love turned back into her." But Mrs. Morel's death fails to break the circle: ". . . his soul could not leave her, wherever she was. Now she was gone abroad into the night, and he was with her still." So we learn from the last page of the book.

Even though dead, Mrs. Morel holds Paul "up, himself." His identity, then, is somehow one with hers. She, however, has gone "abroad in the night"; hence it is with the vast night, much as it terrifies him, that Paul must now begin to feel connected. His mother has passed into the world; will not the world now "be" his mother? "So instead of a release and a deliverance from bondage, the bondage was glorified and made absolute": thus, shrewdly, Jessie Chambers, the original of the Miriam of the novel. " . . . Lawrence handed his mother the laurels of victory," she added. Indeed he did; but it was on the "living" universe that he placed the laurels. His bond with his mother came to be his bond with time and space and with whatever might lie "beyond."

As Daniel Weiss, Frank O'Connor, and others have shown, Freudian theory accounts for a good deal of Paul's story. Indeed, Freud's "The Most Prevalent Form of Degradation in Erotic Life" reads almost like a direct comment on Lawrence's brave and stunning book. And doubtless Lawrence's own connection with his mother, like Paul's, could not easily have been more "oedipal" than it was; it was a classic case. Yet Freudian theory does not explain enough. It leaves untouched the strength of Paul's connection with his mother, the iron in it, and the ease with which it passes, at her death, and indeed (as we shall see) before it, into a mystical worship of the world.

Lawrence's bond with his mother was—no other word—mystical. And it was this, I believe, that made it the unalterable and magically strengthening bond that it was. It was this that made it the seed of a mystical vitalism. Lawrence described this aspect of the relationship in a letter sent to Rachel Annand Taylor in December, 1910:

We knew each other by instinct. She said to my aunt—about me:
"But it has been different with him. He has seemed to be part of me."—And that is the real case. We have been like one, so sensitive to each other that we never needed words. It has been rather terrible and has made me, in some respects, abnormal.
I think this *peculiar fusion of soul* . . . never comes twice in a life-time—*it doesn't seem natural*. When it comes it seems to distribute one's consciousness far abroad from oneself, and one undertands! I think no one has got "Understanding" except through love. (My italics.)

Lawrence concluded: "Nobody can have the soul of me. My mother has had it, and nobody can have it again. Nobody can come into my very self again, and breathe me like an atmosphere."

This letter, so bleak and absolute, has the uncompromising accents of truth. And surely what it reveals is that, whatever else it may have been, Lawrence's bond with his mother was mystical: a shaft into revelation, a numinous enlargement of self. So absolute was it that, Lawrence believed, there could be no going beyond it. Nor could merely personal or, for that matter, sexual relationships seem anything but desolation by comparison. No wonder Paul cannot be satisfied with Miriam or Clara, that he is always wanting "something else." And no wonder his mother seems to him the "pivot" of everything: the "one place in the world that . . . did not melt into unreality." There in the past, so Lawrence must always have felt, was the farthest reach that his soul could go. Why should he then try to break out of the "circle"?

The true problem, rather, was to bring his body into it. This he could not do, of course, so long as his mother was the obvious "pivot" of his soul. And hence Paul is right to try to free himself through sexual intercourse with other women. But it is not other women who then seem to be the new "reality" with which his soul is fused. It is the world. "The highest of all was to melt out into the darkness and sway there, identified with the great Being," Paul feels after intercourse with Miriam. And as for intercourse with Clara: "They had met and included in their meeting the thrust of the manifold grass stems, the cry of the peewit, the wheel of the stars." Together they "know the tremendous living food which carried them always, gave them rest within themselves." So Clara has reason to complain that she is not really there for Paul. None of Lawrence's heroes ever "really loves a woman." Though all passionate lovers, it is the Infinite that they love, "the great Being." They go to a woman as metal goes into a furnace, for a "melting out." [1]

So it was that, seeking to escape his "circle" with his mother through sexual relations, Lawrence found himself in a still greater circle, a circle as large as the world. Trying to leave the filial circle through eroticism, he only expanded and eroticized it. Sex with its tendency to dissolve the ego, to merge the mind with the blood, freed him from any limited personal attachment and, in the words of his letter to Mrs. Taylor, distributed his "consciousness far abroad." In sexual intercourse Lawrence seems to have found himself, not really free from his mother, but precisely where his relation with her had always put him— at the heart of "Understanding." As if by a homing instinct, his body found its way at last, without conscious guilt, into that "peculiar fusion" that his soul had so long enjoyed. And so it was that Lawrence became the messiah of sexual intercourse, of a "wholeness" known only in the blood.

What sexual congress brought into view for Lawrence was not a bodiless realm of the soul but precisely the world as the

[1] At most the woman can become a momentary physical manifestation of the sacred. So it is with Clara when Paul regards her drying her breasts with a towel by the sea: "But she is magnificent, and even bigger than the morning and the sea." As a revelation of the sacred, however, Clara then dims, and Paul becomes dissatisfied again; to him her personality is of little account.

body of the soul: the world as the tremendous living flood that gives the soul rest within itself. In such a *founded* carnal creation, where matter is so necessary to spirit, the body became as real to Lawrence as the soul—as centered and as luminously radiant. And not only did the expanded circle of the soul make room for the body; it was dependent upon the body, which served as its eye or, better, as the hand that felt it. So it was that the long-estranged sensual and spiritual currents in Lawrence finally flowed together. In sexual intercourse, he became whole. At the same instant, he merged with the Whole. Hence the apparent contradiction in Lawrence's later insistence on being "single" and "integral" and, on the other hand, on "melting out." For Lawrence, at least in sexual congress, these two states were one.

Why does Lawrence not make more of this "solution" to his problem in *Sons and Lovers*? The reason, I think, is that he is not yet conscious of it as one. When he was to become conscious of it, he would make more of it than it could easily bear. He would generalize it as a solution for the miseries of all men. And he would pretend or hope that it would yield a more lasting satisfaction than it could, dependent as it was upon passing physical sensation. But meanwhile he merely accepts it as a datum of his experience; he "makes" nothing of it. He enjoys it as a solution before he recognizes it as one. Hence the total absence of surprise in his hero Paul, who suddenly finds himself, in sexual congress, in the midst of a "great Being" without the least sign of astonishment. It is as if he were simply entering his own living room. And, indeed, with Lawrence was this not in a sense the case? The large circle of the great Being is, after all, identical in essence with the filial one; however far the first reaches out to the stars, a Nottinghamshire parlor once accommodated it. The attributes that (according to Mircea Eliade) distinguish the sacred—namely power, reality, being, the founded, and permanence—were, for Lawrence, common to both his mother and the great Being. Lawrence was to be "born" from each, loved by each, kept by each, and his soul was to turn back to find its source in each. Sexual intercourse thus awakened in him only a familiar intuition. So it is that the bud of the Absolute opens in *Sons and Lovers* without surprise or remark.

If Lawrence's bond with his mother was in one sense inescapable, in another it merely prepared the way for what was to become the great bond of his life and the great theme of his work: his sympathy with the world. The metaphysic so casually cast up in *Sons and Lovers* will be elaborated and become all-pervading in the books to follow. On the other hand, the oedipal dilemma as such will simply disappear, a "solution" to it having been found.

Perhaps only in one way did Lawrence's memory of his mother color the concept of Being that otherwise became detached from her. Whenever her death, his own isolation, struck him afresh, his sense of Being was invaded by shadow: the "night" then became more an invitation to death than an assurance that his mother held him up even from there. His notion of Being was thus to oscillate between activity and stillness, flaming life and shadowy death. Now it was a "tremendous living flood"; now the place to enter a "death sleep." As Lawrence said in his poem "At a Loose End," his mother's death threw "a shadow inviolate" into his own "flame of living." When the flame was low, the shadow loomed forth and became the night.[2]

Even apart from this morbid element, Lawrence's erotic experience of Being was never to prove a true redemption. His intuition of a universal life perhaps stitched and sustained him but, as was suggested, could not satisfy him. If it afforded deep security and peace, it did so only on occasion; there was always the need to begin the quest again. Hence the restlessness, the repeated "rebirths," in Lawrence's heroes and heroines. "Being," after all, does not make a satisfactory lover; hard to find, it is still harder to hold on to. Lawrence liked to believe

---

[2] If Paul Morel has a morbid experience of "the great Being" well before his mother's death, it is perhaps out of sexual guilt over his intercourse with Miriam—a young woman who, given her qualities, could only remind him of his mother.

that mysticism could be a permanent state of the soul; but judging from his protagonists, Lawrence must often have found himself waiting, like an empty vessel, to be filled.

Regardless of this, Lawrence's feeling that a "great Being" supported his body and soul was one of the strongest ever to give birth to art. And what rich observation, what passionate conceptions, it sponsored. It is impossible altogether to regret the controlling role of mystical intuition in Lawrence's books. And all the more is this so when one realizes that, far from being an intellectual construction, it was the mainspring of his being: the one thing that gave him the mission to write and the one thing besides that permitted him to be whole.

— 2 —

"It is very different from *Sons and Lovers*," Lawrence wrote of *The Rainbow* (1915): "The Laocoön writhing and shrieking have gone from my new work, and I think there is a bit of stillness, like the wide, still, unseeing eyes of a Venus of Melos." Explaining this last reference, he adds: "There is something in the Greek sculpture that any soul is hungry for—something of the eternal stillness that lies under all movement, under all life, like a source, incorruptible and inexhaustible. It is deeper than change, and struggling. So long I have acknowledged only the struggle, the stream, the change. And now I begin to feel something of the source, the great impersonal which never changes and out of which all change comes." Actually, as we have seen, Lawrence had acknowledged "the great impersonal" even in the midst of the Laocoön writhing of *Sons and Lovers*. And yet *The Rainbow* is indeed "very different." For here the acknowledgement amounts to a continuous radiance. *Sons and Lovers* is charged, even overcharged, with the novelist's problematic psychology. Lawrence wrote the book with his back to the wall. In *The Rainbow*, by contrast, he climbs to a kind of lordly eminence, he writes in a new "clarity of soul." Having discovered that the great visible and travelling world was ready to be the distribution of his soul, he writes now as a man who has his place in the universe. His emotion is measured out in a refulgent rhetoric that half-conceals and half-reveals his "Understanding"—a rhetoric that is like a series of flashes from a hidden blade.

It is the accession of an informing metaphysic to Lawrence's art that explains the differences between *Sons and Lovers* and *The Rainbow*. As a result of the novelist's conscious adoption of his vision, his art now takes on an Apollonian serenity. In *The Rainbow*, Lawrence has become almost Olympian. At the same time, however, he is lyrical, and the book has a soft, organic quality, as if it had blossomed spontaneously out of a nostalgia for eternity. "The hard violent style" of *Sons and Lovers*, so "full of sensation and presentation," as Lawrence described it, here gives way to a luminous language and to a swaying rhythm that is as magnificent and monotonous, as resonant of eternity, as the ebb and tide of the sea.

Among other differences, Lawrence assumes a new relation to his characters and their lives. In *Sons and Lovers* he had rather unwittingly tested his characters by the touchstone of his relationship with his mother; in *The Rainbow*, by contrast, he brings to bear categorically, with the imperious power of a judge, the touchstone of an ideal that combines that magical relationship with Lawrence's pride in his own individuality. On the one hand, he now deliberately sifts his characters, as it were, for the still living coals of his intimacy with his mother, though in metaphysical rather than in personal terms. Every relationship between his characters he now reviews from the high bench of his remembered afternoons with his mother, when he was both himself and not himself, someting cast far abroad. On the other hand, his characters are also tested for that fierce individuality, that concentration and pride of self, that was so bristling in Lawrence himself and that, projected into Paul, would forbid the latter to "give in" after his mother's death. A self, then, that is both "the unanalysable, indefinable reality of individuality," in words from *Psychoanalysis and The Unconscious* (1921), and "a oneness with the infinite," in words from *The Rainbow*—this is the complex conception of the "vital self" that Lawrence now takes as the norm of his fictional world. And searching for its perfect embodiment in *The Rainbow,* he goes through three generations of one family as a pilgrim might wear through three pairs of shoes.

The "vital self"—the term appears now for the first time—is, as Lawrence was later to say in *Psychoanalysis and the Unconscious,* that "individual unit of consciousness and being which arises at the conception of every higher organism." It is the "quick" and "very self" of the individual. A "germinating egg," it grows "on and on to the strange and peculiar complication in unity which never stops" until the individual dies. This "peculiar complication" is indeed complex. In part, it consists of two contrary impulses: one reactive and separative and culminating in the "I"; the other sympathetic and connective and culminating in the sense of the Infinite—that "great Being" of which the self is defined as a "unit." For the rest, the complication consists in the dual activity of the mind and the senses.

If the vital self develops organically—learning separation as well as union, becoming intellectual as well as sensuous—it turns into a "soul." For Lawrence, as for Keats, the earth is a "vale of Soul-making." "How . . . are these sparks which are God to have identity given them," writes Keats, "—so as ever to possess a bliss peculiar to each one's individual existence? How, but by the medium of a world like this?" So, too, for Lawrence the "unit" of the Infinite can approach its great parent, however paradoxically, only by developing all the potentialities of its "individual existence," as an arm can open a door only after its muscles have been developed. The Lawrentian self is Romantic in that it is, at its maximum, a soul that intuits the other world through this one, the Infinite through the flesh as well as the spirit. It is erotic, a "psycho-sensual synthesis" in Kierkegaard's definition of eroticism.

Lawrence's vital ideal of the soul is more complicated (at least in theory) than Keats's, which asks only that the Mind read the Heart in the schoolroom of the World. Lawrence's requires a kind of juggling of four parts, the "I" and the Infinite, the Intellect and the Senses, none of which must be held in the hand too long or be too long in the air; for in the self, as in everything else, the "root of evil," for Lawrence, is the "principle of permanency." No wonder his characters so often fail to measure up to the vital ideal—an ideal he applies to each of them, as if standing them up against a growth chart on a wall. No wonder so few of them are granted the stature of a soul.

The characters of *The Rainbow* fall into categories of failure and success that are to recur in each of Lawrence's succeeding novels. To begin with, there are individuals whose mental development is almost nil. Only their senses are alive—they are human animals. Such are the earliest Brangwen men, all farmers:

In autumn the partridges whirred up, birds in flocks blew like spray across the fallow, rooks appeared on the grey, watery heavens, and flew cawing into the winter. Then the men sat by the fire in the house where the women moved about with surety, and the limbs and the body of the men were impregnated with the day, cattle and earth and vegetation and the sky, the men sat by the fire and their brains were inert, as their blood flowed heavy with the accumulation from the living day.

The vital selves of these men are fixed at the poles of the senses and of sympathy—of sensuous sympathy; the "I" in them, the "individual existence," has never developed. We meet with the same excess and imbalance in a member of the latest generation in the novel, Anthony Schofield, toward whom Ursula, the latest Brangwen heroine, is temporarily attracted. The light in Anthony's eyes—eyes "like the pale grey eyes of a goat"—makes

Ursula's mind go out "like an extinguished thing," leaving her "all senses." Anthony does not "see" a certain beautiful evening because he is "one with it" in sensuous sympathy. Anthony, Ursula decides with finality, has "no soul." There is also a taxi driver whose "face of . . . a quick, strong, wary animal" frightens the same heroine.

Sensual men, these characters are all bonded to time and space. Lawrence, bonded to the Infinite that speaks through time and space, views them with ambivalence. The Brangwen farmers, Anthony, and the taxi driver form a scale of sensual humanity. The first are painted in romantic colors, for at least they stare "towards the source of generation"—a source that, for Lawrence, had intimate connections with that greater "source, incorruptible and inexhaustible," "the eternal stillness that lies under all movement." Anthony is comparatively a creature apart,[3] ignorant of sources. And the taxi driver seems to arouse in both Ursula and Lawrence a shudder of revulsion; he is vital to the exclusion of being a self, a unit of being run wild.

There is next a category of characters who, though awakened from "the drowse of blood-intimacy," fail to develop a proud separateness: characters in a personal limbo. Tom Brangwen, of the first chronicled generation, senses that his "own individuality" awaits him in the larger, social world that lies beyond the farm. He believes, with Lawrence's support, that it depends on his "manhood to preserve and develop" this individuality. But Tom never attains a proud detachment. Superior to his sensuously surcharged forebears, he is capable of mystical "Understanding"—he and his wife Lydia, each a "doorway"

[3] In Ursula's eyes, Anthony is "an isolated creature living in the fulfilment of his own senses." Whether the senses should be regarded as "sympathetic" is ambiguous. Compared to "transcendent desire," sensation entails separation from the world. However, since the sensual man is not burdened with a subjective self, there is also a sense in which he is "one" with the world, as Ursula notes of the very man whom she also views as "isolated."

to the other, enter the infinite together, meeting "to the span of the heavens." Yet Tom remains too puzzled by this experience, too "afraid of the unknown in life," too much a man without a shell, to satisfy Lawrence's or even his own sense of what the individual should be. Tom passes from the impersonality of the blood to the impersonality of "Understanding" without ever becoming personal and individual in the process. He never achieves the kind of quick intelligence, the easy grasp and knowledge of the world, and hence of his own distinctness from it, that Lawrence himself now displays on every page.

Will Brangwen, of the next generation, also fails, for the most part, to be personal and separate. However, Will's impersonality is entirely of the mystical kind. Mystic that Lawrence himself was, he was unsympathetic to any mysticism that, contrary to Romantic mysticism, denied the necessity of a developed "individual unit" of being. Will finds his "absolute" in the "jewelled gloom" of the Lincoln cathedral: " . . . the church lay like a seed in silence, dark before germination, silenced after death. . . . potential with all the noise and transititation of life, the cathedral remained hushed, a great, involved seed. . . ." And so it is with Will himself: "He was aware of some limit to himself, of something unformed in his very being, . . . some folded centres of darkness which would never develop and unfold whilst he was alive in the body." Later—it is a rocking boat of a novel—Will is said to have gained a "purposive self." "Now," Lawrence notes of him, "he had an absolute self—as well as a relative self." In other words, he has learned to be separate and reactive as well as sympathetic and spiritually related to "the great impersonal." But—another wave—this doesn't last, and Will slides into a third category: that of the "drowse of blood-intimacy" with which the Brangwen story begins!

Together with several lesser characters, Tom and Will Brangwen have unformed souls because they are fixed in the sympathetic mode of being. At the other extreme is Anton Skrebensky, who has a nature "detached and isolated," "the nature of an aristocrat." But like other characters in *The Rainbow*, Skrebensky is violated by Lawrence's will to illustrate the *various* failures at attaining a soul in one and the same character; and hence there is also reason to say of him that he is not "reactive" but "sympathetic," a man who is himself unformed because he is consecrated to the "great impersonal"—not of "eternal stillness," in this case, but of the state. It is his ruling belief that "one had to fill one's place in the whole, the great scheme of man's elaborate civilization. . . . The Whole mattered—but the unit, the person, had no importance, except as he represented the Whole." It is almost as if George Eliot had tried to portray Grandcourt and Deronda as the same person. Yet it is clear that, much as Lawrence deplores both types, he prefers the "detached" Skrebensky, so intriguingly aristocratic, to Skrebensky the social "brick." "He went about his duties," Lawrence writes, "giving himself up to them." But "no highest good of the community . . . would give him the vital fulfilment of his soul." "At the bottom of his heart his self, the soul that aspired and had true hope of self-effectuation lay as dead, still-born . . . ." Sensing the absence of vital development in Skrebensky, Ursula is overcome, in his presence, "with slow horror. Where was she? What was this nothingness she felt? The nothingness was Skrebensky." Ursula's final judgment: "He has no soul, no background." Bewilderingly, Lawrence later makes use of Anton's relationship with Ursula to illustrate, on the irrelevant inspiration of the moment, how a man and woman together can pass "into the pristine darkness of paradise, into the original immortality"—quite as if Skrebensky did have an eternal "background." But in the main Skrebensky illustrates the "nothingness" of a Victorian, or social, mode of being.

A surer instance of aristocratic separateness is Will Brangwen's wife, Anna, who fights her husband in an effort to maintain "her own, old sharp self, detached, detached." This "sharp self" is equidistant from blood drowse and the impersonality of "Understanding." It is "absolute," not relative. It exasperates Anna that Will enjoys in church a "dark emotional experience of the Infinite." "She could not get out of the Church the satisfaction he got. The thought of her soul was intimately mixed up with the thought of her own self. Indeed, her soul and her own self were one and the same in her. Whereas he seemed simply to ignore the fact of his own self, almost to refute it." Anna is right about Will; but is she not herself in danger of failing to make a soul because she clings so "fiercely to her known self"? However, Anna proves to have also a capacity for mystical experience, and during her honeymoon she is able to pass with Will into a "poised, unflawed stillness that was beyond time, because it remained the same, inexhaustible, unchanging, unexhausted." Yet Lawrence cannot leave Anna alone; complicated as she already is, he refashions her at the end into a woman lost in a blood trance of breeding, far removed from both the old sharp self and the self of "unflawed stillness."

Only one character in the novel, Anna's daughter Ursula, manages to achieve that "strange and peculiar complication in unity" that is the Laurentian self. She is sharp-minded, freely intelligent; a schoolteacher as Lawrence himself was, she creates a "purposive self," exists as "a separate social individual." "Her real, individual self drew together and became more coherent during these two years of teaching. . . ." She knows "herself different . . . and separate from the great, conflicting universe that was herself." She is an "I," then, an "individual unit" that has conquered its own identity. Yet, precisely because she is more detached than the other characters, she has a greater aptitude for relating to what is not herself. Thus where Anthony Schofield does not see the beauty of the evening—"the moon coming yellow and lovely upon a rosy sky, above the darkening, bluish snow"—because he is one with it, Ursula both "saw it and was one with it." Having made herself a subject, she can take the world as an object. More, she has developed her senses as well as her mind, she is adept at sympathy as well as reaction, and thus she is "one" with the world that she also sees. She is complete: she has a soul.

Ursula's predicament is not being able to find a *man* who has a soul. In Lawrence, a complete unfolding of the original "individual unit" is achieved only in a "conjunction" with another such unit; the supreme melting out into the Infinite comes with sexual intercourse, and intercourse in which the tender spirit as well as the flesh has a part. For Ursula, neither Anthony Schofield nor Anton Skrebensky leads into the "unknown"; both frustrate her Romantic hunger for a wholeness in herself that would give a clue, an opening, to the All:

> . . . a yearning for something unknown came over her, a passion for something she knew not what. She would walk the foreshore alone after dusk, expecting, expecting something, as if she had gone to a rendezvous. The salt, bitter passion of the sea, its indifference to the earth, its swinging, definite motion, its strength, its attack, and its salt burning, seemed to provoke her to a pitch of madness, tantalizing her with vast suggestions of fulfilment. And then, for personification, would come Skrebensky . . . whose soul could not contain her in its waves of strength, nor his breast compel her in burning, salty passion.

It is Paul and Clara again: on the one side, the protagonist who is seeking something vast, he knows not what, and, on the other, the inadequate "representative" of the Infinite.

Meanwhile, however, Ursula catches glimpes of what her life might be. Like both her mother Anna and her grandmother Lydia, she has intuited the "covenant" that forever exists between the "great Being" and each individual. One such moment of revelation comes while she observes, through a microscope in a college laboratory, a moving speck with a gleaming nucleus. This "unit" of being, she perceives,

> intended to be itself. But what self? Suddenly in her mind the world gleamed strangely, with an intense light, like the nucleus of the creature under the microscope. Suddenly she had passed away into an

intensely-gleaming light of knowledge. She could not understand what it all was. She only knew that it was not limited mechanical energy, nor mere purpose of self-preservation and self-assertion. It was a consummation, a being infinite.

It is at this point that Lawrence pens the most teasing of his definitions of the self: "Self was a oneness with the infinite. To be oneself was a supreme, gleaming triumph of infinity." Here Lawrence describes one aspect of the vital self, the sympathetic impulse, as if it were the only one. It was his habit to be extreme, absolute in the moment, to make each of his statements, however partial, a consummation of truth equivalent to the mystical fulfillment he sought. And yet perhaps Lawrence was never more sincere, never more "himself," than when he thus defined the self as "a oneness with the infinite." Was it not precisely this "oneness" that he experienced when, in sexual intercourse, he finally felt integral, complete, a self? Was not his real passion for this moment when, the body and the mind having become a single identity, a *soul*, they found themselves at the same instant "a being infinite," a "consummation"?

However partial Lawrence himself might have been to one side of his ideal, certainly the ideal itself is admirably balanced. Physical and spiritual at once, the "vital self," especially in its fulfillment as soul, was in effect to heal that division between Lawrence's father and mother from which Lawrence himself, as their child, had suffered so greatly—the dichotomy between sensual warmth and proud, puritan selfhood that became internalized in Lawrence owing to his identification with his mother and to his oedipal dilemmas. The Brangwen men with their drowsy blood knowledge are reminiscent of Lawrence's father, who was "one of the sanguine temperament, warm and hearty." Anna Brangwen and the other "aristocrats" of *The Rainbow* grew, in part, out of Lawrence's mother, a woman "proud and unyielding," clever and detached. In Ursula, as in Lawrence himself, these contraries are combined and reconciled. In effect, Lawrence was to become both his father and his mother, to be the marriage they never had. Mental clarity and burning passion, a standing apart and an erotic merging—Lawrence was to want everything that his parents had separately wanted, and if he could not have them in the same moment, except in the miracle of sexual union, then he would have them in succession, would pursue and expound an ethic of dialectical unfolding, of a balance achieved through time. Nothing that either of his parents had excluded from themselves, nothing that Lawrence had ever tried to exclude in his youth, was to be left out of his ideal. It would be, however "strange and peculiar," a complication in unity. It would be Lawrence's intellectual response to the "Understanding" that "everything lies in *being.*"

And yet the vital self proves to be a less satisfactory ideal than its aspects of balance and wholeness seem to promise. "The goal of life," Lawrence writes, "is the coming to perfection of each single individual." But to what perfection can an individual come if, convinced that the principle of permanence is the only root of evil, he must forever be about to abandon the position he is in? And what is continual change if not restlessness and dissatisfaction? Finally Lawrence's vital ideal is "Romantic" in the sense that it pursues a perfection that perpetually eludes it. This in itself may not be a weakness; it may only be a way of keeping life interesting. But what it meant for Lawrence was, in time, exhaustion and impatience with an unfolding that was never, as yet, complete and consummate enough. As Lawrence grew older, he was to speak less and less of going "on and on," more and more of, simply, peace. The sympathetic pole was to gain, the reactive pole to lose, in force of attraction (though in *Lady Chatterley's Lover*, it is true, Mellors is to resign himself easily enough to a six months' separation from pregnant Connie Chatterley). As Lawrence became bitter and tired, he celebrated a mindless "sleep" of being. "The great impersonal which never changes and out of which all change comes" overbalanced the interest that change itself may once have had for him. In the letter on *The Rainbow* from which this phrase comes we may already detect Lawrence's disenchantment with "the struggle, the stream, the change." In keeping with this, there will be in the later work a shifting of the scales, a weighting of the pan of sympathy and the senses, a lightening of the pan of separation and the mind.

– 3 –

In *Women in Love* (1920), Lawrence's ideal of the vital self catches up with the modern industrial world, to which it comes, of course, bearing a sword. There is another difference from *The Rainbow*: *Women in Love* is, as Lawrence himself pointed out, "a novel which took its final shape in the midst of the period of war." ". . . the bitterness of the war," Lawrence said, "may be taken for granted in the characters"—a statement that invites us to take it for granted in Lawrence himself. The chief difference between *The Rainbow* and *Women in Love* is that the first book was written, as was observed, in a kind of nostalgia for eternity, the second under the goad of a historical crisis. *Women in Love* is not so much a "sequel" to *The Rainbow,* in Lawrence's word, as a summary concentration of the novelist's forces—his metaphysic, his rhetoric, his norms for life—as, girding himself up, he comes forward to do battle with the modern world. Where his stance in *The Rainbow* had been almost bardic, in *Women in Love* it is aggressive—Lawrence is now out to change the way men live. In consequence, by comparison with *Women in Love, The Rainbow* is a genial, even a joyful, book, the glowing rhetorical poem of an as yet unembittered young man with an exalted metaphysic. In *Women in Love,* the rhetoric has hardened and become almost brutal; and though the metaphysic is still exalted, it now takes on a terrible aspect as it stands in awful judgment of the Western world.

Owing to this change in pressure, what had been implicit in

the earlier novel becomes hard-edged in *Women in Love* and, at the same time, intensified, given an apocalyptic heat. Thus, for example, the "principle of permanency" has been raised from its covert position in *The Rainbow* and openly proclaimed to be the root of evil in modern civilization—not merely in this or that individual but in all civilized men and women, in the social forms of Western life, and of course spectacularly in the great industrial "machine." In *Women in Love* permanency has become ubiquitous; indeed, here it has a kind of dark, Manichean grandeur. It is locked in a struggle for possession of the world with that bright "principle in the universe to which man turns religiously"—the principle of "life" or creative change. ". . . the first great step in undoing," Lawrence now admonishes, is "the substitution of the mechanical principle for the organic. . . ." And, according to *Women in Love*, so deeply has organic life been subverted in Northern Europe by mechanical repetition and fixity that its culture is now in its final throes. "Those who are timed for destruction," reflects Ursula, "must die now." The end of a phase has come. In line with his organicist ethic, Lawrence now adopts a theory of the inevitable fall of civilizations. Like the human body, civilizations, he now believes, evolve to a point where nothing lies ahead except decay. When this happens, they lose their "organic hold" on "Being" and its principle of change. Life is then "artificially held together by the social mechanism." Ideals that had been alive become as "dead as nails." But since "that which informs it all is there, and can never be lost," namely the "*life* of the universe itself," there is an alternative to shriveling inside a mechanical civilization "as in a tight skin." We can "stare straight at this life that we've brought upon ourselves, and reject it, absolutely smash up the old idols of ourselves."

However, "you've got very badly to want to get rid of the old, before anything new will appear—even in the self." And it is this that accounts for the bitterness and the hysterical exaggeration of *Women in Love*. In this novel Lawrence despairs of the mechanical conservatism of all those millions of Europeans who do not at all want to get rid of the old—indeed, he despairs of everyone he portrays or to which he alludes except Ursula and her new lover, Birkin, the man who, in accordance with the prophecy at the end of *The Rainbow*, has come out of that "Eternity" to which Ursula herself belongs, "a man created by God," to be hers. People "won't fall off the tree when they're ripe," Birkin complains. "They hang on to their old positions when the position is overpast, till they become infested with little worms and dry-rot." The result in *Women in Love* is a seething disintegration in the white Northern "race," a race obsessed by a "desire for destruction," as if by the small, white, hard, barren moon mentioned so frequently in the book.

Introduced into this context of cultural breakdown, the vital self, as might be expected, emerges as an explicit and exigent ideal. More than that, it undergoes a change of lighting. Indeed, it is scarcely recognizable as the same ideal that we found implicit in *The Rainbow*. In part this is due to a new emphasis on its element of "unity." Here, where everything is disintegrating, Lawrence naturally chooses to stress the "integral" nature of the ideal. Then, too, Lawrence seems to have grown a little impatient with duality and oscillation. It is for a "fusion" of the vital components of the self that he now seems to hunger—for the soul, not in its vital development, but in its mystical consummation.

In connection with this, there is a new animus in *Women in Love* against self-conscious individuality. The "sharp, detached self," the personal ego, has now become anathema. There are several explanations for this: the war and the persecution Lawrence suffered in England as the husband of a German wife; his failure to win a religious following among the artists and intellectuals of England; the resistance his wife Frieda seems to have put up to his wish that she merely "represent something"; and his continuing need to be "gone" from himself, "intermingled" like his mother (indeed, with her) in the All. Thus we find Lawrence writing in a letter of 1915: "I am so sick of people: they preserve an evil, bad, separating spirit under the warm cloak of good words. That is intolerable in them." "They all," he adds, "want the same thing: a continuing in this state of disintegration wherein each separate little ego is an independent little principality by itself. . . ." In "The Crown," a turbid and almost rabid essay of the same period, Lawrence traces the war itself to the ego and its permanency. The ego, a "tough entity," a "rind," causes, Lawrence says, the original impulses of the self to thresh unfulfilled beneath it, creating an inner hollowness, a void of death. "This also we enjoy, this being threshed rotten inside. This is sensationalism, reduction of the complex tissue back through rottenness to its elements."[4] This sensationalism has at last, Lawrence continues, become "a collective activity, a war," where "within the great rind of virtue we thresh destruction further and further, till our whole civilization is like a great rind full of corruption."

For Lawrence, the ego is thus the cause of the disintegration of modern man and his civilization; it is the "root" of the evil. With its "will-to-persist," it "neutralizes life." In the chapter called "Diver," Gerald Crich, an industrial magnate, swims in "the pure translucency of the grey, uncreated water" of Willey Water, a lake. It is his element, the neutralization of life that he produces because, an egoist who lives for the "false absolute" of himself, he will be "without bond or connection anywhere, just himself of the watery world." While around him the "purple twigs" are "darkly luminous in the grey air" and the high hedges glow "like living shadows, hovering nearer, coming into creation," he exults in his "separate element," "the still grey water," because it is only there that he can be supreme, feel in "possession of a world to himself." For Lawrence, the sin of the

---

[4] As metaphors of psychological activity, these images of rottenness and threshing are themselves sensational; and they and their counterparts give not only "The Crown" but *Women in Love* a somewhat lurid cast.

ego is thus its denial of the Creation; the egoist would be, not a creature, but the lord of all.

The sensationalism that makes *Women in Love* so strange, so nearly repulsive on first reading, is always "sensation within the ego." The ego here is like a hollow drum that must strike against things, destroying them, in order to resound, to thrill to its own intactness. The more it perceives of the weakness of its adversaries, of everything "other," the securer it feels and the more it exults. So Minette's "inchoate look of a violated slave, whose fulfilment lies in her further and further violation," made Gerald's "nerves quiver with acutely desirable sensation. After all, his was the only will, she was the passive substance of his will." To persist, the ego must continually decreate what would otherwise threaten it—decreate "the vital organic body of life."

It is their common exultation in decreation that unites Ursula's sister Gudrun and Gerald. On first catching sight of Gerald, Gudrun intuits in him his egoistic need to destroy:

His gleaming beauty, maleness, like a young, good-humoured, smiling wolf, did not blind her to the significant, sinister stillness in his bearing, the lurking danger of his unsubdued temper. "His totem is the wolf," she repeated to herself. . . . And then she experienced a keen paroxysm, a transport, as if she had made some incredible discovery, known to nobody else on earth. . . . "Good God!" she exclaimed to herself, "what is this?" And then, a moment after, she was saying assuredly, "I shall know more of that man."

Later, as Gerald holds a "threshing" rabbit at his mercy and Gudrun looks on, her glance reveals a "mocking, white-cruel recognition." "There was a league between them, abhorrent to them both. They were implicated with each other in abhorrent mysteries." Gerald and Gudrun progress together through ever more "subtle thrills of reduction." It is, surely, a macabre view of the ego, itself extreme in its indictment of the ego's extremism. To such had Lawrence's love of a "peculiar fusion of soul," of a distribution "far abroad," combined with his own frustrated will, so badly battered by the wills of others, finally brought him. The egoists in *Women in Love* are all horrible "examples," more subtle as creations but also more absurdly admonitory than George Eliot's. It is in this novel that Lawrence becomes a novelist who, for all the complication in his character portrayals, gives us something less than a picture of "life in its highest complexity."

In reacting against the "reactive" mode of individual being, Lawrence here simplifies or blurs the "complication in unity" that in both *The Rainbow* and *Psychoanalysis and the Unconscious* he attributes to the "original self." If, as Birkin says, the "I" is a "dead letter," if it is an "old formula of the age" that will pass away with the age, what then becomes of the "separatist" component of the vital self? Should it not—as the Victorians had held—be repressed? To get round the implications of his own analysis, Lawrence indulges the fiction of a human being who is "individual" without possessing an ego at all. He had written in "The Crown" that the real "I" is "a blossom," that is, a spontaneous exfoliation of the "great Being" itself, not a self-consistent identity or ego. Now, in *Women in Love*, he turns to this original, impersonal "I" as the only desirable form of individuality. Is this "I" not the same as that "bundle or collection of different perceptions" and impulses that had made Wilde despair of a "form" for the self at all? Is it not what Hume had referred to as precisely the absense of an identity or self? If Lawrence now turns to it not with despair but, on the contrary, with relief, it is not only because he has come to find all fixity "intolerable" but also because he trusts in the cohesion and single identity of the great Being of which the individual is a "unit." But is he not deluding himself in insisting, nonetheless, that this unit has its own unique singleness, incomparable, irreplaceable? "It is not at all the same," Lawrence writes in the essay called "Democracy," "to have personality as to have individuality, though you may not be able to define the difference." You may not indeed.

It is, at any rate, a self-aware identity, a consistent subjectivity, that Lawrence would now strip from the concept of individuality. "At the very last," Birkin instructs Ursula, "one is alone, beyond the influence of love. There is a real impersonal me . . . a naked kind of isolation, an isolated me, that does *not* meet and mingle, and never can." And again: "There is now to come the new day, . . . no longer any of the horrible merging, mingling self-abnegation of love." Separatism, then, is not itself "dead." Lawrence is as much as ever an advocate of "free proud singleness." And yet how can an individuality which consists, not in personality, but only in an upwelling of impersonal "promptings" be free and proud? Birkin wants people "to like the purely individual thing in themselves, which makes them act in singleness." But to know what the purely individual thing is, much less to like it, requires a knowledge of where the self ends and other things begin—requires a self-aware identity. Lawrence appears now to desire individuality without either reaction from the world or independence of the mind. He wants separation without a principle of separation. We can attend to Birkin's speeches only in confusion. It is when we attend to Birkin himself—to his "sharp" and "detached" and self-conscious personality—that we know his words are just words.

Because the now-hated ego belongs, as Lawrence elsewhere observes, "to the conscious or mental-subjective self," there is in *Women in Love* another change in the vital ideal. Instead of a stress on the "complication in unity" of the mind and the senses, there is here an emphasis on their fusion. Self-consciousness cannot be eliminated so long as the mind is allowed to become detached from the surrounding world; the mind must be merged with the senses, paradisally, outside of history. *The Rainbow* had confessed and even insisted that mental development and detachment are natural in human beings and necessary for the unfolding of the soul. In *Women in Love*, by contrast, the separation of the mind from the senses—a separation without which mental development would not be possible—is treated as unnatural, even though the book itself would have been inconceivable without it. Indeed, it is just the crystallization of the mind from the senses that is held responsible for the "Flux of Corruption" in which Western civilization here finds itself. Thousands of years ago, Birkin says, a similar fate had overtaken African civilization: "the relation between the senses and the outspoken mind had broken, leaving the experience all in one sort, mystically sensual." When this occurs, he says, "the soul in intense suffering breaks, breaks away from its organic hold like a leaf that falls." The soul's "organic hold" on "Being" depends, we must conclude, on a fusion of the mind with the senses. Is then the "germinating egg," the original "quick," itself the soul? Is all development in "complication" but a deviation from the unconscious Way? Is not the fetus the best of worshippers? Such would seem to be the view that Lawrence, sore from the battle of life, here finds it tempting to embrace.

Lawrence was repeatedly to argue that the mind is useful as "a great indicator and instument." And Birkin is to say, in the chapter called "Class-Room," that children "are not roused to consciousness. Consciousness comes to them, willy-nilly." And yet, however useful or even inevitable mental consciousness may be, Lawrence believed that it was not essential to the soul. If it could not be eliminated, neither should it be encouraged. "The mind is the dead end of life." And if "everything proceeds from the creative quick outwards . . . ," then even as an "indicator" the mind is supererogatory. And so it is that Lawrence finds himself in *Women in Love* approving of only one form of consciousness: an erotic consciousness that is mental and physical at once. Only this consciousness melts the mind beyond everything "known"; only this consciousness has a "hold" on the life of the universe.

The chapter called "Excurse" is largely devoted to celebrating erotic consciousness. Here Birkin at last achieves his goal of becoming an "inhuman son of God," redeemed from the "sordidness of our humanity." Here, as he comes into paradisal conjunction with Ursula, there falls "a darkness over his mind. The terrible knot of consciousness that had persisted there like an obsession was broken, gone, his life was dissolved in darkness over his limbs and his body." Now his whole being, in which spirit and senses are intermingled, knows itself and everything else "integrally"; his soul itself is now awake, aware. "He seemed to be conscious all over, all his body awake with a single, glimmering awareness, as if he had just come awake, like a thing that is born. . . ." Though no more "mental" than an animal, he is yet aware beyond the limits of the senses. It is a "new universe" that he beholds, a miraculous creation, not merely the sensuous world. He has given himself over to the "deepest physical mind," the "basic mind," where the spirit is undifferentiated from the senses, and where the mind is anything but "outspoken." In this state everything is one knowledge, knowledge is all of the same thing—what Ursula, finding it in "the straight downflow" of Birkin's thighs, thinks of, or simply knows, as "the very stuff of being." "The sense of the awfulness of riches that could never be impaired flooded her mind like a swoon, a death in the most marvellous possession, mystic-sure."

Not surprisingly, erotic consciousness does not last in Birkin and Ursula: in the next chapter, they are as "mental" as before. Indeed, the novel could scarcely have continued to include them, let alone center on them, if they had not so changed, since in "Excurse" they move out of the only mode in which the novel has relevance, the historical. But how Lawrence yearns—as he had in *The Rainbow* while describing the "mystic-sure" honeymoon of Anna and Will—to give us a paradisal pair who seem to have become once and for all "two stark, unknown beings, two utterly strange creatures." Not only "Excurse" betrays this yearning; it is ubiquitous in the novel in the form of the flower as an emblem of paradisal human life. "Why should you always be *doing*?" Ursula asks of Birkin. "I think it is much better to be really patrician, and to do nothing but just be oneself, like a walking flower." And Birkin, he says, quite agrees. In fact, Birkin, taking his turn at expressing Lawrence's philosophy, urges upon Ursula the same ideal of insouciance when he says, in "Moony": "I want you to drop your assertive *will*, your frightened apprehensive self-insistence. . . . I want you to trust yourself so implicitly that you can let yourself go." "I don't mean let yourself go in the Dionysic ecstatic way," he adds. "I want you not to care about yourself, just to be there and not to care about yourself, not to insist—be glad and sure and indifferent." Fairly early in the novel Ursula refers to herself as a "rose of happiness." And in "Excurse" she almost literally becomes a walking flower, with her "over-fine, over-sensitive skin," her "delicate" and "luminous" face, her "complete ease" and "peace." She is "beautiful as a new marvellous flower," "a paradisal flower." And she and Birkin take the "silent delight of flowers in each other."

What havoc the grotesque if arresting metaphor of man as a walking flower plays with Lawrence's ideal of the self as a "dual polarity, positive and negative, of the voluntary and sympathetic nerve centers"! To be "glad and sure and indifferent" is never to feel like an "isolated me" at all; and it is to still all the anxieties of thought. When Lawrence writes in the Foreword that "the creative, spontaneous soul sends forth its promptings of desire and aspiration in us," that "these promptings are our true fate, which is our business to fulfil," and that "a fate dictated from outside, from theory or from circumstance, is a false fate," he is saying, in effect, that man's unconscious mind is his root and stem, indeed his flower, and that any other hold or direction is anticreative. And yet how this seems to imply that mental consciousness, the ego, the dead letter "I," are no more than wisps that with a wave of an insouciant hand can be dispelled forever; how little acknowledgement it makes of the rootedness and hardy persistence of the mind.

Lawrence is the readier to resign us, flower-like, to subterranean promptings because he trusts that these are all paradisal, that the "Dionysic," the frenzied, the sensational, and the corrupt are born only in their *denial*. No more than a flower does the human soul, in Lawrence's view, require the moral supervision of a "conscious or mental-subjective self." The god of the spontaneous self is Apollo. From the "basic mind," Birkin experiences "a pure and magic control." Like the "little flotilla" of daisies that he sets "drifting into the light" in the chapter called "An Island," Birkin and Ursula "drift" in "Excurse" "through the wild, late afternoon, in a beautiful motion that was smiling and transcendent." The "great Being" is a peaceful creature. Indeed, is not permanence, as Heidegger says, the chief characteristic of what we think of as possessing "being"? The "unit" of individual being is, in Lawrence, as self-continuing, as serenely paradisal, as the whole.

If Lawrence wishes to rely on any secondary control, it is not the "indicator" of the "upper" mind but the institution—the word seems just—of marriage. Perfectly balanced as the self is on the great fountain of primal impulse, it yet needs to be balanced also in a "star equilibrium" with another (and always the same) spontaneous self. "Each individual," Lawrence writes in *Psychoanalysis and the Unconscious*, "is vitally dependent" on another individual "for the life circuit." "The perfection of each single individuality" can take place only in a perfected harmony with the beloved, "a harmony which depends on the at-last-clarified singleness of each being, a singleness equilibrized, polarized in one by the counterposing singleness of the other." "I am with him entirely," Birkin says of his cat, Mino, which had been "insisting" to a "poor stray that she shall acknowledge him as a sort of fate, her own fate: because you can see she is fluffy and promiscuous as the wind. . . . He wants superfine stability." "If you admit a unison," Birkin says, "you forfeit all the possibilities of chaos." One would have thought that the "creative, spontaneous soul" was itself proof against the possibilities of chaos; Lawrence's trust in it is not so deep as it seems. Indeed, Birkin claims for marriage what would appear to be due only to the innate cohesion of the great Being itself: "I do think that the world is only held together by the mystic conjunction, the ultimate unison between people—a bond. And the immediate bond is between man and woman."

The truth, I think, is that Lawrence never forgot that what had held him together in his early years was his bond with his mother. For all his love of an "at-last-clarified singleness," he was not a man to stand alone; he needed an "eternal conjunction" with a woman, scented with all the permanence of "being." And yet could any other woman be to him what his mother had been? Could he fuse *with* another woman or only, as it were, with her aid, through "conjunction" with her, specifically through sexual ecstasy? Only the latter would seem to explain Lawrence's insistence on marriage as "a pure balance of two single beings." On the one hand Lawrence wanted, in marriage, to be himself, not merged with some alien personality. Had he not said that, after his mother, no one else could ever come into his soul again? On the other hand, the "self" that he thus wanted to maintain overwhelmingly needed to experience, to reawaken, a "peculiar fusion" with what seemed to lie "far abroad." Starting from where he did, in an attempt to relate mystically to a woman who was in fact to serve only as a convenience to his mysticism, Lawrence could not help seeming confused and contradictory in what he demanded from marriage, not to mention the self. Written into his concept of marriage as a balance of "single beings" was a clause for the sort of personal liberty and independence that he always insisted upon for himself; Laurentian marriage exacts a very-much-alive letter "I"—a letter that, as we have seen, Lawrence otherwise considered dead. And yet, even with regard to marriage, Lawrence was at best equivocal as an exponent of separateness and individuality; for if he wanted separateness from the here and now, from his "beloved," it was for the sake of union with "eternal stillness" and the "far abroad"—with what another personality could only inadequately "represent."

– 4 –

The Plumed Serpent (1926) marks the extreme limit in Lawrence's effort to escape from the "natural" complexity of the self that he himself had both dramatized in his fiction and conceptualized in *Psychoanalysis and the Unconscious* and other essays.

In this novel, which is as ideal and Utopian as *Women in Love* is critical and analytical, the absolute of eternal stillness so overwhelms the foreground that the vital self shrinks to a paltry insignificance. In *The Rainbow*, the "great impersonal which never changes and out of which all change comes," however glowing and absolute, had seemed remote. Thus, though Ursula might belong to eternity, she was nonetheless very much of the earth; and it is there that, at the conclusion, she is striving "to create a new knowledge of Eternity in the flux of Time." Ursula may cry, "I want to go," but she never really attempts to abandon the vital realm. Nor does this realm appear to be a mere veil of illusion; on the contrary, it seems a necessary adjunct to eternity. In *Women in Love*, also, the vital world has a grateful foreground reality. Though Birkin says "I want to be gone out of myself," it is yet an inhuman *earthly* creature that he desires to be; and if Ursula is said to belong "only to the oneness with Birkin, a oneness . . . sounding into the heart of the universe, the heart of reality," this oneness nonetheless seems to strike through the solid earth itself. In *The Plumed Serpent*, by contrast, the proportion between the "great impersonal" and the vital world has altered so greatly that the earth now appears to be but a waiting station for the Infinite. Lawrence has here begun to lose his "organic hold" on the earth itself.

The infinite, instead of bearing up the vital realm, now seems to hang over it or lie, not touching, just underneath. So dazzling is the "dark sun" behind the actual and brilliant sun that it reduces the latter to dullness. Godhead appears tenuously, ethereally, between "the tremors of night and the day." And the Way, which once seemed earthly and paradisal, is now, according to one of the hymns in the book, a "Way / Unseen." In short, the cosmology of *The Plumed Serpent* consists, not of a universe rooted in eternity, but of two adjacent worlds, one temporal, the other eternal.

In consequence, the vital self here ceases to be the "goal" of life. Only so long as the vital realm appeared magnificent, the single manifestation of the great Being, the only arena of "verification," of "oneness with the infinite"—only so long as this was true could Lawrence believe that "the goal of life is the coming to perfection of each single individual." In *The Plumed Serpent*, where Being is a world apart, perfection in *this* realm seems unprofitable. Though Being is now nearer and more accessible as an experience—a matter of going to "sleep"—to reach it requires a withdrawal from vitality, a descent into a different realm. "I have been," says the hero Don Ramon after one of these sleeps, "and I have come back. But I belong there, where I went." It does not leave much to be said for the waking world.

True, such is Lawrence's theoretical coherence that, despite everything, the vital ideal persists even here and is almost as much as ever a touchstone of individual perfection. Kate Leslie, the fortyish Irish heroine who comes to Mexico after the death of her husband, very soon discovers an essential point of Laurentian doctrine: "Man," she reflects, "was not created readymade." "She had thought that each individual had a complete self, a complete soul, an accomplished I. And now she realised as plainly as if she had turned into a new being, that this was not so. Men and women had incomplete selves, made up of bits assembled together loosely and somewhat haphazard. . . . Men to-day were half-made, and women were half-made." "Perfected being or identity," she now perceives, must be created. The vital realm, then, is even here a vale of soul-making. "The soul is . . . a thing you make, like a pattern in a blanket." Its warp is the blood, its woof the spirit.

As in the earlier novels, these "opposites" have in *The Plumed Serpent* generally failed to combine in human beings to create "that centre which is the soul of a man in a man." Indeed, here they are the property, respectively, of the dark and white races. White men are dominated by the "eagle" of the mind and spirit, the darker races by the "snake" of the blood. "White men had had a soul, and lost it"; they had ceased to have a "physical belief" in the "very middle" of their beings. The Indians, on the other hand, display a "curious, radical opposition . . . to the thing we call the spirit." In consequence, they have "heavy," reptilian blood; they squat "helpless outside their own unbuilt selves, unable to win their souls out of the chaos." Indeed, they "belong to a bygone cycle of humanity. They are left behind in a gulf out of which they have never been able to climb. And on to the particular white man's levels they never will be able to climb. They can only follow as servants." Contemplating this dichotomy, Kate envisions a "new conception of human life, that will arise from the fusion of the old blood-and-vertebrate consciousness with the white man's present mental-spiritual consciousness. The sinking of both beings, into a new being."

This looked-for "fusion" is symbolized by the old Aztec figure of the plumed serpent, Quetzalcoatl, the eagle and the snake in one. It is the fusion, erotic and care-erasing, enjoyed by Birkin in "Excurse." But again it must be pointed out that this "sinking . . . into a new being" contradicts the active ideal of *building* a self. Were the "new conception" actually realized by human beings, it would spell the end, not the beginning, of soul making. It is itself—statically, effortlessly—the soul state.

Indeed, is the separate development of the mind and the blood necessary to the Laurentian soul at all? Is development itself necessary? We found reason to doubt that Lawrence believed so in *Women in Love*, and there is even more reason to doubt it here. On the one hand, it is said that the dark races lack the spiritual capacity to develop a soul; on the other, they are shown at various times in soul states, under the direction of the European Don Ramon. "His eyes," we read of one of Ramon's men, "had taken again the peculiar gleaming far-away-ness, suspended between the realities. . . . The boatman, rowing away, was glancing back at the man who stood in the water, and his face, too, had the abstracted, transfigured look of a man perfectly suspended between the world's two strenuous wings of energy." Does it, then, require years of mental development, such as Ursula undertakes in *The Rainbow*, to make a soul, or is a soul what one simply sinks into, as if regressing to some "unconscious" fetal state?

More, Lawrence now favors a view of the soul as somehow removed from vital energies altogether. When he speaks of the "transfigured look" of the man as "suspended between the world's two strenuous wings of energy," he has in mind the spirit and the flesh. Why, then, is the soul said to be suspended "between" them? Why is it not their "fusion"? Don Ramon, preparing for the soul sleep, says: "I, and my soul, we come to thee, Evening Star. Flesh, go thou into the night. Spirit, fare-well, 'tis thy day. Leave me now." Neither, it seems, is necessary to the soul. "I go in last nakedness," Ramon says, "now to the nakedest Star." This is nakedness indeed.

The truth would seem to be that Lawrence has wearied of "the world's two strenuous wings of energy"; they have proved all too strenuous in the years since *The Rainbow*. Accordingly, he is now inclined simply to retreat from vital energies and to take the soul with him. "She wanted to be still," Lawrence writes of Lou Witt in the novella *St. Mawr* (1925): "only that, to be very, very still, and recover her own soul." Such is the dominant mood out of which Lawrence wrote in the twenties. So Somers in *Kangaroo* (1923) declares: "If I am to have a meeting it shall be down, down in the invisible, and the moment I re-emerge [I] shall be alone." Lawrence had had too much of humanity—

of the human "cabbages," of the masses with their "demonish hatred of life," of all those who "break the spirit in the outstanding individuals." He wanted only to be still.

If Don Ramon likes to sleep, it is because he is "nauseated with humanity and the human will." "Mere *personal* contact, mere human contact filled him . . . with disgust." To meet people "on a merely human, personal plane" is, he has found, "disaster." "He had to meet them on another plane, where the contact was different; intangible, remote, and without *intimacy*. His soul was concerned elsewhere. So that the quick of him need not be bound to anybody. The quick of a man must turn to God alone. . . ." "He had gnashed himself almost to pieces," Lawrence writes, "before he had found the way to pass out in himself, in the quick of himself, to the Quick of all being and existence . . . and there, there alone meet with his fellow man." Such a meeting is indeed "without *intimacy*"; in fact it would seem to leave one's "fellow man" behind.

Dislike of "mere human contact" goes so far in *The Plumed Serpent* that Don Ramon is permitted a privilege granted to no other Lawrence protagonist: he is allowed to attain mystical consummation by himself.

And tense like the gush of a soundless fountain, he thrust up and reached down in the invisible dark, convulsed with passion. Till the black waves began to wash over his consciousness, over his mind, waves of darkness broke over his memory, over his being, like an incoming tide, till at last it was full tide, and he trembled, and fell to rest. . . .
He covered his face with his hands, and stood still, in pure unconsciousness, neither hearing nor feeling nor knowing, like a dark seaweed deep in the sea. With no Time and no World, in the deeps that are timeless and worldless.

This is a far and sad cry from Birkin's and Ursula's dual entrance into a "new universe" in "Excurse." It is indeed, as it is called, a "death sleep." Above all, it is the sleep of the spirit, which—beyond "hearing" and "feeling" and "knowing"—lies down in all its sores and tatters and forgets the human world that has so filled it with disgust. The eternal "now" thus entered is, we are told, "wingless"; it is a "Snake." It is, in other words, a healing sea of "plasm." And thus it is appropriate that Ramon's design of the Quetzalcoatl symbol should be, not in fact a plumed serpent, but an "eagle within the ring of a serpent that had its tail in its mouth."

And yet so weak now is Lawrence's will to struggle and resist that the whole waking world, blood and all, seems to him a mere phantom. "We have to shut our eyes," Ramon says, "and sink down, sink away from the surface, away, like shadows. . . ." And elsewhere Lawrence editorializes: "we must give up the assembled self, the daily I, and putting off ourselves one after the other, meet unconscious in the Morning Star." The vital self is thus derogated to a fabrication; it is something merely "assembled." When awake in the "daily I," Ramon says, men but go "from dream to dream, in the hope of a perfect dream." "Only the sleep that is dreamless breathes I Am!" As for the vital realm, how much better it seems down in the depths where there is "no Time and no World." For Ramon, there is but one reality—"the infinite room that lies inside the axis of our wheeling space."

What had once been a species of Romanticism, treasuring the connection of this world with the next, thus becomes in *The Plumed Serpent* a tired desire to be gone altogether "beyond the individualism of the body," gone into some universal plasma that will sink the mind below all hurt. And yet so nauseated is Lawrence with everything actual and near that even this plasma he chooses to think of as "ethereal." And so it is that his mystical vitalism separates in *The Plumed Serpent* into a vitalism that is merely a painful "dream" and a mysticism that places a man "between" the only energies that, waking, he is able to discern. In *Sons and Lovers,* "real living" had been Paul's sense of warmth while working in his mother's presence; it had been the "shimmering protoplasm in the leaves and everywhere." Here it has shriveled to a "deep sleep" that carries no troubling dreams. Paul had turned with courage toward "the faintly humming, glowing town," even though what held him up had been cast into the night; now Lawrence himself seems to turn to the night as, after all, the lesser of the terrors. In works written after *The Plumed Serpent,* Lawrence will prize again "the great rose of Space," delight once more in the flowers that "are loved into being between the sun and the earth." But meanwhile he has had his fill of the "tremendous living flood"; it has not given him the "rest" it had promised.

-- 5 --

Lawrence's chief problem as a novelist was, as he admitted, that human beings bored him—and, as he said, "you can't have fiction without human beings." Lawrence was always hard on his characters, exacting from them a perfection that he himself lacked and was either disgusted with them or indifferent toward them if they failed to attain it. As personalities, they are all *non grata*; and yet only as personalities can they exist in the pages of his books. There he is, in each of his novels, hovering over his cast, repelled by their actions as by the scurryings of insects. How he would like to sweep the whole lot away! In the chapter called "Sunday Evening" in *Women in Love* Ursula (as Lawrence) reflects:

But what a joy! What a gladness to think that whatever humanity did, it could not seize hold of the kingdom of death, to nullify that. The sea they turned into a murderous alley and a soiled road of commerce, disputed like the dirty land of a city every inch of it. The air they claimed too, shared it up, parcelled it out to certain owners, they trespassed in the air to fight for it. Everything was gone, walled in, with spikes on top of the walls, and one must ignominiously creep between the spiky walls through a labyrinth of life.

But the great dark, illimitable kingdom of death, there humanity was put to scorn. So much they could do upon earth, the multifarious little gods that they were. But the kingdom of death put them all to scorn, they dwindled into their true vulgar silliness in face of it.

It is not a happy vision for a novelist. Powerful, bitter, scornful, repulsed, it is acid for a satirist or fuel for the fire of an Old Testament prophet. Lawrence's characters are all at the unfair disadvantage of having to justify their existence to their author. Unless they happen to be Laurentians, he will say of them—as Birkin says of the guests at the Crichs' wedding party—that "essentially, they don't exist, they aren't there": "They jingle and giggle. It would be much better if they were just wiped out."

In a famous letter on *The Rainbow*, Lawrence wrote: ". . . that which is physic—non-human, in humanity, is more interesting to me than the old-fashioned human element—which causes one to conceive a character in a certain moral scheme and make him consistent. The certain moral scheme is what I object to." And yet a certain moral scheme and consistency of character are not necessarily correlatives. The characters in the first half of *Sons and Lovers*, for example, are highly individual and coherent; but no one would say of them that they were conceived in a certain moral scheme. In truth it is personality itself that Lawrence objects to. With everything "merely" human he is impatient. His novels are all searches for that "new conception of human life" of which Kate Leslie speaks in *The Plumed Serpent*. And this, since it moves man on into the "unknown," Lawrence prefers to think of as "inhuman." Most of Lawrence's characters are either examples of the "old" conception, dragged up onto the shore of the novel to illustrate the putridness of the "old-fashioned human element," or, like Ursula and Kate Leslie, representatives of Lawrence's own soul in its quest for a consummate and "intolerable accession into being"—characters before the flashing body of the sea, crying "I want to go."

After *Sons and Lovers*, Lawrence's characterizations become tendentious. *Sons and Lovers*, especially the first half, is as natural as breathing. The characters appear to live and feel as real people live and feel. The novel gives us the great pleasure of blended recognition and illumination. Consider the passage in which Walter Morel watches his wife imitate his "once handsome bearing": "He saw again the passion she had had for him. It blazed upon her for a moment. He was shy, rather scared, and humble. Yet again he felt his old glow. And then immediately he felt the ruin he had made during these years. He wanted to bustle about, to run away from it." The truth of this is undoubtable, perfect. It is creatively generous; Lawrence himself, as a personality, is not in it. Is there anything comparable to it in Lawrence's later work? There is at least one delightfully free moment—free from the strain of a "new conception," though not from touching human interest—in Chapter IV of *The Rainbow,* when Tom Brangwen finds his newly wed daughter Anna "turning blissfully at the handle" of the mangle he has given her, and the servant Tilly beside her exclaiming:

"My word, that's a natty little thing! That'll save you luggin' your inside out. That's the latest contraption, that is."
And Anna turned away at the handle, with great gusto of possession. Then she let Tilly have a turn.
"It fair runs by itself," said Tilly, turning on and on. "Your clothes'll nip out on to th'line."

But is not almost everything else in *The Rainbow,* and still more of the later books, itself being run through a mangle? That the handle is in this case also turned "with great gusto of possession" serves to redeem the books, but it does not make them less like aesthetic machines.

Lawrence held to a mimetic theory of the novel, conceiving the genre to be a kind of automaton that, no matter how badly the novelist tampered with it, would nonetheless tell the truth. "Let me hear," he writes in "The Novel," "what the novel says. As for the novelist, he is usually a dribbling liar." ". . . in a novel," he adds, "there's always a tom-cat, a black tom-cat that pounces on the white dove of the Word, if the dove doesn't watch it. . . ." (Yet goodness knows there are novels of Lawrence's in which we wait in vain for the tomcat to pounce.) Still,

Lawrence held to this view insecurely and equivocally. Thus, if he attacks Joyce and Proust and Dorothy Richardson, it is precisely because they are content to be realists—because they present things merely as they are. The response that they evoke in readers, he says, is "that's just how I feel myself." And to this he objects, not that people do not in fact feel that way, but that they ought not to; they ought *not* to be so self-conscious and analytical. Lawrence's tom, then, is not the common beast of things as they happen to be but an exotic creature that, truth to tell, could scarcely be expected to appear in any fiction except Lawrence's own—a cat of his own philosophy. "The man in the novel," he says, "must be 'quick.' And this means one thing . . . : it means he must have a quick relatedness to all the other things in the novel: snow, bed-bugs, sunshine, the phallus, trains, silk-hats, cats, sorrow," etc. If we balk at this "must," if we object that most men are not livingly related to all things, Lawrence would doubtless answer, "So much the worse for them."

In Lawrence's hands, the novel becomes a light to show the way. "It's got," he said of the form, "to have the courage to tackle new propositions without using abstractions; it's got to present us with new, really new feelings, a whole line of new emotion, which will get us out of the emotional rut." Nor, despite this disavowal of abstractions, did Lawrence object to philosophy in the novel: "It seems to me it was the greatest pity in the world," he said, "when philosophy and fiction got split." All that Lawrence required of the novel was that the "purpose" in it, the "philosophy," not be "at outs with the passional inspiration." What, however, is this "passional inspiration"? Can a "whole line of new emotion" expect to be more than fantasy? Lawrence came close to handing over the novel to the unsatisfied impulses of his soul—to reducing it to a medium for compensating the "sordidness" of life. ". . . only artists," says Birkin, "produce for each other the world that is fit to live in." There is truth in this, but it is a perilous as well as a wonderful truth, and so disgusted with the actual world was Lawrence that he wrote, on the whole, in indifference to the peril. He did not care how absurd some of his own "passional" passages were, so long as they formed, for him, a world that was fit to live in.

What troubles the waters of Lawrence's novels is his anxiety to break free of the narrow channels of "character" and swim out into the sea of erotic impulse. Though Lawrence had much to say in praise of "singleness," he suffered from it terribly. He can never express enough contempt for personality. "Never trust for one moment any individual who has an unmistakable *personality*," he writes in "Democracy." "He is sure to be a life-traitor." "Life," for Lawrence, is the psycho-sensual synthesis of eroticism, which dissolves all "character"; life is passion and wonder, change and peace—it is anything, in human beings, except "the self-conscious ego." And so, against the grain of the novel, Lawrence tried to portray, not persons, but impersonal forces of the body and the spirit. "In every great novel," he writes, "who is the hero all the time? Not any of the characters, but some unnamed and nameless flame behind them all"—"the God-mystery within us." After *Sons and Lovers*, Lawrence sought to portray the vital "quick" in "whose action the individual is unrecognisable." "You mustn't look in my novel," he said of *The Rainbow*, "for the old stable *ego*—of the character." Yet is this not as much as to say that we must not look for human beings as we know them? Is this not to say that we must expect, not a novel, but a fantasia of the unconscious?

In Lawrence's work the novel becomes a kind of choreography of psychic changes. Of course, Lawrence does not in fact simply dissolve the "stable *ego*," "the individual." He was, for all we have said, too much the novelist for that. He chose to work in the novel form, he loved it, indeed he did magnificently in it, for all his faults. There is enough observation of "personalities" and "mere" human activity in Lawrence's work to nourish a shoal of lesser novelists. And yet how Lawrence chafed at the materials that the form itself seemed to dictate. Without doubt Lawrence recognized "the old stable *ego*" in everyone he knew.

Would he have cried out so against it if he had not? But, no, he would not write about *that*, except grudgingly and in order to condemn it. He would only care to write about "an odd sort of fluid, changing, grotesque or beautiful relatedness." Character is not what everyone else supposes it is; it is really something marvelous and strange; it is really a happy release from the anxious and confining ego. "Character is a curious thing," Lawrence writes in "The Novel." "It is the flame of a man, which burns brighter or dimmer, bluer or yellower or redder, rising or sinking or flaring according to the draughts of circumstance and the changing air of life, changing itself continually, yet remaining one single, separate flame, flickering in a strange world. . . ." To Gudrun, Gerald is not "like a man" but an "incarnation, a great phase of life." All Lawrence's characters burn at an intensity that, with a change of just one degree, allows them to flare into incarnations. "Reaction" and "sympathy," conceived as "promptings" from the "beyond," rise and fall in them, all, as Lawrence says, to some rhythm never before known in the novel. They are like strange organisms, now contracting, now unfolding, on the floor of a sea that each aches both to reject and to swallow.

"*All* emotions," Lawrence writes, "go to the achieving of a living relationship between a human being and the other human being or thing he becomes purely related to." And he adds: "If the novelist puts his thumb in the pan, for love, tenderness, sweetness, peace, then he commits an immoral act: he *prevents* the possibility of a pure relationship . . . : and he makes inevitable the horrible reaction, when he lets his thumb go, towards hate and brutality, cruelty and destruction." It was to Lawrence's good as a novelist that the vital self was to him a thing of "duality and change." His major characters do display "*all* emotions," and they are the more human and recognizable for that. The problem, however, is that they tend to display them programmatically. They seem to wash about internally, to be full of hatred now and "luminous" with paradisal peace next, chiefly because Lawrence will not permit them, any more than he must, to remain at rest in the "old stable *ego*." Lawrence may not put his thumb on the pans, but he does set them to rocking rather wildly. His characters do not act on their own; they are acted upon by their author's vision. In Lawrence's novels it is not the psychology that is compelling but the spectacle, grand and poetic, of human emotions in a curious dance beneath the "travelling stars."

If Lawrence's view of the vital self as a "polarity" encouraged excessive changes in his characters at the same time that it harmonized with actual human psychology, his rival view of the self as ideally a "fusion" simply turned them into fantasies. Will and Anna on their honeymoon, Birkin and Ursula in "Excurse," Kate Leslie and Don Ramon in the coils of the Snake of the now, are characters who present us with "really new feelings" indeed. They are so far out of the "emotional rut" of actual human experience that no one can take them seriously. They are characters in whom, for a while, Lawrence himself sleeps away the cares of this world. They are unbelievable, and sometimes foolish, precisely to the extent that they are Laurentian. It is to this "sleep" that Lawrence would bring all of his characters; here is the "new conception" for which he has found himself willing to stay here and "persist and persist for ever," rather than resign himself to the death that "is beyond our sullying." Yet once he has maneuvered a special few into the paradisal dimension, he ceases to have anything to say to us. We are forced to leave him there, dreaming, alone.

How much more credible than the "intolerable accessions" of the later books are Paul Morel's unconscious discoveries of "the great Being" in *Sons and Lovers*. In Paul, erotic mystical intuition seems no more than the wake of his sexual excitement; it *follows* his psychology and experience. In the later books, by contrast, this intuitive "Understanding" becomes an idea, a knowledge (of the "unknown" though it may be) that is deliberately pursued. The heroes and heroines are herded into it because Lawrence himself is anxious once again to be there.

It is unfortunate, I think, that Lawrence's novels are curious and maimed just where fiction is, after all, morally crucial and influential: in its depiction of human beings. Yet it must be said again that even in the most extreme of Lawrence's novels, such as *The Plumed Serpent* (I shall say nothing, however, for the second part of *The Man Who Died*), there is enough brilliantly observed and livingly presented human and natural reality to make them absorbing and beautiful works. Even failing this, Lawrence gives us, in compensation for what we may regret in him, and as a rule, an intense and sensuously magnificent vision, a vision that does indeed answer to the Romantic needs of the soul.

VI.   *The Politics of Being*

Lawrence's politics represent his attempt to adjust his metaphysic of a universal spontaneity to his hatred of the "democratic mob." The attempt, it must be said, was unsuccessful; for the two ingredients will not blend. Yet certainly it constitutes (in the terminology of *Kangaroo*) an extraordinary "thought-adventure."

"It was in 1915," Lawrence writes in *Kangaroo,* that "the old world ended." No one who had "really consciously lived" through the collapse of London in the winter 1915-1916, he continues, "can believe again absolutely in democracy." Yet it cannot be said that the war disillusioned Lawrence himself with democracy; for democracy, to Lawrence, had never been an ideal. Neither had all the other ideals that (according to Lilly, the autobiographical figure of *Aaron's Rod*) it was no longer possible to believe in: "The ideal of love, the ideal that it is better to give than to receive, the ideal of liberty . . . the ideal of the sanctity of human life . . . the ideal of sacrifice for a cause, the ideal of unity and unanimity. . . ." The "old world" had ended for Lawrence when he discovered that his bond with his mother was his destiny. It was then that he imagined, or that there opened up for him, a "spontaneous creative universe" of creatures alternately vitally isolated and mystically united—a universe in which there is neither need nor space for ideals. For Lawrence, the war was, in this connection, merely a "conclusive" Apocalypse, a final proof of the insignificance of the "old world."

The real lesson of the war for Lawrence lay elsewhere: in its revelation of the power of the mob. "From 1916 to 1919," he writes in *Kangaroo*, "a wave of criminal lust rose and possessed England, there was a reign of terror, under a set of indecent bullies like Bottomley of *John Bull* and other bottom-dog members of the House of Commons." "The torture," he adds, "was steadily applied, during those years after Asquith fell, to break the independent soul in any man who would not hunt with the criminal mob."

The word "hunt" directs us to Lawrence's fundamental source of grievance: the persecution he endured as the English husband of a German wife. Unfortunately, this persecution drove Lawrence, already proudly isolated, even further into himself, so that he was "like a man on a plank in a shipwreck," the plank being "his own individual self." No wonder that, in the fiction he wrote after the war, Lawrence would claim that "the self is absolute. It may be relative to everything else in the universe. But to itself it is an absolute." But of course not even this idea was new to the Lawrence of the war and postwar years; only the note of desperate insistence was new. The important effects of the persecution were, first, to turn Lawrence, in his own words, into "a sort of human bomb, black inside, and primed," and, second, to leave him terrified of mob rule. Violently, the war threw Lawrence up against the question of power, giving him an interest in it at once furious and fascinated. During the war, he had been humiliated by power; afterward, in reaction, he would be seduced by it.

In *Aaron's Rod* (1922)—the first of Lawrence's fictional ventures at a new politics—Lawrence rather tentatively and apologetically shows his interest, his hardly disguised personal interest, in the exercise of power. Now Lawrence had never denied the necessity of power—in fact, in "The Crown" he had identified the "dark" pole of Being itself with power (associating the "light" pole with love). He had often insisted on the necessary duality and equilibrium of the tiger and the lamb in human nature. What is new, in *Aaron's Rod*, is the surprising declaration that the love urge is now spent, the lamb a fat old sheep that would be better off dead: ". . . the mode of our being is such that we can only live and have our being whilst we are implicit in one of the great dynamic modes. We *must* either love, or rule. And once the love-mode changes, as change it must, for we are worn out and becoming evil in its persistence, then the other mode will take place in us. And there will be profound, profound obedience in place of this love-crying, obedience to the incalculable power-urge."

The "power-urge," writes Lawrence in his essay "Blessed Are the Powerful," "comes to us, we know not how, from beyond." Genuine power, he says, is not will, still less money or position, but the "proud gate" of the soul, the strength of life in a man: the charge he carries of the Absolute. This power "is like electricity, it has different degrees. Men are powerful or powerless, more or less. . . . And the communion of power will always be a communion in inequality." Lilly, in *Aaron's Rod*, obliquely reveals—one would say betrays, but Lawrence is hiding nothing —the origin of this conviction of metaphysical inequality in the author's painful experiences during the war. "You've got to have a sort of slavery again," he says. "People are not *men*: they are insects and instruments, and their destiny is slavery. They are too many for me, and so what I think is ineffectual. But ultimately they will be brought to agree—after sufficient extermination—and then they will elect for themselves a proper and healthy and energetic slavery." No doubt there is consciously enjoyed perversity in this, and we may indeed detect here the ticking of "a sort of human bomb." Nevertheless, Lawrence is serious, never more so, in suggesting that some men are destined for slavery, others for leadership, and that there must be "a real committal of the life-issue of inferior beings to the responsibility of a superior being": "a sort of voluntary self-gift" ("more or less" voluntary, he qualifies) and "a voluntary acceptance. For it's no pretty gift, after all." "But once made," Lilly observes, "it must be held fast by genuine power. . . . Permanent and very efficacious power"—that is, "of course," military power.

Yet the moment anyone takes him seriously, Lilly cries: ". . . one can easily make a fool of you." Obviously he feels a little uneasy about his politics of slavery, perhaps a little shamefaced. Setting a pattern of ambivalent oscillation that will be repeated in *Kangaroo* and *The Plumed Serpent*, he declares: "I think every man is a sacred and holy individual, *never* to be violated. I think there is only one thing I hate to the verge of madness, and that is *bullying*. To see any living creature *bullied*, in *any* way, almost makes a murderer of me." The statement itself is tense with incipient contradiction: the murderous impulse against bullies who are also, supposedly, "sacred and holy" individuals. And certainly there would seem to exist a tension between Lilly's passionate individualism and his advocacy of the slavery of the many to the few. Lilly, however, denies any self-contradiction. "I don't go back on what I said before," he explains to Aaron Sisson. "I do believe that every man must fulfill his own soul, every woman must be herself, herself only, not some man's instrument, or some embodied theory." It is just that men and women must fulfill their souls through voluntary submission to the metaphysically powerful! "You'll never get it," protests Aaron. "You will," Lilly replies, "when all men want it. All men say, they want a leader. Then let them in their souls submit to some greater soul than theirs." Lilly's belief in the inviolability of the individual thus paralyzes him as a leader; until men are ready to submit to such men as himself, he can do nothing but burn and talk. In consequence, *Aaron's Rod* leaves us feeling suspended in air, and also feeling that Lawrence himself is suspended, hoping where he has no reason to hope. The "insects and instruments," the "mass-bullies, the individual Judases"—is it these who will someday voluntarily submit to superior men? Lawrence is divided, in *Aaron's Rod*, between denigration and flattery of the masses, between black despair and febrile hope.

The check that Lawrence's reverence for the individual places on his manifest hunger for power in *Aaron's Rod* virtually disappears in *Kangaroo* (1923). As this novel reminds us, the precinct of Laurentian individuality is the "central self, the isolate, absolute self," which is God-given and divine in substance. But according to Somers, the protagonist of *Kangaroo*, "The bulk of mankind haven't got any central selves. . . ." There is therefore nothing in them to violate. Since they have no selves to submit, voluntary self-submission can scarcely be expected of them—nor does Lawrence any longer seem to expect it. There is, instead, a new note of compassionate paternalism:

> Most men bruise themselves to death trying to fight and overcome their own new, life-born needs, life's ever-strange new imperatives. . . . [Note the contradiction here. They have no central selves, yet they have "life-born needs."] Life is cruel—and above all things man needs to be reassured and suggested into his new issues. And he needs to be relieved from this terrible responsibility of governing himself when he doesn't know what he wants, and has no aim towards which to govern himself. Man again needs a father. . . . Man needs a quiet, gentle father who uses his authority in the name of living life, and who is absolutely stern against anti-life.

This statement is made, not by Somers, an uprooted, "classless" Englishman, but by Kangaroo, the leader of a nationalist movement in Australia. Somers, however, approves of the totalitarian character of Kangaroo's politics. Indeed, Lawrence—never one to place himself second—lets it be known that Kangaroo has derived most of his ideas from Somers's essays.

Nevertheless, Somers differs from Kangaroo in his interpretation of power. To Kangaroo, power is of the spirit: it is love. To Somers, on the other hand, power is of the blood, "darkly" metaphysical. "I know your love," he says. "Working everything from the spirit, from the head. You work the lower self as an instrument of the spirit. Now it is time for the spirit to leave us again; it is time for the Son of Man to depart, and leave us dark, in front of the unspoken God: who is just beyond the dark threshold of the lower self, my lower self."[1] ("My," here, is not so much proprietary as defensive; for Somers, as uneasy as Lilly, more than a little suspects that his views may strike others as nonsense.)

Somers, though more intrigued by Kangaroo, is actually more tolerant of the less personally threatening Willie Struthers, the leader of a "matey" Australian Socialist movement. Mate love had always attracted Lawrence; socialism, however, simply bored him. Here was idealism at its last gasp, perhaps the "logically inevitable next step," as Lilly concedes, but nonetheless the last step just before the dead end. Like his disagreement with Kangaroo's Nationalism, however, Somers's disagreement with Struthers's Socialism is fundamentally a dispute as to the nature of power. There is in the socialist mentality, Mannheim has observed, "a glorification of the material aspects of existence, which were formerly experienced merely as negative and obstructive factors"; and to Lawrence, too, they are merely nega-

---

[1] What is astonishing is that Somers does not yet seem to have been in "communication" with this "great dark God"—in which, however, he has such confidence and of which he has so much to say. In Chapter IX, he reflects "that before mankind would accept any man for a king, and before Harriet [his wife] would ever accept him, Richard Lovat, as a lord and master, he . . . must open the door of his soul and let in a dark Lord and Master for himself, the dark god he had sensed outside the door." This is not encouraging. And one hundred pages later, Somers, it seems, has yet "to turn to the old dark gods, who had waited so long in the outer dark." Moreover, Somers holds conflicting ideas about the dark God. On the one hand, the God passion appears to be a kind of various and continuous fountain of impulse. Open the gate of the lower self, Somers says, and "sometimes in rushes Thor . . . or Bacchus comes mysteriously through . . . ; or it is Venus. . . . All the gods." On the other hand, the dark God seems to give only one new "prompting" every few generations, or even centuries. (Thus the old Christian ideals are not mistaken; they are merely dead, having lived their natural life.) And what Somers wants to establish is, of course, not a continual play of various impulse but a "new life-form."

tive, if not obstructive. "All this political socialism," complains Somers,"—all politics, in fact,—have conspired to make money the only god." If Somers wants "the men with the real passion for life, . . . for *living* and not for *having*," to "seize control of the material possessions," it is to "safeguard the world from all the masses who want to seize material possessions for themselves, blindly," and not of course, so that the supreme few can enjoy these possessions themselves. These last will enjoy one thing only: the pride of God's presence at the "lower" door. It was because socialism located *its* god, as Mannheim said, "within the framework of history" that Lawrence could never take a real interest in it.

Indeed, Somers is inclined to be critical even about the mateyness of Struthers's Socialism. As in the case of the Nationalist movement, he balks at a politics of love. "Absolute lovers," he reflects, "always smash one another," and, in any case, ". . . human beings *can't* absolutely love one another," for ". . . every individuality is bound to react at some time against every other individuality, without exception—or else lose its own integrity. . . ." True, ". . . the human heart must have an absolute." But only one absolute will satisfy it: "The God who is the source of all passion."

The "God-passion" itself is "polarized," as we have seen. It prompts every individual to both pride and submission, power and love. Once again, "every individuality is bound to react . . . against every other individuality, without exception. . . ." Yet if this is true, then the effort to keep the many in a state of submission would constitute a violation of their natures. To bring his Spontaneous State into line with his metaphysic, Lawrence is thus forced to deny that the vital self exists in most men, at the same time that, in rejecting love as an absolute, he insists that it is present, holy and inviolable.

The truth is that, when power is in question, Lawrence is finally prepared to champion only the individuality of the few. It is the protection of the outstanding individuals, not the fulfillment of the many, that he has at heart. Though he observes in *Kangaroo* that "the purest lesson our era has taught is that man, at his highest, is an individual, single, isolate, alone, in direct soul-communication with the unknown God, which prompts within him," it is clearly his own high individual value, rather than that of the "criminal" or centerless many, for which he has a passionate regard. Significantly, it is only when Somers is personally threatened with self-obliteration by love, whether political or personal, that he shrinks aways and takes a ringing stand on the inviolate and absolute character of the soul. When he thinks of the "foul, dense, carrion-eating mob," he is not nearly so particular about insisting on individuality.

There are, then, two Lawrences: a totalitarian politician of power and submission, and a metaphysician of "individual being"; and the only way to understand their apparently peaceful co-existence is to see that the first has the submission of "others" in mind, the second his own inviolability. Thus the metaphysician will say in "The Reality of Peace": "The very division of mankind into two halves, the humble and the proud, is death. Unless we pull off the old badges and become ourselves, single and new, we are divided unto death," whereas, in the very same essay, the totalitarian will say: ". . . alas! the slaves have got the upper hand. Nevertheless, it only needs that we go forth with whips, like the old chieftain. Swords will not frighten them, they are too many. At all costs the herd of nullity must be subdued."

Just what a Laurentian State would be like, God-uttered and shaped, is illustrated in *The Plumed Serpent,* where for the first time a Laurentian hero becomes a social leader. Don Ramon's Quetzalcoatl society (established after some trickery and calculation—which is to say, not quite "spontaneously") embodies the two principles of the "new" state that Lawrence had outlined to Bertrand Russell in 1915: ". . . . the idea is . . . that the highest understanding must dictate for the lower understandings. And . . . the highest aim of the government is the highest good of the *soul*, of the individual, the fulfilment in the Infinite, in the

Absolute." The Laurentian State is thus—in words Kangaroo uses of his Nationalist program—a "kind of Church, with the profound reverence for life . . . as the motive power." And despite both Kangaroo's and Somers's disclaimers in this regard, its purpose is the salvation of souls, their fulfillment in the Absolute—that and, of course, the protection of the "outstanding individuals" from the masses who, according to *The Plumed Serpent* also, have no "centre, no real I," only "a raging black hole, like the middle of a maelstrom." To create and thus save the souls of the masses, the "few individuals" in the world are (we now perceive in *The Plumed Serpent*) obliged not only to present themselves as masters of life *and death*, but to prescribe the content of their subjects' minds and the forms of their public rituals—to indoctrinate them with an explanatory myth of reality.

"When I hear modern people complain of being lonely," Lawrence wrote in his last book, *Apocalypse*, "then I know what has happened. They have lost the Cosmos." And insofar as the Quetzalcoatl government is generous, it aims to give men mystery and "let the world live again" in their eyes; it means to give them togetherness with one another and the universe. To this end Don Ramon revives—or, more accurately, reinvents—an ancient Aztec myth of the cosmos, literally reissuing it in installments, the so-called hymns of Quetzalcoatl, which he has printed up by the hundreds. These hymns serve to connect the people emotionally and imaginatively with the world. To effect the ultimate goal of his religion, the fulfillment of the individual in the Infinite, Ramon also invents rituals, the purpose of which is to lead the individual beyond myth, as we have already seen in his own case, into the dark and "infinite room that lies inside the axis of our wheeling space." Ramon thus makes himself master of both his subjects' waking consciousness and their mystical sleep—he is indeed "lord of the day and night." It is in this sense that the Laurentian State is totalitarian: a total if gently nourishing governance of human life.

Predictably, however, Ramon's government is gentle only so long as men freely submit to it. In fact, those who do not submit are declared "less than men" and "not good enough for the light of the sun." In the notorious passage depicting the ritual execution of five "rebels," Lawrence illustrates what it means to be (in Kangaroo's words) "absolutely stern against anti-life." Lawrence is tough and unabashedly candid about the motive for these killings: "If men that are men will live, men that are less than men must be put away, lest they multiply too much." Far from constituting a lapse, as others have suggested, the scene is the logical outcome of Lawrence's most pressing reason for pursuing power in the first place—namely to become the master of men like those who had once overmastered him. As for its inhumanity, Lawrence had long before vehemently rejected the values that the word *humanity* implies. The execution is a not surprising outcome of Lawrence's substitution of justice to the metaphysical life principle (or the outstanding few) for the democratic ideal of justice to the individual. In *Sea and Sardinia* (1921), Lawrence remarked of two convicts whom he had seen chained together among a Sicilian crowd: "It is a great mistake to abolish the death penalty. If I were dictator, I should order the old one to be hung at once. I should have judges with sensitive, living hearts: not abstract intellects. And because the instinctive heart recognized a man as evil, I would have that man destroyed. Quickly. Because good warm life is now in danger." Here we see the same metaphysical "justice" at work. In both instances Lawrence flagrantly betrays his own words: "I think every man is a sacred and holy individual, *never* to be violated."

In sum, to make his ideal of the self consistent with his political needs Lawrence revised it "into two halves, the humble and the proud." Feeling it necessary to declare the death of love, he failed to see that the "humble gate" of the self, on which his politics relied, is, after all, precisely the gate of love. Nor did Lawrence acknowledge that men who should find themselves ready to make a voluntary obeisance to "higher" men would already have admitted the dark God into their souls—or where should they find the grace to submit? But in that case they should be truly "individual" at last, "in direct soul-communication with the unknown God"; they should not need a man of "Understanding" to guide them. On the other hand, if the masses lack souls—as Lawrence, in his desperation, sometimes thought—then they cannot be helped, only herded. But Lawrence could not accede to this. He was a savior, not a shepherd, and his centerless masses, so badly in need of a soulful leader, must of necessity have souls themselves, deep answering unto deep.

In trying to extract a politics from his metaphysic, Lawrence thus came up with a tangle of cross-assumptions. The truth is that it was a mistake for Lawrence to design a politics at all, for a Laurentian politics is a contradiction in terms. If there is indeed a "deep God," if He is indeed the spontaneous self of each man, then there should be no need for a politics of any kind. Holding all individuals "separate and yet sustained in accord," the deep God would resolve the political world into a harmony of perfected beings. Left alone, untormented, Lawrence might never have made his disastrous literary foray into politics. Goaded as he was, however, he dreamed of a State in which no one should really be left alone and in which the bullying of those who resist submission would be done, for a change, by outstanding individuals like himself.

VII. *Oliver & Constance / John Thomas & Lady Jane*

In *Lady Chatterley's Lover* (1928), Lawrence's last full-length novel, his vitalism reasserts its original wholesomeness. Indeed, it was never so lovely and peaceful, so nearly idyllic, as in this book by a dying vitalist. Here the morbidity of *The Plumed Serpent* has passed over like a shadowing cloud, leaving a profound and life-affirming tenderness. *Tenderness* was, in fact, one of the three projected titles of the book; and perhaps it is the most felicitous of the three. For the tenderness of this novel, so overwhelming, so surprising in view of the preceding work, is its great achievement: an emotion self-luminous, gentle yet exalted.

It is, to begin with, an aesthetic tenderness, the overflow of delighted senses, the grace of a sensibility exquisitely open to the physical poetry of the world. It is this tenderness that hears and reports "the tinkle as of tiny water-bells" of John's Well, that lingers over the first violets "that smelled sweet and cold, sweet and cold," that sees the daffodils "rustling and fluttering and shivering, so bright and alive" and the "thick-clustered primroses no longer shy." And the tenderness of the book is physical as well: the glow that radiates from the sense of touch, from the aroused blood, lights many of its pages. But what is new, here, in the range of Lawrence's tenderness—new enough to be almost revolutionary—is a quite human tenderness, that is, a moral one. Hitherto Lawrence had allowed in his scheme of salvation little place for the milder Eros, for love not experienced in extremity—in sensual or mystical floods of "ineffable riches." But in *Lady Chatterley's Lover* he has brought together, for the first time, the two great streams of sensuality and affection. Here compassion and passion become subtle translations of each other, as when Mellors, seeing a tear fall onto Connie's wrist, stands up and moves away from the pheasant coop at which he had been working, "for suddenly he was aware of the old flame shooting and leaping up in his loins, that he had hoped was quiescent for ever." It is a high moment in Lawrence's art, this moment of passionate tenderness; with St. Augustine, it says *I want you to be.*

To be sure, there is bitterness, too, in *Lady Chatterley's Lover.* It is Mellors who says of "the Cliffords and Berthas": "Tender to them? Yea, even then the tenderest thing you could do for them, perhaps, would be to give them death. They can't live. They only frustrate life. . . . Death ought to be sweet to them. And I ought to be allowed to shoot them." This, of course, is the old, the too-familiar Laurentian arrogance—so virulent a combination of egoism and fear of the world. Lawrence, as in his earlier fiction of the twenties, is still writing with the blood of the wounds he received from the "indecent bullies" of wartime England—the spies outside the window, the officials at induction centers, the censors of his books. In Mellors, as in "the man who died," there is a curious sense of having been hurt too deeply to want to live any longer, though life nonetheless—as in that shooting up of "the old flame" in his loins—renews him. ". . . I ought to be allowed to shoot them"—these are the words of a man too blisteringly proud to forget an injury, a man liable to be wounded, when wounded at all, to the very quick.

Lawrence's characteristic antipathy to the individual *person,* to that "vile entity," the ego, is also much in evidence in the book. True, the expert witnesses at the British trial of the novel spoke of Lady Chatterley and Mellors as one speaks of actual persons one has known—a tribute to these characters' humanity. Mr. Griffith-Jones, in the opening address for the prosecution, had sounded the challenge:

> it [the unexpurgated novel] goes on to give us a little, and you may think it gives us very little, about the characters of the people mentioned; the heroine, if I may so describe her, Lady Chatterley, and the hero, if I may so describe him, the gamekeeper, are, you think, little more than bodies, bodies which continually have sexual intercourse with one another.

"Bodies which continually have sexual intercourse" is of course nonsense, and the tone of this puts one off. Still, was the witness who said, "I think . . . Connie Chatterley and Mellors . . . are extremely closely and intimately drawn" any nearer to the truth? Or Mr. Gardiner of the defense when he spoke of the hero and heroine as being "in love" and of Lawrence's concern that men and women "re-establish personal relationships"? Or the witnesses who said, severally, that the book stresses "the real value and integrity of personal relations," that Lawrence intended to establish a "spiritual relationship between persons," that he tried "to tell the story of two people . . . and their personal feelings, and an attempt by these two people to break through into personal fulfillment," and that the novel recommends "a right and full relationship"? In a word, no. The vocabulary is all wrong—much too conventional and, in terms of the novel, outdated. It was Lawrence, after all, who said in "A Propos of *Lady Chatterley's Lover*": "We have abstracted men and women into separate personalities—personalities being isolated units, incapable of togetherness . . ."; who insisted that "the sex activity is . . . in some way hostile to the mental, *personal* relationship between man and woman"; who spoke of the ego, the assertive, identifying core of the person, as "false" and "evil"; and who thought the "modern cult of personality" simply "fatal for marriage." What misled the witnesses, perhaps, was not only their desire to rescue Lawrence's novel but the novelty of its enterprise—namely, the creation of a pastoral tragi-comedy, a romance, not of human individuals, but of human *organisms*. The difference is a decisive one.

In the oversimplified polarity between the mechanical and the organic in *Lady Chatterley's Lover*—as in all of Lawrence— the personal, the ideal, the mental, are all linked to the first and the body and its "emotions" (the only authentic emotions, according to Lawrence) to the second. It is precisely the opposite of the "quest for identity" characteristic of our own day, the anxious search for a coherent sense of self, that is exemplified first by Mellors and then by Connie, both of whom pursue, instead, the anonymity of organic being. Since consciousness and names identify and thus fix and deaden, they are eschewed. Connie, at first, is puzzled by Mellors' "queer, persistent wanting her, when there was nothing between them, when he never really spoke to her." Yet it is she who earlier reflects, in connection with a father for the child she desires: "It was not a question of love; it was a question of *a man*. Why, one might even rather hate him, personally. . . . This business concerned another part of oneself." The sight of Mellors's half-naked body hits her in the impersonal "middle" of her own—evidently that other "part" of herself with which mating is concerned. And, significantly, she neglects to ask his name until late in the book. Just as he thinks of her as "the woman," so she is content to think of him as "the man."

"He! He! What name do you call him by? You only say *he*," said Hilda.

"I've never called him by any name: nor he me: which is curious, when you come to think of it. Unless we say Lady Jane and John Thomas."

Being a "democracy of touch," a love of and for the body, Laurentian love, here as before, does not recognize persons. "Perhaps he wasn't quite individual enough," Connie reflects of Mellors; "he might be the same with any woman. . . . It really wasn't personal. She was only really a female to him." But it is just this impersonality that she comes to value: "She could feel in the same world with her the man, the nameless man, moving on beautiful feet, beautiful in the phallic mystery."

Moreover, as from his earlier heroines Lawrence exacts from Connie the obliteration of her personality, insofar, that is, as she is to represent the beloved—"Self! Self! Self!" especially in women, being the particular object of his (as of Mellors's) nausea and loathing. Thus, for Lawrence, Connie is "herself," she is what she really ought to be, only when—the "quick of all her plasm" having been touched—"she was gone, she was not, and she was born: a woman." For it is then that she finally dies as a person and is born as a "strange," "nameless," "beautiful" organic being. The aim of this passage, as of the one that gives us Mellors "motionless, and in the invisible flame of another consciousness"— that of the "basic, physical mind"—is to embody the transcendent "reality of peace" that issues from organic "togetherness." Peace is, indeed, the cardinal desire in *Lady Chatterley's Lover*—not love, not even tenderness, certainly not joy, but organic peace. And peace for Lawrence is escape from "the sense of menace and fear" that he always associated with "the feeling of individualism and personality." Here once again —as had first been the case in *Women in Love*—individuality is to being what evil is to good.

This, of course, could have been predicted—the rankling bitterness, the virulence against the "others," especially insofar as they are distinct personalities, with edges sharp and (for Lawrence) lethal as blades. Yet the tenderness of *Lady Chatterley's Lover* is all the more, and not the less, remarkable for the bitterness that qualifies it. It assumes an aspect of unquenchable life assertion. It is as if Lawrence, despite the longing for a "death sleep" so frankly expressed in *The Plumed Serpent*, yet found "good warm life" irresistible, for all its pain. The tender quality of the book has the wonderful authority of an *unwanted* recovery; it seems to be an earnest that life, given time, will prove to be its own physician.

The most surprising and important sign of this healing, the most gratifying gift we could have received from a dying Lawrence, is the *sub rosa* triumph, for all the stress on anonymity, of "the old-fashioned human element" in the book. For Mellors and Connie do indeed come through as personalities—Connie so winsomely that, with Lawrence, our impulse is to call her Connie, not Constance or Lady Chatterley. What moves us, for example, in the scene already referred to, when Mellors's tender passion is aroused at his perception of Connie's misery, is his involuntary, humane response to her life, not as a "strange" or "inhuman" being, but as a suffering person. And then there is the remarkable letter from Mellors that concludes the novel— so "human" a letter to come from a Lawrence protagonist, so much the expression of a "daily I" that looks forward to loving in the daily world.

If things go on as they are, there's nothing lies in the future but death and destruction, for these industrial masses. I feel my inside turn to water sometimes, and there you are, going to have a child by me. But never mind. All the bad times that ever have been, haven't been able to blow the crocus out: not even the love of women. So they won't be able to blow out my wanting you, nor the little glow there is between you and me. We'll be together next year.

Would Birkin have been capable of such a letter—Birkin with his irritable Salvator Mundi touch, his shrill insistence to Ursula that there "is a real impersonal me," "an isolated me, that does *not* meet and mingle, and never can," "and it is there I would want to meet you. . . " ? Though Birkin wants a love more delicate than fierce, he wants it "mindlessly in darkness"; Ursula is to him less a person than a creature "mystically-physically satisfying." By contrast, when Mellors writes to Connie, "Never mind about Sir Clifford. . . . He can't really do anything to you. Wait, he will want to get rid of you at last. . . . ," it is quite as if he thought of her, person that she is, as at least a friend, someone to reassure and to help.

From the point of view of Lawrence's beliefs, there is in this

novel an even more astonishing victory of what the author liked
to patronize as the old-fashioned human element: the quite
lively presence of those two scandalous, unique characters in
distinguished English fiction, John Thomas and Lady Jane.
How unexpected, after the esoteric rhetoric of *Women in Love*
and *The Plumed Serpent*, this humanization of the sexual organs! Up to this point, to go with his "nonhuman people,"
Lawrence had propounded a queer "electric" or "fiery" or awesomely "paradisal" sexuality. But now, into this lovely, warm
lull, before the solemn sexual ponderosities of *The Man Who
Died*, come humor, lightheartedness, erotic gaiety. In Mellors's
personifications of his and Connie's sexual organs there is an
almost youthful jollity. At the same time, Mellors and Connie
are near to being forlorn in nothing so much as this, that they
come to seem secondary, even in their own eyes, to their sexual
organs, which appear to have a fuller humanity than their own.
Is Mellors weary of will, can he not tolerate Connie's? Never
mind: John Thomas, admirable fellow, has a "will of his own."
Mellors, again, may be sour, but John Thomas "comes up
smilin'." And if Mellors's occupation is low, John Thomas is a
"gentleman"—even knighted. If Mellors and Connie cannot yet
get married, John Thomas is free to marry Lady Jane:

> He fastened fluffy young oak-sprays round her breasts, sticking in
> tufts of bluebells and campion: and in her navel he poised a pink
> campion flower, and in her maiden-hair were forget-me-nots and
> woodruff.
> "That's you in all your glory!" he said. "Lady Jane, at her wedding
> with John Thomas."

This "lad," moreover, "cheeky" as he is, has in this novel the
last word: "John Thomas says good night to Lady Jane, a little
droopingly, but with a hopeful heart." The dehumanization of
Mellors and Connie is thus inversely proportional to the humanization of their sexual organs. "This is John Thomas mar-
ryin' Lady Jane," Mellors says again. "An' we mun let Constance
an' Oliver go their ways."

The creation of John Thomas and Lady Jane—and *John Thomas and Lady Jane* was Lawrence's favorite of the projected titles—thus reflects a deep ambivalence. On the one hand, it implies the rejection, the insignificance, of Constance and Oliver, two human *persons*. On the other hand, it personalizes the human body just where—given Lawrence's wish to dehumanize the human being—we might have expected the greatest stress on a nonhuman organic quality. What Lawrence had for so long scorned and repudiated re-enters his fiction, blatantly and affirmatively, at the place where it could least have been anticipated. And what this seems to signify is precisely what is revealed by the almost tangible tenderness in the novel: a new acquiescence to the conditions of life and the inescapable complexity of human nature. *Lady Chatterley's Lover* is, like *Middlemarch*, a book that stands out in its author's canon as the work which admits, both in the sense of confesses and gives entry to, truths and realities otherwise resisted and denied.

Lawrence's long flight from personality had always been, in part, an effort to keep himself separate from others so as to be free to face toward the "beyond" where his mother had become "intermingled." And this is to say that his ethic of an impersonal individualism was, even from the first, the result and sinecure of a somewhat morbid mysticism. Not surprisingly, then, in *Lady Chatterley's Lover* the morbid desire for a world that is "other" and the horror of personality ease concurrently. The mists of "distribution" clear, leaving an immediate world that, though endangered, nevertheless contains beauty, ecstasy, tenderness, companionship, even a little gaiety and humor. The novel of Lawrence's in which personality enjoys its greatest triumph is also the book in which the vital world is most lovingly described, most cherished for its own sake—as if it were, after all, the only world we have. Unlike Birkin, Mellors does not tug at the tethers of daily human consciousness. The mystical translations or "births" are largely reserved for Connie, as if only from a woman's point of view could Lawrence now feel free to fantasize about an inner, vital eternality. (The attempt from the male point of view in *The Man Who Died* proves embarrassing.)

By comparison with *The Plumed Serpent, Lady Chatterley's Lover* displays a sudden and inevitably somewhat sad access of realism—a fall back into this world. Not that it is right to judge, as has been done, that the utopian Lawrence has here been stoned, as it were, into silence. Though *Lady Chatterley's Lover* contains enough sense of the real state of the world, and of the sheer hopelessness of hope, to scuttle a novel like *The Plumed Serpent*, the Lawrence of the political novels and of *Apocalypse* (1931) nonetheless finds his voice in it. He manages to sketch in both the activity and the political structure appropriate to paradise. Thus Fourier's and Morris's dream of pleasurable work is here dreamed again by Mellors, as he imagines a world where play is the prime activity. Of working men he says: "They ought to learn to be naked and handsome, and to sing in a mass and dance the old group dances, and carve the stools they sit on, and embroider their own emblems. . . . They should be alive and frisky, and acknowledge the great god Pan." And as for the politics of paradise, they are curiously like Clifford Chatterley's in appearance, so that when Clifford speaks, one often has the illusion that he is echoing earlier Laurentian political heroes, as when he says: ". . . today education is one of the bad substitutes for a circus. What is wrong today is that we've . . . poisoned our masses with a little education." Mellors's politics are Clifford's, however, only as transformed by a metaphysic of innate power and understanding in the highest men. Mellors, of course, is the true aristocrat in *Lady Chatterley's Lover*. He possesses a higher vital intelligence and a more majestic soul than Clifford; and that reference to the masses and *their* great god Pan illustrates his consciousness of his own superiority. ("The few can go in for the higher cults if they like," he allows. "But let the mass be forever pagan.") In the army, he himself had felt a blood subjection to a natural aristocrat, a Colonel, "a very intelligent man: . . . a passionate man in his way." "I lived under his spell while I was with him," Mellors says. "I sort of let him run my life. And I never regret it." And now he easily sounds masterful, even proprietary, in planning his utopia, as when he says, "An' I'd get my men to wear different clothes."

No, the Lawrence of *Lady Chatterley's Lover* has not relinquished his dreams of a metaphysical utopia, a Godly earth. He has, however, lost much of the confidence and hope that floated *The Plumed Serpent* out of the range of all likelihood. So long as a "power" stands beyond human beings—so *Lady Chatterley's Lover* suggests—perhaps humanity cannot lie beyond redemption. But our redemption, Lawrence now seems to feel, is too great a burden for one man. At least it is too much for Mellors.

It is true that Mellors enjoys in the novel a limited victory— a victory that we may take as allegorized by one of Lawrence's late paintings, *Eve Regaining Paradise*, which shows "Eve dodging back into Paradise, between Adam and the Angel at the gate, who are having a fight about it." In the novel, too, "fate" is flouted, an illusion; the Fall is not irredeemable. "Bit by bit" we can "drop the whole industrial life, an' go back"— back from Tevershall and Stacks Gate, the Satanic mills, and back from Wragby, the Heartbreak House of culture, to the garden, and be once again the "old Adam and the old Eve," "the sons of god with the daughters of men." But meanwhile the Angel at the gate proves formidable. The powerful Clifford, an Angel only in his and the world's regard, embodies not only personality and ego, but Science (engineering), Art (in his own stories, his love of Proust and the ordered emotions of Racine), Goodness ("Suddenly he had become almost wistfully moral, seeing himself the incarnation of good . . ."), Spirituality ("Belive me, whatever God there is is slowly eliminating the guts and alimentary system from the human being to evolve a higher, more spiritual being"), Work ("a certain remarkable inhuman force. . . . In business he was quite inhuman"), and Rule ("And what we need to take up now is whips, not swords"). And he has the key to the park gate.

Mellors and Connie will enjoy together, despite Clifford and despite their own saddening knowledge of things as they are, a primal delight, a paradisal innocence. Indeed, they enjoy it even in Clifford's park, though at the last they are locked out of it, and must love elsewhere. They will triumph; and yet how entrenched and extensive Clifford's fallen world is. "It won't disappear," Mellors is brought to admit. "I'd wipe the machines off the face of the earth again, and end the industrial epoch absolutely," he says, sounding like the old Lawrence. "But since I can't," he adds, "an' nobody can, I'd better hold my peace, an' try an' live my own life . . ."—which is exactly what he does.

Forced to leave Clifford's park, Mellors falls into a kind of dormancy until he and Connie can live together openly.[1] It is an honest and moving ending. Mellors waits at once in gratitude, sadness, and hope. He is grateful that, despite Clifford's world, Connie exists and is his own, and that the crocus will still come up. He is sad because he knows his powerlessness only too well. Yet he is hopeful, withal, because John Thomas, who is "himself," is still cheerful at heart. Nowhere else in Lawrence's conclusions do we find so rich, so likely, a blend of emotions. And what it suggests is that shortly before his death, and however reluctantly, Lawrence, relenting, acquiesced to an imperfect world.

[1] A similar "seasonal" rhythm of separation and togetherness—evidently a variant on the concept of "polarity" and "equilibrium"—appears later in *The Man Who Died*.

VIII. *Lawrence and Forster in Italy*

In the first two decades of the present century, Lawrence and Forster together constituted—constituted rather than effected—a revolution in English culture. Metaphysical writers both, they sought to restore, after the depletions of the previous century, a sense of wonder to the body of the world, including, of course, the human body. What both deplored in English culture was the divorce between ideation and impulse, the typically denatured, mechanical, ungiving, sterile character of the Englishmen of their day—and the fact that the magnificence of the physical world, as well as the music straining through it, had lost, in England, its power to pique, exalt, and bless.

This is to say that Lawrence and Forster passionately opposed the culture endorsed—if not quite typified—by George Eliot: a culture that placed itself above life, an overwhelmingly social, moral, and intellectual culture: a provincial colony of duty, conventionality, science, work, and charity isolated (so these post-Victorians thought) in a world actually pouring with vitality, and instinct with mysterious power. Both writers sought to reconstitute the sensuous self as an inhabitant of a universe of desire. They sought the larger world, the greater emotions, the "marvellous piercing transcendence" known to the Romantics, then lost for a time, a grown-over path. They unlocked doors, threw open windows, announced a new day.

Though Lawrence and Forster in Italy were two distinct writers, each turned to it as a country where vitality had not yet been subverted by civilization—as a place where it was still possible to be "whole man alive." As the Romantics themselves had done—and also, to a degree, that elusive Victorian, Browning—they went to Italy to be themselves. And, doing so, they left England behind or, at most, brought it with them as one brings a half to its completing half.

George Eliot in Italy, even in fifteenth-century Italy, had been Victorian England abroad, ensconced in her own set principles. She had managed to impose even on turbulent Renaissance life the lesson that the "highest" life of all is "a conscious voluntary sacrifice." Over the noise of the crowds in her Florentine streets rings the familiar, the inevitable theme: "Every bond of your life is a debt." Like the Savonarola whom it portrays, *Romola* takes its stand on "a great negation": the annulment of the creaturely ego. What it affirms is "the others"—that is, whatever is not humanly immediate and concrete; for each of the others, of course, must also deny himself while affirming others, so that no one is left self-affirmed, no one is firmly rooted in being. By contrast, Lawrence and Forster in Italy are Englishmen who reach for the roots of the self in desire. And desire itself, they believe, is a root that pierces into the heart of the world.

In Lawrence's case, it is true, self-realization was finally to prove hard to distinguish from a kind of self-abdication; for Lawrence came almost to prefer the root to the flower. And yet there is a very substantial Lawrence who believed that "the great *desire* is that each single individual shall be incommutably himself, spontaneous and single, that he shall not in any way be reduced to a term, a unit of any Whole"—a Lawrence who conceived of a *blossoming* self. We are therefore entitled to say

that, where George Eliot is a novelist of self-extrusion, Lawrence and Forster are both novelists of self-occupancy. To each
of them, carnality was not merely a condition but a component
of the self. Indeed, the body's mysterious vitality and emotions
formed, in their view, the very majesty of life.

There thus comes an end, in their pages, to the morality of
self-alienation that had formed the rock of the Victorian ethos.
To George Eliot, salvation had meant redemption from the undying worm of the bodily ego. In the pale if fervent realm of the
spirit—there alone lay goodness and peace. To Lawrence and
Forster, on the other hand, though no less salvationists, redemption is achieved precisely in and through the body, the first and
nearest home of the spirit. And charity, with them, begins at
home. The self is a living creature, not to be murdered. In fact,
the body is nearer the divine sources than the mind. Not that
the spirit, the mental matrix, can be ignored; indeed, the spirit
is inseparable from the body. Everything is important. Nothing
created is meant to be undone. It all hangs together, all of it is
wonderful. If there is "Eternity," it is to be sought "in the flux
of Time," not outside of it. Individual wholeness, the whole of
the world: these are the things worthy of our reverence.

Lawrence and the early Forster differed, however, in their
conception of the whole human being. Each conceived wholeness as dialectical, yet differently. In Lawrence the "contest"
between the flesh and the spirit climaxed in "consummations"
of unity, as in the jumping of a spark between two nodes. In
Forster, by contrast, with his ethic of "proportion," there is
simply a balancing in the course of time, the scales weighted
now toward helping others, now toward carnality, and so on.
"Don't *begin* with proportion," says his spokesman, Margaret
Schlegel. "Let proportion come in as a last resource, when the
better things have failed. . . ." Then, too, both writers conceived
wholeness, alternatively, as something quiescent, as a rainbow
and not the lightning's unifying dance. Yet in distinction from

the liquid Laurentian "fusion," completeness of this kind in Forster comes only when all the strings of the self are struck at once, in harmony.

Lawrence and Forster varied also in their view of the role or condition of mind in a complete and fulfilled human nature. They agreed, to be sure, in setting intuition above intelligence —a valuation indispensable for even the vaguest of vitalists. But where Forster granted a place, indeed an important function, to intelligence, Lawrence was uncertain of its necessity. He was ready, at most, to restrict its service to that of preparing the leap into instinct. Lawrence seems really to have believed that instinct or intuition is still powerful enough in human beings to act as a mind. A fate "dictated" entirely by the "feelings"—this was his ideal of human life. "The only thing a man has to trust to in coming to himself," Lawrence writes, "is his desire and his impulse." "The rare, superfine whispering of the new direction" is the only true "intelligence." We may "steer by the delicacy of adjusted understanding, and our will is the strength that serves us in this"; but the peace we seek—the peace which is the only "reality"—is a "sleep upon impulse." In Forster, by contrast, the mind, awake upon impulse, stirs and flies free with a vigor of its own; it is alert "in faith," not asleep "in faith." Lawrence's longing was to run the mind into the blood, as one mixes all the colors into white. In Forster, by contrast, mind, soul, and body, like the layered bands of a rainbow, remain delicately distinct. There is, in him, no rage for unconsciousness, no melting pot.

To become Laurentian, Lawrence, of course, did not need Italy. But unlike most things in this world, Italy agreed with him. Italy itself, so to speak, was very nearly Laurentian. The pagan idea of the self—betrayed though it is by modern Italy, as Italy itself had been betrayed by Northern machinery—was a lesson, Lawrence believed, that Italy could still supply to the English. Here they could find, not merely warmth, but the warmth of life.

It was partly to point this lesson that Lawrence wrote *Twilight in Italy* (1916), a "travel" book that could almost have been labeled an essay on man. *Twilight in Italy* is yet another of Lawrence's books advocating the "two ways"—those of the senses and the spirit. Congruent with these opposite "ways," Lawrence says, are two kinds of self: the Italian or pagan self, with its kingly and sensual "I"; and the Northern or Christian self, which is really a "Not-Self." Though the Italians had once climbed up from a pagan nature to the summit of the Christian spirit, later they slid back and remained in the fertile valleys, exulting only in the fulfillment of the ego, assuming "all power and glory unto the self." Having also reached the summit, the Northern races, by contrast, remained there, where the holy dove of the mind and soul rises free from the tree line of the senses and where the vastness of what lies beyond the self smites its natural pride.

The self, then, can move and have its being in and between two opposite Infinites—one within, the other without. By now, however, both the pagan and the Christian self, Lawrence says, have gone numb: neither Infinite is magical any longer. His conclusion: both must be revitalized.

The Lawrence of *Twilight in Italy* is thus ostensibly the Lawrence who conceives of completeness in terms of dynamic polarity. "It is past the time," he writes,

to cease seeking one Infinite, ignoring, striving to eliminate the other. The Infinite is twofold, . . . the Dark and the Light, the Senses and the Mind, the Soul and the Spirit, the self and the not-self, the Eagle and the Dove, the Tiger and the Lamb. The consummation of man is twofold, in the Self and Selflessness. By great retrogression back to the source of darkness in me, the Self, deep in the senses, I arrive at the Original, Creative Infinite. By projection forth from myelf, by the elimination of my absolute sensual self, I arrive at the Ultimate Infinite, Oneness in the Spirit. There are two Infinites, twofold approach to God. And man must know both.

Is life, then, to be an incoherent oscillation between extremes, or is it to be whole as well as complete? Now, the idea of unity commands Lawrence's intellect; it is even sovereign over his predilection for extremity—indeed, in him it is a form of extremity; and so we find Lawrence going on to insist that "there exists a relation" between the two Infinites—a relation he names, none too helpfully, "the Holy Ghost." Perhaps inevitably, his efforts to explain this concept arouse the suspicion that he is groping in the dark. The Holy Ghost is an "intervention" of some kind. It doesn't confuse the two Infinites—that would result in "nullity"; instead it yokes them, somehow, into "One Whole." How two extremes without a middle can add up to a whole, Lawrence does not and perhaps cannot elucidate; he can only point, as always, into the shadows of mysticism, where, unfortunately, those who are not adepts can perceive nothing but an absence of light.

In any case, *Twilight in Italy*—like all of Lawrence—swerves toward unity of a lesser kind: toward the powerful single magnet of the dark sensuous pole. The book really bespeaks regret only for the death of the sensual Infinite. It is about this that Lawrence feels the ache of loss. Significantly, in the passage just quoted, he makes the Spirit the *antithesis* of the Soul—a parsing that seems to rob the spirit of any special accent.

Elsewhere in Lawrence, as we have seen, the soul itself is the complete and coherent quick of the human being, the "center" where neither Spirit nor Blood is excluded. It is the only unit that pulses with the "unknown." In its presence, there would thus be no call to project the self forth into an "Ultimate Infinite." Indeed, this would undo the soul. So convinced was Lawrence that the soul was inextricably part of the body that he chose to identify it with the blood. ". . . the blood," he said, "is the substance of the soul, and of the deepest consciousness." Why, then, does he insist on a polarity that sends one reeling out into "the not-self"? The truth would seem to be that, partial as Lawrence was to the "darkness," to "the Original, Creative Infinite," he was yet English enough to be dismayed by examples of lethargy in the Italian blood. Of the "blood sleep" of a Bavarian peasant he notes: ". . . this heat of physical experience, becomes at length a bondage, at last a crucifixion." It was probably in reaction against this *excess* of the blood (of blood which here seems to be less than "the substance of the soul"!) that Lawrence urged the need for recurrent "elimination" of the "absolute sensual self." As time went on, he would urge increasingly the "elimination" of the split between the spirit and the senses. Snapping from extreme to extreme as he does in *Twilight in Italy*, he bypasses altogether the fusion that even here he appears to desire.

The reason Lawrence seeks "fusion" is that he wants to escape the tearing loneliness of the mind. And he knows that he can find what he wants within the "universal blood." Yet it is not quite or not only this he wants either. After all, there is "supremacy," his "individuality," to consider. And this he is too proud, too intense—in truth too much a settled self—to relinquish. Lawrence's theory shifts and turns about as one or the other of these contrary needs gains ascendancy. Yet the need for "togetherness" preponderates, and even "individuality," as we have seen, he prized as a way of keeping his soul free for its liaison with the Infinite.

As we pursue Lawrence in Italy, Lawrence grows more frustrated, more bitter; and in consequence his preference for the sensual becomes more manifest. In *The Lost Girl* (1920), Italy is portrayed, splendidly, as a wild, romantic region of the sensual Infinite. At the same time that the novel registers Lawrence's own shock before the savage landscape he so stunningly describes, and also his unease before Italian "blood sleep," it lays bare the intense glamour that extreme sensuality always possessed for him, the depth of his longing for self-loss. The Italian hero, Cicio, and the landscape blend into one overpowering, ambivalently exciting lover as they compel Cicio's wife, Alvina, the English heroine who has come to live in Italy, toward unconsciousness and the sleep of the spirit. Cicio has upon Alvina this kind of effect: "Her eyes were wide and neutral and submissive, with a new awful submission as if she had lost her soul. So she looked up at him, like a victim." In the same way, the "flood of light on dazzling white snow tops, glimmering and marvellous in the evanescent night," "the pallid valley-bed away below," the "scrubby, blue-dark foot-hills with twiggy trees," all "magical," seem to extinguish her "very being," to send her "completely unconscious." Sometimes she feels "a wild, terrible happiness" while thinking that "No one would ever find her. She had gone beyond the world into the pre-world, she had re-opened on the old eternity." A "savage hardness" comes into her heart; she begins to find it only too easy to believe that the "fierce, savage gods" were "the true gods."

Like Kate Leslie of *The Plumed Serpent*, Alvina "yields" one day and revolts the next, not knowing whether to lie down in the sun and "swoon for ever unconscious" or leave Cicio, leave Italy, once and for all. She thus expresses Lawrence's own hesitation before the spiritual darkness of the sensual pole. Yet Alvina cannot bring herself to leave Cicio: her need to sleep upon impulse is too great. The whole novel seems to be struggling, *suffering*, on the brink of an "awful submission." A peasant in it is said to have "seemed to see," when in England, "a fairness, a luminousness in the northern soul, something free, touched with divinity." But this freedom and fairness are rendered, in *The Lost Girl*, only to be found wanting. The book expresses a terrible hunger for some utter sensual consummation.

In Lawrence's last book on life in pagan Italy, *Etruscan Places* (1932), the vacillation has ended. Here (to all appearances) it is only the "absolute sensual self" that man *must* know. As in *Lady Chatterley's Lover*, we meet with the suggestion of a former paradise (the Etruscan past of "phallic consciousness") and of a subsequent fall (the Roman intervention and the Italian present). And "mental and spiritual consciousness" is, again, the satanic power involved. That Infinite of "selflessness" which it was once so wrong to ignore—how contemptuous Lawrence is of it now. "There seems to have been in the Etruscan instinct," he writes, "a real desire to preserve the natural humour of life. And that is a task surely more worthy, and even much more difficult in the long run, than conquering the world or sacrificing the self or saving the immortal soul." The new note is scoffing, bitter. A great civilization has waned, and with it the secret of life: intimacy with the "Original, Creative Infinite." "The old religion" represented "the profound attempt of man to harmonize himself with nature, and hold his own and come to flower in the great seething of life." And in such a cosmology there is no safety, no attraction, no profit, in the Selfless Infinite. It is the world of the Tiger.

So it was that Italy, at first half-resisted, became, if not the home, then the *lost* home of Lawrence's soul.

In Forster, too, Italy is the antitype of England; but here the polarization is less extreme. Although Forster and Lawrence both thought and wrote in dialectical terms, Forster's imagination was less theoretical than Lawrence's, more moderated by observation, less exigent, world-wrestling, apocalyptic. The reason is not—as might at first appear—a greater diffidence, but a clearer window onto the world. Lawrence storms experience with his own crackling and contradictory needs; Forster, by contrast, delicately hovers over it, often an amused, frequently a passionate, and occasionally a sentimental, ironist. And when he is something other than ironic, when he is direct and lyrical, he is the rainbow, not the storm.

Where Italy confronts Lawrence's Alvina with an absolute either/or—she must either lose her "soul" in "awful submission" or return to England and luminousness—it constitutes, for Forster, an invitation to full humanity. In *The Lost Girl*, what had been negligible in England—namely, the sensual "Infinite"— becomes jolting and irresistible in Italy. By contrast, in Forster's *Where Angels Fear to Tread* (1905) and *A Room with a View* (1908), Italy simply charms open the airless English soul. Hypocrisy, Respectability, Practicality, Dullness—these musty English draperies, these middle-class shutters, are flung aside. As the Italian world with its beauty, distances, and spontaneous people clears the fog from the Northern soul, inner distances open up, the body wakens as from a sleep, the majesty of the earth springs into view. There is in these books no strapping either/or, no simple turnabout of values. They are essentially works of mediation. If they bring England to Italy, they also bring Italy to England. The ideal of human character implicit in them is what Schiller—in his *Letters on the Aesthetic Education of Man* —calls "the cultured man": the man "who makes a friend of Nature and respects her freedom while merely curbing her caprice."

Drafted first but rewritten and published after *Where Angels Fear to Tread, A Room with a View* is, of the two, much the easier in its attitude toward Nature. Indeed, the book is so radiant, so unguarded a celebration of desire, that it lies open to the charge of being "romantic" in the rosy coloring of the word; it is a very young man's novel, though coruscatingly clever and wisely sensitive all the same. Here, if events are capricious, Nature is not; there is apparently nothing in its "freedom" that needs curbing. Instinct is "reality," desire is "holy": it is, it would seem, as simple as that.

Here Italy is Nature's unmixed and wholesome realm. With apparent approval, Forster observes: "all feelings grow to passions in the South." Not even a murder in a piazza seems reprehensible; after all, was it not openly and passionately lived? More, Italy is "the most graceful nation in Europe"; it betrays an "eternal league . . . with youth"; an Italian driver is Phaeton, his girl friend, Persephone. Italy is Fiesole and a profusion of violets, it is soul-expanding distance and airy views. The English heroine, Lucy Honeychurch, having broken out of her English respectability while on a stay in Florence, returns there with her husband after being spurned in England, and hears the Arno "bearing down the snows of winter into the Mediterranean." In short, Italy is Erotic Pastoral, though pastoral often bracingly touched by a light comic breeze.

Still, as the note of comedy itself implies, *A Room with a*

View is not wholly given over to Impulse. It combines without effort the "radiance that lies behind all civilization" with the luminous freedom that Lawrence's peasant had seemed to see in the Northern soul. Significantly, the spokesman for Italy and its league with passion and youth is not an Italian but a philosophical Englishman, and an aged one at that, Mr. Emerson. In a sense, it is true, Italy speaks here for itself—but only in a sense. ". . . they see everything," a perceptive English character remarks of the Italians, "and they know what we want before we know it ourselves." Nonetheless, they do not articulate it. It is Mr. Emerson who interprets and justifies what the Italians see and hence, for Lucy, brings a bow to the arrow of desire. Impossible to imagine an Italian in this novel announcing, as Mr. Emerson does, that "the Garden of Eden is really yet to come. We shall enter it when we no longer despise our bodies," or that "love is of the body; not the body, but of the body." Though "life is very glorious," he says, it is "difficult," and a clear mind helps. "Truth counts. . . ." It is Lawrence's view of the intellect as an "indicator," but without his profound mistrust of "ideas."

In *Where Angels Fear to Tread*, Nature is again befriended, her freedom again respected. Here, however, her freedom is complicated by caprice. Some of the savagery assailing Alvina in the Italian landscape breaks out in Gino Carella—an Italian who, unlike those of *A Room with a View*, is brought into the foreground, where his "freedom" shows its faults. To his English wife, Lilia, Gino is coolly unfaithful, cruel in his lack of "chivalry." We see in him that "brutality so common in Italians." The human counterpart of the sea of violets that floods the little wood below Monteriano, Gino lives in happy disregard of cultivated rows, of high-principled limits. Forster, himself "chivalrous," finally rises against him:

It would have been well if he had been as strict over his own behaviour as he was over [Lilia's]. But the incongruity never occurred to him for a moment. His morality was that of the average Latin. . . . Of course, had Lilia been different—had she asserted herself and got a grip on his character—he might possibly—though not probably—have been made a better husband as well as a better man. . . .

This is bringing Italy to England indeed.

The mediation in this novel is forlorn in the sense that, failing to take root in any of the characters, it blossoms only at the level of inference. In *A Room with a View*, Nature and Truth are in perfect accord; here their relation is upset by the claims of a third ideal, that of Character. In consequence, the "gloriousness" of life is less apparent than its "difficulty." Life becomes a juggling act that none of the characters is up to. The fullness of humanity is broken up, as by a prism, into individuals who manage to be only its partial representatives.

Thus Gino, as we have seen, is strong in Nature but weak in Character; he is also muddled in Mind. The English hero, Philip Herriton, though wonderfully clear-sighted, is weak in both Character and Nature. Only the English heroine, Caroline Abbot, approaches the ideal of human completeness. She is "strict" over her own behavior, has a "commendable intelligence," and proves susceptible to the "radiance that lies behind all civilization." It is she who perceives the majestic naturalness of Gino's love for his son; and she comes to love Gino "body and soul." Unlike Lucy Honeychurch, however, Caroline has no sage to lead her to see "the holiness of direct desire." She is more than a little ashamed of her love for Gino and thinks of his worship of her as "saving" her from her desire for him. She is strong in Character and even in Nature, but short on Truth.

In *Where Angels Fear to Tread*, in sharp contrast to *A Room with a View*, the English characters return to England in defeat, leaving Italy to the Italians. "Life was greater than he had supposed," concludes Philip, "but it was even less complete." And yet Forster's novel does not insist upon the necessity of incompleteness. If in this case the difficulty of being complete proves insurmountable, it is largely because the English characters, young as they are, have come to Italy too late. Nature and Character can be reconciled both with each other and with Truth; but if the conditioning of a culture that makes too much of Character lies deep, if Truth has no forceful spokesman, then at best there can be only a deadlock among these forces. Such is the painful situation that the novel describes. In the name of "the cultured man," it laments the overcultured. It pays a sad respect to the power of a culture bent not on curbing but on breaking Nature, by showing how irreparable its damage can be.

It is, then, somewhere between George Eliot and Lawrence in Italy that Forster takes up his position. As we saw in an earlier chapter, George Eliot and Lawrence both subscribed—George Eliot decidedly, Lawrence somewhat cloudily—to an absolute either/or. And in a passage in *Etruscan Places*, as often in Lawrence, we come upon the terms of this dichotomy: "It seems as if the power of resistance to life . . . : a power which must needs be moral, or carry morality with it, as a cloak for its inner ugliness: would always succeed in destroying the natural flowering of life." While George Eliot, as we saw, took her stand on morality, or "resistance to life," Lawrence took his on "the natural flowering." And yet the stand is in each case a troubled one. In *Romola* and *The Lost Girl*, the enshrined necessities— of "resistance" and of "flowering," respectively—*impale* the heroines. If Romola and Alvina "submit," it is reluctantly and with a sense of violation. And so it is that each book admits the attractiveness of what it would reject. Each demonstrates the unnaturalness of the exclusion it urges. The importance of Forster's early novels as "bright books" and "guides" to life is that they testify to the possibility of a complete human nature. They do not strive to eliminate any portion of what has been humanly given. They attempt to harmonize, not to cull and choose. With Mill, they would cultivate and unfold the elements of human nature, so as to make of humanity "a noble and beautiful object of contemplation."

PART THREE

E. M. Forster

IX. The Personal Self

How does an individualist fare in an age of imperialism, of technocracy, of mass movements? The question answers itself. Forster was a man unhappy in his faiths. They isolated him, and though they may have supported him, they also required his support. Standing on the self as if it were a last stand, he defied, in the main, both the political and the metaphysical seductions that elsewhere in the twentieth century have combined to crush the individual.

And yet Forster's belief in individualism and in what, for him, individualism involves, "the importance of personal relationships and the private life," was not a deep one. It was stubborn rather than strong and referred, for a sanction, to the pleasures of his own life, not to an "objective" philosophy. Forster's two highest values—that of the Person and of what he himself calls Romance—blossomed unlooked-for in his childhood and his youth at Cambridge. They were spontaneous and organic and, of course, all the more irresistible for that. Forster's feeling for the Romance of life, which is the intuitive connection of the near with the far and of the moment with all time, evidently sprang from his early life in the English countryside. Writers "love, and ought to love," he says, "beauty and charm and the passage of the seasons. . . ." Of the house in Hertfordshire in which he lived as a child with his mother, Forster has said: "I took it to my heart and hoped . . . that I should live and die there. We were out of it in ten years. The impressions received there remained and still glow . . . and have given me a slant upon society and history. It is a middle-class slant, atavistic. . . ." Forster's Romantic view of the Person as one who gives glimpses of the eternal, of the majesty of life, seems to owe something to the fact that his bond with his mother (his father having died when Forster was still a boy) was especially close. Forster was not a Lawrence, with a mystical fatality, an indomitable need to be distributed abroad, stemming from a strong early attachment. But he was, like Wordsworth, a man whose soul was early entwined with "enduring things— / With life and nature," and with at least one other human being known as a dear and mysterious Presence.

This bud of Romance seems to have opened fully in the atmosphere, the "magic quality," of Cambridge. In his biography of Goldsworthy Lowes Dickinson, Forster gives an idea of the nature of this "magic": "Body and spirit, reason and emotion, work and play, architecture and scenery, laughter and seriousness, life and art—these pairs," he says, "which are elsewhere contrasted," were "fused" at Cambridge into one. "People and books reinforced one another, intelligence joined hands with affection, speculation became a passion, and discussion was made profound by love." Such a place would indeed satisfy Romance, which is a hunger to feel the continuity of all things. "When Goldie speaks of this magic fusion," Forster notes, "he illumines more careers than his own. . . ."

So long as a full biography of Forster himself remains to be written, we can only guess at the private origins of his beliefs; perhaps we could only guess in any case. The point to note, however, is that these origins are private; they spring from a life, not from an intellect picking and choosing among traditions. Of course the same can be said of the origins of George Eliot's and Lawrence's beliefs. But neither of these other writers was content to rest upon his origins. Provoked perhaps by guilt, each raged to make a system of his beliefs, to throw them over everyone and everything as the very net of universal necessity. Forster's beliefs also carry menace, but they do not come forth in a mail of passionate argument. They move lightly, even laconically. There is an intellectual paleness about them, a vulnerability—which is not to say that they lack assurance. Indeed, it is just Forster's easiness with them that explains their briskness and feathery touch.

Apart from this, there was enough of a Voltaire in Forster to keep him shy of attempting an intellectually formidable Romanticism. His values, he seems to have sensed, were better left alone, the natural products that they were, then taken apart and subjected to the microscope, with perhaps the consequence that they could never be put together again. If Forster lacked George Eliot's and Lawrence's passion to justify a childhood bliss by means of system, he also lacked the intellectual credulity that allowed them to erect one. He keeps his skeptical mind away from his beliefs as one keeps a candle away from precious family papers. He indulged his sensibility, not necessarily out of weakness before the truth but because it seemed to him in itself a truth of supreme importance. He liked to quote Keats on the holiness of the heart's affections.[1]

When Forster does have reason to doubt his faiths, as at the end of *Howards End* and in *A Passage to India*, they falter or fail him, as we shall see. But for the most part he simply uses them naturally, as, without questioning them, one uses one's legs to walk. Forster does not attempt to make his beliefs appear philosophically absolute; to him, they simply *are* absolute. Forster's work gives the impression of conviction without passionate certitude, of a belief more spontaneous than profound. Forster feels that the world—that time and eternity intermixed

---

[1] Or misquote or paraphrase. In *The Longest Journey* he speaks of "the holiness of the heart's imagination."

—is sacred, but he does not attempt to give a religious accounting for this. To him the sacredness is simply something sensed, as one senses the presence of the moon by the lightness of the sky. What he says about it, even what he renders of it, will persuade no one, not even aesthetically—for we find in Forster none of the hypnotic suggestion of a Lawrence. Forster writes not so much from a desire to create significance as from a feeling that he knows what is significant and what is not. His voice lacks the volume that George Eliot's and Lawrence's gained from their wish to prove (to themselves as much as to others) the exact truth of what they had to say. In lyrical moments, Forster, too, can ring the bell of finality, enjoying its deep-resonance. But for the most part he seems content just to know that the rope lies in his hands.

— 2 —

For Forster, as for Lawrence, not only the cosmos but the human individual can become what Eliade calls a hierophany: a manifestation of the sacred. Hence the association of George Emerson, in *A Room with a View*, with Greek gods—those earliest "human" hierophanies of Western culture. Hence Caroline Abbott's manifestation to Philip Herriton, in *Where Angels Fear to Tread*, as a "goddess," as one of those forms "inadequate for the things they have shown." Hence, too, in the same novel, the hierophany of Gino Carella's baby, who seems "to reflect light" and who strikes Caroline Abbott as a "glorious . . . fact." Gino himself is described as "mysterious and terrible" as well as "majestic." After all, he has behind him a country "that's upset people from the beginning of the world."

Yet so mild is Forster's perception of the sacred in individuals that it proves consonant with a sense of the virtue, the daily support and propriety, of "personal relationships and the private life." Forster is not teased and tormented, as Lawrence is, by a sense of the incommensurateness between the sacred and its human "representatives." Caroline's physical presence may be "inadequate" for the glory it shows, but it is not offered as a painful inadequacy. The soul may shine in the Infinite, the form of a baby may "reflect" it, but neither is obliterated by the light. For Forster, self is not a "oneness with the infinite" but rather partakes of it, gently, without shock. Wherever it came from, it is now here, its tendrils wrapped around present things. ". . . we have souls," says the "profoundly religious" Mr. Emerson of *A Room with a View*. "I cannot say how they came nor whither they go, but we have them. . . ." Such is Forster's note, a note of easy acceptance.

In keeping, the Forsterian soul has ballast and stability; it does not, like the Laurentian soul, cry to enter the "beyond." It belongs to people, as against using them—and people, in Forster, therefore have some glory in their own right. ". . . people," Lucy Honeychurch observes, "are more glorious" than "art and books and music," and though Lawrence would agree, he would want to add that there is something even more glorious, the "great Being" of which people are only units. Forster himself will come to this point in the last pages of *Howards End*, and in *A Passage to India* he will seem to doubt that the individual is even so much as a unit.[2] But for the most part his first four novels take pleasure in the existence of individuals as such.

In Lawrence, the "daily I," thin as it is, blots out the whole of the Infinite. It must dissolve before the sacred can appear. The Romantic connection for Lawrence lies between the individual but "impersonal" human organism and the great Being of the cosmos. In Forster, by contrast, the Romantic experience is impossible without "the little thing that says 'I' " in "the middle of the head." It is from the deep well of its memories, its associations with "enduring things," that the stars become visible. To Lawrence, the principle of life in the universe consisted in change and renewal. Whatever held still, for him, ceased to "be."

---

[2] *A Passage to India*—a work occupying in Forster's canon almost the place held by *Middlemarch* in George Eliot's—must be excepted from most of the generalizations in this chapter.

The fixity of the ego, especially, was a bolting of the vital gates. In Forster, by extreme contrast, Romance feeds on stillness and permanence. For both writers, to be sure, as for thinkers generally, the chief attribute of *being* is that it continues, endures. But where in Lawrence *being* endures in change—is what endures by changing—in Forster *being* is rather what is collected in order to be present to itself. The Laurentian self is like a flame licking up from an Infinite fire, the Forsterian self like a telescope that, having an extension of its own, can perceive an infinite extension.

The "I" is thus the nucleus of Forsterian Romance. Unless it exists, stable and consistent, opened upon its past and its psychology, which together comprise its depth, the individual can know nothing of the depth of the cosmos itself. Unless it is real to itself, it will not sense the larger reality that contains it. It is for this reason that, as we noted earlier, "Truth counts" in Forster. The Laurentian self, since it is one with the Infinite, needs no mediation from the mind; rather, it needs to get the mind out of the way. The Forsterian self, being rather a medium through which the Infinite is sensed, needs to be clear to itself, in self-aware subjectivity, as a pond needs to be clear before one can see its depths. Those of "cloudy" mind, like Agnes Pembroke of *The Longest Journey,* are pronounced "unreal," and certainly they are far from feeling that the reality around them is Romantic.

In Forster, as in Lawrence, one separates the sheep from the goats by the criterion of connection. In George Eliot, too, it is awareness of a "larger life" beyond "narrow" self that makes the difference between salvation and damnation. But in both George Eliot and Lawrence, one leaves one's personal self in order to enter the larger life. The self stays on legitimately in George Eliot only in the charitable form of sympathy; in Lawrence, only in the form of a mystically kindled, sentient "unit" of being. In Forster, by contrast, the sheep are those who, though far from self-obsessed, enjoy a lucid possession of their own inner reality. They are selves opened up to themselves, rooms with views: such are Caroline Abbott, Lucy Honey-church, Mr. Emerson, Stephen Wonham, Margaret Schlegel, and still others. ". . . man is an odd, sad creature as yet," Forster writes in *Howards End,* "intent on pilfering the earth, and heed-less of the growths within himself. He cannot be bored about psychology. He leaves it to the specialist, which is as if he should leave his dinner to be eaten by a steam-engine." And he adds of Margaret Schlegel: ". . . Margaret has succeeded—so far as suc-cess is yet possible. She does understand herself, she has some rudimentary control over her own growth." The goats, in For-ster, are those who, being closed rooms to themselves, have no "I" with which to connect with others: characters like Mrs. Herriton, Charlotte Bartlett, Herbert Pembroke, and Henry Wilcox.

The Forsterian Person is a room with a view not only of his inner growths but of the world as itself a growth. The "I," having found its own mysterious dimensions, begins to suspect that they mirror those of the surrounding world. When Mar-garet reflects: "But in public who shall express the unseen ade-quately? It is private life that holds out the mirror to infinity; personal intercourse, and that alone, that ever hints at a person-ality beyond our daily vision," she is arguing one mystery from the only other mystery she knows. The window of the self faces not only in but out. And since it faces, inevitably, on a world of matter, it finds there the depth, the mysterious presence, the gathering, in Parmenides's words, of "itself in itself from itself," and at the same time the openness, that it knows within. Thus is born the Romantic universe, which consists, once again, in a phrase from Lawrence's *Rainbow,* in a "knowledge of Eternity in the flux of Time"—or, relatedly, in a knowledge of Infinity in the poignant distances of Space.

In Forster, the personalization of the self thus involves a per-sonalization of the universe. As the self opens to itself, the world opens to it, too. As the self grows more precious to itself, as it understands its own mystery and its own order better, it finds itself the inhabitant of a precious and mysteriously ordered world. The personal self is thus the antithesis of egoism, which in Forster, as in Lawrence and George Eliot, is narrow and blind. Yet the personal self is nonetheless a consistent identity, an individual "I." It is the self, not in its abdication from itself, but in its discovery of its likeness with the world.

– 3 –

Wherever he lives, the Forsterian Person finds himself a passenger in a vessel that, though material, is nonetheless sailing "towards eternity." Reverence for everything—affection; at worst tolerance—flows from his knowledge that he is a part of a sacred whole: so Margaret Schlegel displays "a profound vivacity, a continual and sincere response to all that she encountered in her path through life." Often, love as well is born, an act at once of inner and outer connection, "the building of the rainbow bridge" between the flesh and the spirit, and between Person and Person. Truth, too, becomes important, as the discovery of the laws of a holy reality. And, since everything must be reverenced, since all things partake of the whole, proportion should be kept, harmony maintained, among the parts. So it happens that Romance itself, reverence, affection, love, truth, and proportion are all aspects of the Forsterian Person. Until *Howards End,* Forster's fourth novel, proportion will not be insisted upon, except for the proportion between "inner" and "outer," and matter and spirit, implicit in Romance itself. Nor, at any time, will love, since for Forster physical sex posed problems.[3]

[3] P. N. Furbank, whom Forster chose to be his biographer, writes: "He achieved physical sex very late and found it easier with people outside his own social class, and it remained a kind of private magic for him—an almost unattainable blessing, for which another person was mainly a pretext. He valued sex for its power to release his own capacities for tenderness and devotion, but he never expected an *equal* sexual relationship." Furbank adds that Forster "never showed any wish to set up house" with any of the men to whom he made love. See "The Personality of E. M. Forster," *Encounter,* November, 1970.

But reverence, affection, and truth are all essential to the Person, as of course is the Romance they serve and attend.

We find at least these minimal components in, for example, Stewart Ansell of *The Longest Journey*. Ansell is a sexless philosopher, but he is nonetheless a Person. We can imagine Lawrence asking of him, as he did of Forster: "Why can't he take a woman and fight clear to his own basic, primal being? Because he knows that self-realisation is not his ultimate desire." Forster's implicit response is that "primal being" is not hidden away in the sexual organs; it lives wherever the spirit touches a truth. In fact, self-realization *is* Ansell's desire, but the self he wants realized is not, as it were, confined to the cells. For Forster, Ansell is of the sheep simply in being both "serious and truthful." To be serious, we learn, is to be "convinced that our life is a state of some importance, and our earth not a place to beat time on." It is, in other words, to apprehend the sacredness of experience, of reality. Seriousness is thus a condition for Romance—as, also, its result. As for being truthful, it is to struggle against inner muddle, especially the cant of "respectable" feeling. Ansell's very profession is the discovery of truth. Yet to define the two terms this way is to miss the connection between them. If Ansell is serious, it is because he sees the truth of life, which is its Romance; and if he is truthful, it is because he feels the seriousness of truth.

Since to be "serious and truthful" is to be, ipso facto, a Romantic, we should find in Ansell a passion of attachment to a person or a place or to some other partly physical thing; he should feel the "burden of the Mystery," in Wordsworth's phrase, in something here below. And this we do find in his love of books and their truthful words and in his fondness for Rickie Elliot, the book's troubled and rather weak and muddled hero. Dry and intellectual as Ansell is, the cherishing Romantic intuition lives within him. It is in fact Ansell who speaks most directly and reverently about this intuition: "If you ask me what the Spirit of Life is, or to what it is attached, I can't tell you. I only tell you, watch for it. Myself, I've found it in books. Some people find it out of doors or in each other. Never mind. It's the same spirit, and I trust myself to know it anywhere, and to use it rightly." What Ansell finds in his books is "philosophy," which "lies behind everything." It leads the mind out to the edges of the known:

> . . . [Rickie] sat on the edge of the table and watched his clever friend [Ansell] draw within the square a circle, and within the circle a square, and inside that another circle, and inside that another square.
> "Why will you do that?"
> No answer.
> "Are they real?"
> "The inside one is—the one in the middle of everything, that there's never room enough to draw."

Philosophy, in short, is steeped in Romance. Ansell, we're told, "looked up at the dome [in the British Museum] as other men look at the sky." It is, for Forster, much the same.

Yet Ansell finds "the Spirit of Life" in Rickie as well. Forster's Persons, though not always lovers, are always passionate friends. Ansell passes by the Cnidian Demeter in the British Museum, knowing that it represents a power "he could not cope with, nor, as yet, understand." But he does love Rickie Elliot, as the latter, with grateful shock, perceives:

> MY DEAR STEWART,—You couldn't know. I didn't know for a moment. But this letter of yours is the most wonderful thing that has ever happened to me yet—more wonderful (I don't exaggerate) than the moment Agnes promised to marry me. I always knew you liked me, but I never knew how much until this letter. Up to now I think we have been too much like the strong heroes in books who feel so much and say so little, and feel all the more for saying so little. Now that's over and we shall never be that kind of an ass again. We've hit—by accident—upon something permanent. You've written to me, "I hate the woman who will be your wife," and I write back, "Hate her. Can't I love you both?" She will never come between us, Stewart . . . because our friendship has now passed beyond intervention. No third person could break it. . . . the thing is registered.

"Something permanent"—it is the heart of the Romantic intuition, the identification of the enduring with the universally real. And Ansell's love does last, however unworthy Rickie becomes of it. If Ansell seems brutally cold when Rickie ceases to be serious, it is because he cares about Rickie too much to act as if nothing has changed. And it is Ansell who, when he sees a chance to win Rickie back to seriousness, strikes out, as he predicted, "like any ploughboy."

So it is that truth and seriousness are the primal ingredients of the Forsterian Person. They are themselves sufficient means to the Romantic ends of experiencing the Spirit of Life and the holiness of the heart's affections.

— 4 —

Forster's agnosticism, writes Frederick Crews in his book *E. M. Forster: The Perils of Humanism*, "is complicated by romantic evasions, by . . . a thwarted fascination with the Absolute." But Forster is centrally and openly Romantic, and it would be truer to say that his Romanticism was sometimes hindered by his agnosticism, feeble as the latter was. Forster was not so much fascinated with the Absolute as, day by day, its familiar; and his love for it was thwarted only in the sense that its mystery proved gratefully indissoluble—an explained universe was not at all what he desired. Far from being a scattering of "romantic evasions," Romance in Forster is the axis of the world. Life is "unmanageable," Forster writes in *Howards End*, "because it is a romance, and its essence is romantic beauty." Forsterian seriousness is founded upon this perception; Forsterian comedy is a laugh at those who fail to share it. Romance is at once the ontology and the justification of the Forsterian universe. The novels would not hold together without it. Nor, without it, would Forster have been moved to write them. The intuition they all enshrine is that of being centered in a significant if elusive whole,[4] the quintessential Romantic sensation.

[4] Romance is so much a matter of reaching for significance, of listening to whispers, of merely *sensing* the ultimate, that it can neither be

In Forster, Romance, Time's love for Eternity, pervades almost everything. And it is in consequence of this that the Forsterian Person, though he must indeed be Romantic, yet has a range of Romantic experience to choose from. It is enough to have found the Spirit of Life in this or that to have entered the Romantic cosmos. If Forster is much more tolerant than Lawrence, far more catholic in his sympathies, it is because, unlike Lawrence, he does not expect each of his characters to seek the "knowledge of Eternity" in a single manner. For Lawrence, sex was the chief, almost the only, gate, and it was strait, a delicate process of dodging the "mental" in order to arrive in the paradise of the mystical and physical. Love of nature, though perfected in Lawrence himself, is secondary in his characters; they make no point of it. By contrast, consider Margaret's reassurance to her sister Helen—who wonders if it is "some awful, appalling, criminal defect" that she cannot love a man—that there are many gates, all of them beautiful:

"It is only that people are far more different than is pretended. All over the world men and women are worrying because they cannot develop as they are supposed to develop. Here and there they have the matter out, and it comforts them. Don't fret yourself, Helen. Develop what you have; love your child. I do not love children. I am thankful to have none. I can play with their beauty and charm, but that is all—nothing real, not one scrap of what there ought to be. And others—others go farther still, and move outside humanity altogether. A place, as well as a person, may catch the glow. Don't you see that all this leads to comfort in the end? It is part of the battle against sameness. Differences—eternal differences, planted by God in a single family, so that there may always be colour; sorrow perhaps, but colour in the daily grey. . . . Don't drag in the personal when it will not come."

In Forster simply to be a person is to be in the midst of Romance. "Romance only dies with life," Forster says in *Where Angels Fear to Tread*. "No pair of pincers will ever pull it out

---

proven nor refuted. Indeed, it can scarcely be presented in prose: it is just its indefiniteness, its will-o'-the-wisp quality that makes it difficult to distinguish from an "evasion." By contrast, Laurentian metaphysics will, I think, appear to be either undeniable or wholly imaginary.

of us." Whatever gives hints of permanence or distance, whatever seems to have a depth that can never quite be plumbed, whatever is both of time and outside of it, will be Romantic; and hence Romance will lie all about and be known often and variously within. It is this that allows for "differences," for a changeable and unambitious Spirit of Life. Where the Laurentian "consummation" aspires to conflate all "Being" in a single experience, Forsterian Romance is an unanxiously limited and ever shifting intuition of mysterious "essence."

For Forster, as we have seen, Romance may awaken in philosophy. And of course it may awaken in love, which opens the emotions as philosophy opens thought. So Lucy Honeychurch feels that "in gaining the man she loved, she would gain something for the whole world." In other words, she would help to confirm the Romantic essence of reality—an essence obscured by the words and actions of "the vast armies of the benighted, who follow neither the heart nor the brain." "Marry him," Mr. Emerson tells her, referring to his son George; "it is one of the moments for which the world was made." The world, then, was made for Romance; in Forster it has, and needs, no other justification. "When love comes, that is reality," Mr. Emerson also says. Defined by Romance, reality is what continues indefinitely, and love is a sense of having entered a realm of emotion without genesis or destruction, some psychological essence. In popular romance, of course, this is expressed as "eternal love," and the youthful Forster is not writing far from this level.

Published only a year after *A Room with a View*, *The Longest Journey* is a curious successor, for it is as distrustful of romantic love as the former is enthusiastic. Will not love, this novel questions, mark the end and not the beginning of Romantic experience? Marriage is now suspected as a closing of the gates. Of course, marriage to an Agnes Pembroke *would* close them, and the novel comes to no final judgment on the subject. It only remarks that marriage is apt to make a man a hostage to convention. The strongest bonds in the novel, and the enduring ones, are those between men. But Romance is deflected from heterosexual love still more upon human regeneration and the pastoral life—the last appearing, in its natural fertility, the proper setting for the first.

"It's something rather outside that makes one marry, if you follow me," says rustic Stephen Wonham: "not exactly oneself." It is the Romantic world that desires human regeneration; it is in love with everything that continues. Stephen will follow the natural current of things; he will acquiesce to what is expected. But it is what he wants as well. After all, discontinuation of any kind is death. "Are there many local words?" Rickie asks him as they journey by wagon through Wiltshire.

> "There have been."
> "I suppose they die out."
> The conversation turned curiously. In the tone of one who replies, he said, "I expect that some time or other I shall marry."

Having a child is, for Stephen, a Romantic connection with the future, an indefinite continuation, the more poignant for being indefinite. Of course Stephen, not Rickie, is the Romantic hero of the book, and above all because he will perpetuate—make permanent—the race. The difference between their fates, the glory of the one, the waste of the other, is emblematized in a scene toward the end of the novel. In Rickie's presence, Stephen sets fire to a piece of paper, then lays it "flower-like" on a stream:

> Gravel and tremulous weeds leapt into sight, and then the flower sailed into deep water, and up leapt the two arches of a bridge. It'll strike!" they cried; "no, it won't; it's chosen the left," and one arch became a fairy tunnel, dropping diamonds. Then it vanished for Rickie; but Stephen, who knelt in the water, declared that it was still afloat, far through the arch, burning as if it would burn forever.

Life ("unmanageable because it is a romance") has chosen to perpetuate itself on the left, through the bastard Stephen; and it has chosen well, since, of the two, only Stephen is securely Romantic ("one arch became a fairy tunnel, dropping diamonds"). Rickie, deformed from birth like his father, will die out. Stephen alone kneels in the on-going stream, standing on his knees like the Cnidus Demeter. Rickie had earlier caught Stephen "by the knees and saved his life." Rickie himself will die when a train, symbol of an unromantic age, runs over his knees. Romance, in Forster, thus has its superintending ways, and though it does not amount to quite the Terror of the reign of necessity in Lawrence and George Eliot, it proves a formidable antagonist to those who doubt or defy it. Relenting a little, however, as if in view of Rickie's fitful deferences to it, Romance permits Rickie, and itself, a minor triumph when Stephen collects Rickie's stories for posthumous publication. Art, too, after all, regenerates, and in its own way burns "as if it would burn forever."

The earth, with its own renewals, its soul-opening views, its "rallying-points" for the spirit, its seas that gather in the rivers, its places softened and deepened by history, is an inevitable object for Romance, and Forster makes much of it in all four of his early novels. The best places are those that, like Howards End, with its whispering tree, speak of an eternal "now." So the little dell near Cambridge is for Rickie a "holy place," because "inside . . . it was neither June nor January. The chalk walls barred out the seasons, and the fir-trees did not seem to feel their passage." The dell thus becomes a natural "rallying-point" for Rickie, and "all he had read, all he had hoped for, all he had loved, seemed to quiver in its enchanted air." Or the best places are those that lead the mind through distance into the indefiniteness of Infinity. Margaret is enchanted by the view at Oniton Grange: "Then she turned westward, to gaze at the swirling gold. Just where the river rounded the hill the sun caught it. Fairyland must lie above the bend. . . ." Then there is the view from the Purbeck Hills in the same novel:

How many villages appear in this view! How many castles! How many churches, vanished or triumphant! How many ships, railways, and roads! What incredible variety of men working beneath that lucent sky to what final end? The reason fails, like a wave on the Swanage beach; the imagination swells, spreads, and deepens, until it . . . encircles England.

It is from the same vantage point that, a little later, England appears "alive, throbbing through all her estuaries, crying for joy through the mouths of all her gulls. . . ." England is a ship of souls "with all the brave world's fleet accompanying her towards eternity." Here England, vast, alive, sustaining, enduring, virtually becomes the Romantic cosmos itself.

Perhaps no novelist has made so much of views as Forster. Not that he excels at describing them. His severely economical style will scarcely permit him to particularize them; he does not, like Lawrence, paint them boldly on the page. But at least Forster's psychology is sound; as George Emerson points out in *A Room with a View*, the magic of views does not depend on their detail: "all that matters in them" is "distance and air." It is these that conduct the spirit to the Infinite. In Forster, they also tend to spring the inner Infinite of love. It is thus unfortunate for Caroline Abbott that she first sees Gino at a distance, in a room in which "the light . . . was soft and large, as from some gracious, noble opening." "The vista of the landing and the two open doors made him both remote and significant, . . . intimate and unapproachable at the same time." He is near enough to be apprehended sensuously, remote enough to be mysterious: it "astride the parapet, with one foot in the loggia and the other is a Romantic distance. A little later, Gino sits near Caroline dangling into the view"—again a purely Romantic position; Caroline is by now romantically attached to him, to her very English shame. Then, too, Lucy Honeychurch, though she first feels emotionally opened to George Emerson on a bridge over the swirling water of the Arno, with its mysterious progress "out to the sea," becomes irrevocably attached only when she sees him against a view. "It makes such a difference," she later says innocently, before she knows she is in love, "when you see a person with beautiful things behind him unexpectedly."

More, views in Forster tend to divinize those who are seen against them. The universal element in the setting, the suggestion of an Infinity continuous with the known and near, exposes, as it were, the universal in the individual. Glory is shed from one to the other. So Lucy "more than ever" reminds Cecil Vyse of a "Leonardo" when she stands between him and the light among "the flower-clad Alps," with "immeasurable plains behind her," her features "shadowed by fantastic rock." She rejects his proposal of marriage, but for him "the things that really mattered were unshaken." (Pater, we recall, had found in *La Giaconda* the suggestion "of a perpetual life, sweeping together ten thousand experiences," a Romantic fancy.) Then, in *Where Angels Fear to Tread*, it is Philip Herriton's memory of Gino's baby "sprawling on the knees of Miss Abbott, shining and naked, with twenty miles of view behind him" that makes him wonder whether he is right to abduct the infant to England. Is not the baby, at least in its setting, and as revealed by it, something too glorious to treat as a counter in a fight between the English and the Italians? (According to the symbolism of the scene in which the baby dies in its spill from a carriage, it would have "disappeared" in England into a "great rut"—that is, into respectability.) Later, Philip undergoes "conversion" to seriousness when he beholds Caroline's eyes as she tries to comfort the grief-stricken Gino, "eyes full of infinite pity and full of majesty, as if they discerned the boundaries of sorrow, and saw unimaginable tracts beyond." Here is the same process reversed, the divinity of the human figure evoking an immensity of view.

Truth, love, friendship, procreation, art, the earth and its views—these, then, are the chief Romantic forms and objects in Forster. Their availibility and likelihood in life itself explain why Forster finds it possible to say, in all truth and seriousness, that "poetry, not prose, lies at the core."

– 5 –

Forster's first three novels are all stories of Romantic education. As Robert Warshow noted, Forster's method "is to confront his characters with situations for which their moral preconceptions have left them unprepared; the tensions and readjustments that result from these confrontations make up the novel." The "moral preconceptions" are rationalizations for respectability and worldly success; the "readjustments" are conversions to the view that poetry, not prose, lies at the core.[5] The protagonist deepens upon himself, becoming a Person. And the more he becomes a Person, the more he inhabits a world of Romance.

In two of these novels, *A Room with a View* and *The Longest Journey*, Romance has its way; it is imperial. After all, is not the great earth itself, not to mention the sky, its ally? And what power has the empty practical man, so muddled and, indeed, impractical, against the Person, so deeply rooted in reality? "We must drink it," Forster says of the "teacup of experience"—the empirical cup that makes us "quite sane, efficient, quite experienced, and quite useless to God or man"—"or we shall die. But we need not drink it always. Here is our problem and our salvation." Yet this concession to the prose of life is hardly made in good faith. In the same novel, *The Longest Journey*, a teacup of the worldly Mrs. Failing's is literally broken by a piece of chalk—by the earth and all its Romance; and so it ought to be, suggests the novel. In fact there is no "problem" either here or in *A Room with a View*. Lucy Honeychurch and Stephen Wonham will not even be invited to tea; and this is just as well for all concerned, since these Romantic youngsters are not only too unconventional but too real and glorious for suburban drawing rooms. But no matter: the world is larger than Tunbridge Wells or Sawston thinks. There is Italy, there is pastoral England; and in these places the Romantic can drink all he wants of what Ansell calls "the wine of life."

In *Where Angels Fear to Tread*, by contrast, it is Sawston, not Romance, that proves imperial. For Philip and Caroline, abortive Romantics both, Romance flares, then dies: "all the wonderful things are over." Philip and Caroline return to Sawston

[5] In Rickie Elliott's case, of course, the readjustment proves unsuccessful: disastrously, Rickie fails to discard his idealization of his mother for the varied and actual spiritual "coin" of Romance.

and its prose and teacups almost as to a death in life. "I and my life must be where I live," Caroline unhappily recognizes; and she has in her too much of Sawston to try and live elsewhere. Here, then, there is no "salvation"; Caroline must drink the tea and drink it always. It is an "inevitable" ending, given Philip's and Caroline's weaknesses, but it has no universal reference. Romance will live elsewhere, Sawston is not the world.

What, though, if Sawston *were* the world? What if London itself were to be the only England of the future? What then would become of Romance? Would not all the wonderful things be over for everyone? In Forster's fourth novel, *Howards End*, this possibility, indeed probability, overtakes Forster's confidence in Romance, his reliance on it as the triumphant Spirit of Life. Romance, after all, cannot flourish without Persons, and what is there in London or its suburbs to nuture Persons? Nor can Romance thrive where the old earth is covered over with temporary dwellings, or its views blanked out by road dust and densely populated, uniform suburbs. *Howards End* is the largest and most important of Forster's early novels because it is the only one in which Romance stands in fear and dismay before the fact of the modern world. Choked in the fumes of a civilization that is speeding by it, it ceases to dream, to enjoy a vegetable stupor, and realizes that it is becoming obsolete. Shortly, it will no longer find it possible to go off in a corner; London is "creeping." The sheep will not be able to leave the goats for greener pastures. There will be no pastures; indeed, there will no sheep, for the conditions necessary for producing them will have been annihilated. What is Romance to do? In *Howards End*, it does what suits and becomes it. It turns heroic. It breaks in upon the world of prose, proselytizes, tries to deflect its gray, unthinking course. And in the process it exacts from its adherents a strenuous ideal reminiscent of Greek measure and proportion.

That only certain places are conducive to Romance was implicit in Forster's novels from the first. London, briefly visited by Stephen Wonham in *The Longest Journey*, had proved a place of failing physique and shallow intellect; Stephen was right to return to Wiltshire, of which Forster says: "Here is the heart of our island: the Chilterns, the North Downs, the South Downs radiate hence. The fibres of England unite in Wiltshire, and did we condescend to worship her, here we should erect our national shrine." As this suggests, the Forsterian Romance of place has, in England if not in Italy, a national cast: the island itself is so perfect a Romantic object, a ship in the eternal sea, large enough to swell the imagination but not so large as to escape it. And yet the Romance of place is not confined to national boundaries. What is fundamental to it, as was observed, is a suggestion either of eternity or of infinity.

To suggest the first, a place must be still and quiet, as if so deeply rooted in time that the present could not shake it. It must seem to have endured a great age, as an earnest of its foundation in being: what "is" is what endures. It should appear innocent of change, especially of newfangleness, or to have absorbed it confidently, as a pond absorbs a tossed pebble. Such a place is Howards End, tucked away in Hertfordshire. The house has been altered—a kitchen added, a paddock converted into a garage—but its character is evidently what it always was. The place even shows something like a will to resist change. A rockery is put in by Evie Wilcox, with Alpine trees; it fails and is overcome by an English meadow. Henry Wilcox fills in a gap in the hedge where Miss Avery has passed on her chores for many years; the gap reasserts itself. And Margaret, standing in the "rural interior" of Miss Avery's farmhouse, grasps what remains the same in all the changes of country life, has her knowledge of Eternity in the flux of Time:

Here had lived an elder race, to which we look back with disquietude. The country which we visit at week-ends was really a home to it, and the graver sides of life, the deaths, the partings, the yearnings for love, have their deepest expression in the heart of the fields. All was not sadness. . . . It was the presence of sadness at all that surprised Margaret, and ended by giving her a feeling of completeness. In these

English farms, if anywhere, one might see life steadily and see it whole, group in one vision its transitoriness and its eternal youth, connect—connect without bitterness until all men are brothers.

Oniton Grange, away on the Welsh border, has also its mirroring pool of the past—the ruined castle on its grounds. Old religion speaks in the "rounded Druids" nearby; old passion in the ruined castle itself, for here Anglo-Saxon fought Kelt. "I love this place. I love Shropshire," the Romantic Margaret says. "Ah, dear . . . what a comfort to have arrived!" Romance wants the present *to be*, and knows no other way to ascertain that it does than to divine in it the authentication of centuries of living.

As for infinitude, a Romantic place needs no more to suggest it than openness, a sense of space. Situated among fields and low hills, Howards End affords no picturesquely extensive views; but it is intimate to the earth and the sky, and Margaret, after a day there, feels enlarged when she returns in the evening to London:

Her evening was pleasant. The sense of flux which had haunted her all the year disappeared for a time. She forgot the luggage and the motor-cars, and the hurrying men who know so much and connect so little. She recaptured the sense of space, which is the basis of all earthly beauty, and, starting from Howards End, she attempted to realize England. She failed—visions do not come when we try, though they may come through trying. But an unexpected love of the island awoke in her, connecting on this side with the joys of the flesh, on that with the inconceivable.

Oniton, too, has its spatial Romance—its river rounding the hill, mentioned before, and a "poetry" of "carelessly modelled masses" in the nearby hills. Romance affirms the immediate in space, but desires from it, as from time, a hint of the illimitability of its mode. The near must meet the far, the moment perpetual time. The only home for the soul is what, in its loving grasp of time and space, it can manage to hold together in a single instant.

So Romance has its delicate conditions. And what sends shud-

E. M. Forster

ders through it in *Howards End* is the careless destruction of these conditions by commerce and cosmopolitanism.

The center of these, as of a spreading disease, is London. London is here the antitype of the Romantic world. The latter is the intuited unity of all things; London is "eternal formlessness," "chaos." The Romantic world peacefully whispers of perma-and indifferent, streaming away—streaming, streaming for ever" nence; London is "continual flux," "all the qualities, good, bad, Life in London is described as follows:

> Over two years passed, and the Schlegel household continued to lead its life of cultured but not ignoble ease, still swimming gracefully on the grey tides of London. Concerts and plays swept past them, money had been spent and renewed, reputations won and lost, and the city herself, emblematic of their lives, rose and fell in a continual flux, while her shallows washed more widely against the hills of Surrey and over the fields of Hertfordshire. This famous building had arisen, that was doomed. . . . And month by month the roads smelt more strongly of petrol, and were more difficult to cross, and human beings heard each other speak with greater difficulty, breathed less of the air, and saw less of the sky.

It is a deft profile of the modern city. "One visualizes it as a track of quivering grey," Forster says of London, intelligent without purpose, and excitable without love; as a spirit that has altered before it can be chronicled; as a heart that certainly beats, but with no pulsation of humanity." At Howards End, Margaret finds a place where all men might be brothers; London is a place of crowds, and harmless Leonard Bast frightens those whom he passes on its streets. Romance exalts the spirit with intimations of the Infinite; London is but "a caricature of infinity." Could one merge with it? "Margaret's own faith held firm. She knew the human soul will be merged, if it be merged at all, with the stars and the sea." London is "a foretaste of [the] nomadic civilization which is altering human nature so profoundly. . . ." When it is all the civilization that there is, "trees and meadows and mountains will only be a spectacle, and the binding force that they once exercised on character must be entrusted to Love alone. May Love be equal to the task!"

The problem facing Romance in *Howards End* is only in part the disappearance of a "binding" rural life; equally endangered is the existence of the Person. The Wilcoxes "breed like rabbits": they are the future; and the Wilcoxes represent, not the Person, with his hallowing subjectivity, but what Nietzsche called "the objective man." "He is only an instrument—he is a *mirror* . . . ," Nietzsche says of the type in *Beyond Good and Evil*; "he is not an 'end in himself.' . . . He waits until something comes along and then spreads himself out delicately, so that even faint footprints and the slipping by of ghostly creatures shall not be lost to his surface. . . . Whatever 'person' is left in him seems accidental to him, often arbitrary, even more often disturbing." So of Henry Wilcox, a rubber magnate, Forster says, "As soon as he had taken up a business, his obtuseness vanished. He profited by the slightest indications. . . ." He and his son Charles are best "when serving on committees." Yet about their own psychology they are, in Nietzsche's words, "unsubtle and careless." They are "heedless of the growths" within. ". . . if you could pierce through him," says Helen of the type, "you'd find panic and emptiness in the middle'—"Never the 'I'." Having no conquered subjectivity, no inner stillness, can such a man know Eternity in the flux of Time? "As is man to the Universe, so was the mind of Mr. Wilcox to the minds of some men—a concentrated light upon a tiny spot, a little Ten Minutes moving self-contained through its appointed years. No Pagan he, who lives for the Now, and may be wiser than all philosophers. He lived for the five minutes that have past, and the five to come; he had the business mind." The Wilcoxes are of a piece with the London they have helped to create—formless, prolific, continually in flux as they buy and sell houses, colonize and bleed Africa, motor through an England that they travel too fast to see.

If London and the Wilcoxes are the future, the Romantic is indeed a threatened species. "Life's going to be melted down, all over the world," Helen observes at the end of the book; and "Margaret knew that her sister spoke truly." What, then, can the Romantic do? Short of despairing, he can do but one thing: dare the future by helping the objective man to his soul. He must enter the market place, not to denounce it, but to change it. No longer a refugee from suburbia, he must try to give color to its "daily grey."

Romance has inherently, we noted, its aspect of proportion: "Only connect . . . ," the epigraph of *Howards End*, had been Forster's motto from the first. But here the sphere of proportion dramatically expands, enlarged by the heat of a new necessity. In *A Room with a View* and *The Longest Journey*, the objective man could safely be barred out from Romance—though, in truth, it was he who did the barring; he could be abandoned to his suburban fold. But here where all England is becoming suburbia, the Romantic must try to include the objective man in his net of connections. He must try to reconcile, not merely time and eternity, space and infinity, the mind and desire, but more humble if also more recalcitrant opposites: character and personal relations, art and politics, business and "the unseen," idealism and practicality, imagination and the daily grey, energy and sensitivity. None of these can be ignored: all must be united. And if in the process Forster's ideal of the Person loses a little of its former purity, still it is the heavier and the more valuable for that, as when lead is added to crystal. It will be forced to make some compromise with "men as they are"; but better that than being a defeatist or a "barren theorist." It will allow a measure of daily grey; but better that than being "effeminate" of soul.

So Margaret Schlegel consents to read the prose of life and even professes to find some virtue in it. Referring to marriage settlements, death duties, telegrams, and the like, she says: "This outer life, though obviously horrid, often seems the real one—there's grit in it. It does breed character. Do personal relations lead to sloppiness in the end?" "Neatness, obedience, and discipline"—is the Wilcox character really contemptible? Not so: "Without their spirit, life might never have moved out of protoplasm. More and more do I refuse to draw my income and sneer at those who guarantee it." The Wilcoxes, observes the gnomic Miss Avery, do "keep a place going. . . . Yes, it is just that." So the practical man seems finally to get his due in Forster, and the greatest compliment paid to him is that Margaret, Romantic though she is, emulates some of his qualities.

In Margaret, the Delphian ideal, "Nothing in excess," is heroically renewed, though interpreted to signify: Nothing for too long. According to *Howards End*, the mean can be achieved only through time, like the cutting of the big meadow at the end of the book, the whirring blades "encompassing with narrowing circles the sacred center of the field"; for there is nothing, after all, *between* the opposites of life, and at best the Person can only balance as he goes:

All vistas close in the unseen—no one doubts it—but Helen closed them rather too quickly for [Margaret's] taste. At every turn of speech one was confronted with reality and the absolute. . . . she felt that there was something a little unbalanced in the mind that so readily sheds the visible. The business man who assumes that this life is everything, and the mystic who asserts that it is nothing, fail, on this side and on that, to hit the truth. "Yes, I see, dear; it's about halfway between," Aunt Juley had hazarded in earlier years. No; truth, being alive, was not halfway between anything. It was only to be found by continuous excursions into either realm, and though proportion is the final secret, to espouse it at the outset is to insure sterility.

Only prigs, Margaret points out, would "*begin* with proportion." "Life's very difficult and full of surprises. . . . To be humble and kind, to go straight ahead, to love people rather than pity them, to remember the submerged—well, one can't do all these things at once, worse luck, because they're so contradictory. It's then that proportion comes in. . . ." So one can keep to an ideal of proportion but not to the mean itself. In contrast to the wych-elm at Howards End, which has "strength and adventure in its roots, but in its utmost fingers tenderness," and lives virtually out of time, the human effort after reconciliation must be active, patient, untiring. It is, precisely, an ideal.

There are, however, at least two areas in which the mean can be maintained. One of these is economic. Wealth and poverty: neither is desirable. The poor are crushed by the wealthy, and the wealthy have more than a fair share. So Margaret, at the end, "intends to diminish her income by half during the next ten years" (an exemplary touch that has about it a suggestion of Shaw). And love, of course, is an even more important constant, since love is itself a form of connection. "Without it," Margaret reflects, "we are meaningless fragments, half monks, half beasts, unconnected arches that have never joined into a man." We are reminded, by this, of Lawrence and his ideal of erotic fusion; but as Margaret later contemplates the "noblest" love, "where man and woman, having lost themselves in sex, desire to lose sex itself in comradeship," we are reminded also of Jane Austen. That Forster can bring both to mind indicates how much of proportion lies in his own ideal.

So Margaret becomes a new sort of protagonist in Forster, a heroine of reconciliation and proportion. It may almost be said (Forster almost says it) that proportion in her is inborn—her German heritage, through her father, having "warmed her blood," her English heritage, through her mother, having "cooled her brain." Yet Margaret, all the same, holds proportion before her as an ideal. She is *determined* to be neither sloppy nor brutal, not to consist of "meaningless fragments"; she is consecrated to establishing "truer relationships" on this side of the grave. In short, she is indeed, for all her disdain of "the heroic outfit," a heroine. "You mean to keep proportion, and that's heroic, it's Greek . . . ," says her sister. Margaret, with her "profound vivacity" and clear, noble life, reminds us of Plato's belief that God gave gymnastics and music together, and that the human being who can blend them into harmony will be "a greater darling of the Muses than the legendary hero who first put together all the strings of the lyre."

Yet to what end does Margaret become, in Mill's words for the fully developed human being, "a noble and beautiful object of contemplation"? Doubtless proportion is an intrinsic good, its own reward; but Margaret intends to do more than enjoy it. She means to inculcate it, and so make the world safe for Romance. Indeed, so far as we can see, the future of Romance depends on her—on people like her, if there are others like her. She carries its fragile destiny, and it is over swirling waters that she carries it. Margaret has thus an importance beyond herself. Admirable though she is to contemplate, darling of the Muses though she is, we must yet regard her as a failure if she cannot change Henry Wilcox, the objective man. We must view her as the bearer of a torch that is flickering and dying out in her hand. We must see her as having failed in her mission.

And so, in fact, are we forced to view her. As the champion of Romance, Margaret fails. She enters the market place and spreads her wares and the Wilcoxes of commerce and cosmopolitanism pass by without seeing them, so darkened are they by their overbright "Ten Minutes" of mind. In truth, she could not but fail, given the objective man as Forster portrays him. But Forster does not know that she fails, or rather will not admit it. And the novel is, accordingly, false and confused.

There are, it may be argued, three outcomes, three endings to this large and glowing but finally muddled book: one false, one unacknowledged, one merely wishful. The false and favored ending, the feigned triumph of Romance over Imperialism, is based on the premise that the objective man can be taught to "connect." When Margaret announces her intention to marry Henry, Helen, sounding the battle cry, exclaims: "Go on and fight with him and help him." And from this point on, we are encouraged to believe that she can. Certainly Margaret herself is all confidence. "Mature as he was," she reflects, "she might yet be able to help him to the building of the rainbow bridge that should connect the prose in us with the passion." Again, in a scene that must make us shudder in retrospect, she puts "a hand on either shoulder" and looks "deeply into the black bright eyes. What was behind their competent stare? She knew, but was not disquieted." Later, when she discovers that Henry was unfaithful to his first wife, she seems disquieted indeed, but this too she can accept with assurance: "Henry's inner life had long laid open to her—his intellectual confusion, his obtuseness to personal influence, his strong but furtive passions. Should she refuse him because his outer life corresponded?" She will not; she is "not a barren theorist." "Henry must have it as he liked, for she loved him, and some day she would use her love to make him a better man."

And by the end of the novel Henry is indeed improved. "Broken" by his son's indictment and consequent imprisonment for manslaughter, Henry reemerges, in the final chapter, after, as it were, a larval period of fourteen months, a new and better man. Before, he could not be brought to admit that he was partly responsible for the downfall of both Leonard Bast, the young man on whom Charles Wilcox had brought a fatal heart attack by striking him with the flat of a sword, and Leonard's wife Jacky, with whom Henry had been unfaithful to Ruth Wilcox. Now, however, ". . . he worries dreadfully about his part of the tangle." He has, moreover, learned to "understand . . . and to forgive" Helen Schlegel, and even to accept her child, illegitimate though it is (and Leonard's besides). There he is, at the end, disengaging himself from Margaret's embrace, to greet the two of them "with a smile." Henry, in short, having been "broken" as an objective man, reemerges a Person.

It is Margaret who is given credit for this improvement. "What a change—and all through you!" observes Helen. "You! You did it all, sweetest, though you are too stupid to see." It had been Margaret's idea to live at Howards End with both Helen and Henry, enemies though these two were. ". . . you picked up the pieces, and made us a home. Can't it strike you—even for a moment—that your life has been heroic? Can't you remember the two months after Charles's arrest, when you be-

gan to act, and did all?" ". . . things that I can't phrase have
helped me," Margaret replies mysteriously. Are there, then,
Romantic or mystical powers abroad? Uncannily, Howards End
will go to Margaret, the arch Romantic, just as the first Mrs.
Wilcox had wished it to. Is Ruth Wilcox not even now the
ruling Spirit of the place? Are they not all "only fragments of
that woman's mind"? "She knows everything. She is everything,"
Margaret had earlier remarked. "She is the house, and the tree
that leans over it." Margaret herself will leave the house to
Helen's child, the offspring, propitiously, of an idealist and a
Child of earth. No wonder Margaret has moments when she
feels that Howards End is "peculiarly our own." Is not Howards
End the time-steeped England of Romance? Is it not the England that was, is even now, and always shall be? "The field's
cut!" cries Helen in the last paragraph of the book—"the big
meadow! We've seen to the very end, and it'll be such a crop of
hay as never!" Earlier Forster had asked whether England belongs "to those who have moulded her and made her feared by
other hands, or to those who had added nothing to her power,
but have somehow seen her, seen the whole island at once, lying
as a jewel in a silver sea." And now his question has been answered; England belongs, not to her Imperialists, but to her
Romantics. Indeed, to make matters perfect, have not Helen
and Henry moved toward the mean from their opposite excesses
(idealism, materialism) to join with Margaret, the Person at the
"sacred centre"? Is not all now for the best? "I didn't do wrong,
did I?" Henry asks. "You didn't, darling," Margaret replies.
"Nothing has been done wrong."

"There was something uncanny in her triumph," reflects
Margaret. "She, who had never expected to conquer anyone,
had charged straight through these Wilcoxes and broken up
their lives." This, surely, is a peculiar "triumph" for one who
had not *meant* to conquer. Why does Forster speak of it as a
"triumph" at all? He would seem to admit by it that Margaret
has been at war with the Wilcoxes all along. But Margaret had

appeared to marry Henry, not to declare war on him; she had set out to improve him, not to defeat him. What Forster's insistence on her triumph confesses is that, if Margaret still wishes to live with Henry, she has no choice but to defeat him. The only way to make him "a better man" is to remake him, beginning, as it were, from scratch.

Indeed, we are led by Margaret's flattered sense of having triumphed to wonder whether her compromise with "men as they are" had ever been in good faith. Margaret had claimed to admire the Wilcox "character." Was it, then, only with a view to changing it—or, as it now seems, to destroying it? In truth, Margaret had counted on being able to teach Henry to "connect"; she had accepted him only on this basis. She did not know that the objective man, by definition, cannot connect. Did Forster himself not know it? He offers hope, at first, like a man who has hope to spare. But the novel describes his own, as well as Margaret's, disillusionment.

Both Margaret and Forster seem to take back, by the end, anything good they have said for the Imperial type. Margaret herself is allowed to make the important point. When Henry refuses to let the pregnant Helen spend a night at Howards End, Margaret explodes:

"You shall see the connection if it kills you, Henry! You have had a mistress—I forgave you. My sister has a lover—you drive her from the house. Do you see the connection? Stupid, hypocritical, cruel—oh, contemptible!—a man who insults his wife when she's alive and cants with her memory when she's dead. A man who ruins a woman for his pleasure, and casts her off to ruin other men. And gives bad financial advice [words of Henry's had caused Leonard to leave his job], and then says he is not responsible. These, man, are you.[6] You can't recognize them, because you cannot connect. . . . No one has ever told you what you are—muddled, criminally muddled.

"You cannot connect": this is final, and fatal to Forster's hopes

[6] I have quoted, here, from the Vintage Books edition (New York, 1956). In the Edward Arnold edition (London, 1947), this sentence reads: "These men are you."

for Romance. Margaret does not repent her words: "Her speech to him seemed perfect. She would not have altered a word. It had to be uttered once in a life, to adjust the lopsidedness of the world. It was spoken not only to her husband, but to thousands of men like him—a protest against the inner darkness in high places that comes with a commercial age." Henry, then, cannot connect, and if he is nonetheless able to connect in the last chapter, he is not the same character. Forster, framing in his own way a protest against darkness in high places in a commercial age, had made Henry a caricature of the objective man from the first. With Margaret's denunciation of Henry, Forster then fixes him in the caricature almost vindictively, as if setting him alive in concrete. Let him suffer as what he is, the novelist seems to say, if he refuses to be anything better. It does no good, then, for Forster later to release him; he merely seems to be introducing a new character.

If the Imperial man had once seemed to possess "character," Forster will take this away from him, too. The type will seem not only unable to improve; it will seem worthless as what it is. Henry crumbles, Charles causes a man to die: can this be character? Is to be "hypocritical, cruel" to have character? Not so. It is Margaret, the conqueror, who has "grit." It is Leonard, the Romantic wanderer of the hills, who has "character":

He never confused the past. He remained alive, and blessed are those who live, if it is only to a sense of sinfulness. The anodyne of muddledom, by which most men blur and blend their mistakes, never passed Leonard's lips—
> And if I drink oblivion of a day,
> So shorten I the stature of my soul.

It is a hard saying, and a hard man [Meredith] wrote it, but it lies at the foot of all character.

Indeed, the Wilcoxes will come to seem worse than merely lacking in character; they will seem to be downright destructive. "Healthy, ever in motion," Forster will say of the Imperial type,

it "hopes to inherit the earth. It breeds as quickly as the yeoman, and as soundly; strong is the temptation to acclaim it as a
super-yeoman, who carries his country's virtue overseas. But the
Imperialist is not what he thinks or seems. He is a destroyer."
We can only complain that Forster himself had seemed to give
way to the temptation to acclaim the Imperialist, and that the
Imperialist is not what Forster himself had seemed to think.

So in reality it has been a war, and the book's "soldier" and
"sword" motif has meant more than we had guessed. All the
same, it would be wrong to conclude that Margaret is a victor.
If Forster presents her as one, it is only to persuade himself that
there is hope for heroic Romance. The fact is that Margaret
does far less than Forster gives her credit for. When Henry announces "I'm broken—I'm ended," Forster says of her: "No sudden warmth arose in her. She did not see that to break him was
her only hope." But Henry has, after all, just admitted to being
"broken." It is not up to Margaret to "break him." Forster so
badly wants to make the outcome seem *her* triumph that he
does not attend to the facts of his own plot. The truth is that the
Wilcox men defeat themselves—or that Forster himself defeats
Henry for the sake of a daybreak denouement. Are we then to
assume that the Imperialist inevitably destroys himself—that
the "thousands of men" like Henry will all, at some time, sham-
ble up to some Margaret, broken? Forster is not so unreasonable
as to suggest it. And so Romance seems merely to triumph here
on a fluke. It is awarded the round on a technicality; but it is
clear that it is destined for defeat.

With this ending, Forster merely pampers his noble fears. The
logic of his book requires—hard as it would have been to bear—
a conclusion of desperation and defeat. And this ending is in
fact incorporated in the novel, however abortively, at the end
of Chapter Thirty-Nine. Here Margaret decides to leave for
Germany with her pregnant sister. If a Wilcox cannot connect,
then there can be no future for Romance in England; and Henry—Margaret herself has said it—cannot connect. "In the past

year she had grown so fond of England that to leave it was a real grief. Yet what detained her? No doubt Henry would pardon her outburst, and go on blustering and muddling into a ripe old age. But what was the good?" Indeed, there can be no good, if England and the Imperialist are as Forster has portrayed them. Romance must migrate, it must go into exile.

Not that Germany is a haven for the Romantic. Life, once again, is "going to be melted down, all over the world"; and Germany, the novel has suggested, is every bit as imperial as England. Nonetheless, its blood is warm; it has an "interest in the universal"; it represents "the good, the beautiful, the true, as opposed to the respectable, the pretty, the adequate." And so it is at least fitting that the Romantic should go there. Appositely, it was a German and another Schlegel, Friedrich, who—as Arthur O. Lovejoy observes—"launched upon its impetuous career through nineteenth-century criticism and philosophy" the term "romantic."

Forster, having first forced us to see that Romance is doomed in England, and then having concealed this conclusion in a rosy mist, cannot leave it at that. As if doubting the substantiality of Margaret's "triumph," he provides Romance with a double indemnity. Let us suppose, he seems to say, that a Wilcox cannot be changed. Even so, could not the earth be "beating time"? Could there not still be such a crop of hay as never? If "England's hope" does not lie in Margaret, then might it not lie in the descendents of her yeoman class, who even now keep "to the life of daylight"? They breed quickly too, Forster assures us; and "clumsily they carry forward the torch of the sun, until such time as the nation sees fit to take it up." Leonard comes from such stock, or very near it; and Howards End will go to his son. So, then, if she has done nothing else, Margaret has at least accomplished that—she has at least been a midwife for the yeomanry. Wild as this is as a venture at optimism, Forster reaches even further in the final pages, finally offering us hope without troubling to indicate any basis for it. "All the signs are against it now," Margaret says, "but I can't help hoping, and very early in the morning in the garden I feel that our house is the future as well as the past." "Logically," she knows, places like Oniton and Howards End "had no right to be alive"—but why not "hope . . . in the weakness of logic?" To such wishful clinging and stubbornness of faith have Forster's apprehensions reduced him.

The collapse of the novel into confusion and feeble trust is not the only concession Forster makes to the Wilcox type. Having found that combat is useless, he becomes disenchanted with the broad and heroic pursuit of proportion. Why struggle to connect with "men as they are" if they represent the negation of Romance? Indeed, from the point of view of Romance, the objective man is not even real: "Alas!" Margaret feels, "that Henry should fade away as reality emerged, and only her love for him should remain clear, stamped with his image like the cameos we rescue out of dreams." In her disgust with the Imperialists of the seen, Margaret retreats to the unseen; disillusioned with materialism, she rebounds from matter itself. Thus, after Henry's failure to connect and Leonard's death, her "soul retires within, to float upon the bosom of a deeper stream" and have "communion with the dead." It alters its focus "until trivial things are blurred." "Leonard's death brought her to the goal"—as if this had been her objective all along. Is Leonard's death, then, trivial? It is indeed if "life and death" are "anything and everything, except this ordered insanity," this "jangle of causes and effects."

So it is that Margaret appears to change roles with Helen: having formerly criticized her sister for being "high-handed" with the seen, she herself now discounts its actuality, while it is Helen who exclaims, in the final words of the book, over the cutting of the field. Margaret, in the last chapter, is "absent" when Helen addresses her. In the fourteen months since Leonard's death, she has grown "less talkative." She sits quietly, sewing. If the circular cutting of the meadow fails to excite her, she yet catches glimpses of "diviner wheels." Helen assures us that she has seen Margaret "loving Henry, and understanding him better daily," and though we have no reason to doubt this, how remote Margaret seems, nonetheless, from anything merely human and companionable. Forster seems scarcely to know how far from "heroic" she appears in these closing pages—how much she has come to resemble the wych-elm in her still and halcyon "communion with the dead." And perhaps the reason is that Forster himself is finding unwitting rest in her withdrawal. Significantly, in his next novel, *A Passage to India,* he will *begin* with the suspicion that the "jangle of causes and effects" is only an evil dream. By then he will openly have abdicated Romance, with its balance between the seen and the unseen, as if vacating a blighted area, and have turned for refuge to the spaceless and timeless regions of the mystical.

In Margaret's transformation from a darling of the Muses to a priestess of the unseen we may thus detect a confession of despair over the future of Romance. Like the remoteness from "daily life" of the first Mrs. Wilcox, whom Margaret has come to resemble, it tells us that very likely there will be no full humanity in the England of tomorrow: no golden proportion, no heroic purpose, no hope on this side of the grave. There will be, instead, for the special few, only a waiting before the gates of the All, passive "communion with the dead." In *Howards End,* Forster secretly turns from England's future to the eternal, surrendering daily life to the Wilcoxes of the world.

– 6 –

Forster's position as a moralist is roughly at the median between George Eliot's and Lawrence's. In George Eliot, the moral absolute is the human collective, right and wrong being almost totally referred to it. In Lawrence, by extreme contrast, the "moral" absolute is universal change. In George Eliot, again,

all conduct ought to be ethical—literally a "being led" to the
right by principle. In Lawrence, on the other hand, all life
ought to be spontaneous, the play of a universal fountain. Forster differs from both by taking the Person as the moral absolute.
And since the Person is at the meridian between other Persons
and nature, his morality consists in reconciling daily human
duties with his love of the eternal and the infinite.

In Forster there is as little question of living for others as for
the "pristine" unconscious in the self. One lives, rather, for the
connections one makes—with others, with one's past, with the
natural world. Claims must be balanced; here nothing is absolute except proportion itself. In *A Room with a View*, Mr.
Emerson and his son learn that the cottage they have rented had
originally been promised to the gentle Miss Alans. Should they
write to Miss Alans and offer the cottage? Or should they send
them "to the wall"? To the wall it must be. George observes:

"There is a certain amount of kindness, just as there is a certain
amount of light. . . . We cast a shadow on something wherever we
stand, and it is no good moving from place to place to save things;
because the shadow always follows. Choose a place where you won't
do very much harm, and stand in it for all you are worth, facing the
sunshine."

Compare Dinah Morris in *Adam Bede*: ". . . all my peace and
joy have come from having no life of my own, no wants, no
wishes for myself, and living only in God and those of his
creatures whose sorrows and joys he has given me to know." In
George Eliot, the letter would have been sent off to the Miss
Alans who—so gratefully!—would have refused the offer, having
no wants, no wishes, for themselves. And in Lawrence? The two
old spinsters would "essentially" not exist at all. They would
long ago have forfeited their right to the sunshine. One recalls
the much younger spinster Banford, on whom a tree is felled,
fatally, by the Laurentian hero in *The Fox*. It is, we are made to
feel, no great loss.

Forster's books reconcile George Eliot's overwhelming fear

of harming others with Lawrence's feeling that ethical right and wrong are insignificant beside the sacredness of life itself. For Forster, the "we" is a false absolute; yet, like Mill, he wishes to give others—other individuals—their due. So Stephen Wonham in *The Longest Journey* will not, he says, play loose with women, for that "would be harming some one else." But Forster departs from Mill and George Eliot alike, and joins forces with Lawrence, when he goes on to imply that, if not society, then some larger whole is sacred. In *Where Angels Fear to Tread*, Caroline Abbott, exemplifying an ethical frame of mind, wishes to "save" Gino's baby from the "contagion" of his father, a "cruel, vicious fellow." Her point of view changes, however, when she observes Gino's awesomely natural love for his son, a love exalted by his Romantic comprehension "that physical and spiritual life may stream out of him for ever." In consequence, Caroline loses her "comfortable sense of virtue"; she sees that she is "in the presence of something greater than right or wrong." So, too, in *A Room with a View*, Mr. Beebe predicts that when Lucy's life becomes as wonderful as her music, "then we shall have her heroically good, heroically bad—too heroic, perhaps, to be good or bad." As a final instance, Stephen Wonham is, in Rickie's view, "a law to himself, and rightly": he is "great enough to despise our small moralities."

Yet if Stephen despises small moralities, he does not, as we have seen, despise morality itself. If morality is essentially the justice of our relations to other beings, then, of course, neither Forster nor Lawrence can be said to despise it. ". . . let us now realize," Lawrence writes in *Psychoanalysis and the Unconscious*, "that we cannot proceed to order the path of our own unconscious without vitally deranging the life-flow of those connected with us. If you disturb the current at one pole, it must be disturbed at the other. Here is a new moral aspect to life." Yet, again, it is just what we ordinarily think of as morality—supervising principle, idealism—that, in Lawrence's view, deranges "the life-flow." Proper behavior is spontaneous; the "creative, spontaneous soul" is the only touchstone of the right; "nothing that comes from the deep, passional soul is bad, or can be bad." It is thus only the vital "unconscious" that one ought to reverence in others; it is this and this alone that one must not despise.

In Forster, by contrast, it is the human and personal center that is held sacred: the intuitive and conscious nucleus of connections. Unlike Lawrence, Forster is tender to the entire human being, since all of the human being goes to create the sacred sphere of Romance. Forster reverences not less than Lawrence but more; and this further part embraces what George Eliot also thought it our duty to reverence, in others if not in ourselves: the vulnerable consciousness, the feeling heart, of the human being.

– 7 –

Forster's acceptance of both man's sensuous and spiritual powers would seem to place him at least theoretically at an advantage over George Eliot and Lawrence as a novelist, if only because he does not come to his characters bearing knives, in an attempt to "enlarge" them by reducing them from what they already are. Of the three, Forster alone stands unequivocally for what Schiller called "*totality* of characacter," "fullness of form with fullness of content," "the possibility of a nature that is both sensuous and rational."

Burdened as Forster was, moreover, by what Lionel Trilling, in his book *E. M. Forster*, calls "moral realism," he was not nearly so liable as George Eliot to divide good and evil among his characters, making the good too good and the bad—well, perhaps she does not exaggerate the bad. Forster had, in this regard, an advantage even over Lawrence, though the latter had also his share of what Forster, in *The Longest Journey*, names "the Primal Curse, which is not . . . the knowledge of good and

evil, but the knowledge of good-and-evil." How reassuring Lawrence is, for example, when in *Women in Love* his Ursula, after
displaying her instinctive creativeness by saying that she does
not want to destroy a paper lantern with a deathly "white cuttle-
fish" that has terrified Gudrun, nonetheless shows "merely" human pique at Gudrun's insistence that Ursula exchange one of
her own lovely lamps for it: ". . . she could not help feeling
rather resentful at the way in which Gudrun and Gerald should
assume a right over her, a precedence." The moment before,
while showing her creativity, she had threatened to be no more
than an "incarnation" of a "great phase of life"; that she then
reveals resentment redresses the balance, apprising us that Lawrence has not lost sight of her as a human being.

In point of fact, however, Forster does not prove superior to
these other novelists at characterization. Forster, too, had to
run the gauntlet of his idealism, and sometimes did not make
it through. From some of his characters he demanded a perfection of harmony, a settledness in a "wonderful" world of
Romance, that actual human beings could scarcely, or rarely,
match. Forster can be as sentimental about Romance as George
Eliot often is about "the nobler emotions, which make mankind
desire the social right," or Lawrence about "the creative, spontaneous soul," and "loins," and "the very stuff of being." Where
Lawrence's characters are sometimes overcolored, even purple,
and George Eliot's mellowed and misted over by "precious seeing," Forster's can be too purely lambent, too translucent to the
light of Romance.

Not only do the middle three of Forster's five novels end as
weakly as George Eliot's, with the same atmosphere of a smiling
lie. His novels, like both George Eliot's and Lawrence's, can be
false in patches well before the end. One thinks of Caroline
Abbott in her appearance as a perhaps too majestic goddess, of
Gino as a too majestic father, of George Emerson as a "radiant,"
muscular god, of Stephen Wonham as an almost cutely difficile
pastoral figure. And Forster's need for a "world fit to live in,"

in Lawrence's phrase, causes him to bring about at least one reform as unlikely as Gwendolen Harleth's: Henry Wilcox's last-minute change into a Person who has done nothing wrong.

Forster's characters are often sharper of line than either George Eliot's or Lawrence's. More than theirs, his pen impales; more even than George Eliot's, it has a comic incisiveness. Yet, by the same token, his characters seem less substantial than theirs, and are harder to hold in the memory. Unlike his sentimentality, this would seem to owe little to his idealism—unless to his impatience with "men as they are." Forster's goats are usually stereotyped; there are two main groups, the aesthetes and the philistines, and within these groups the characters are virtually interchangeable. And as for his major Romantic characters—Mr. Emerson, Stephen Wonham, Margaret Schlegel— his tendency is not so much to present as to celebrate them. The characterization of Margaret is doubtless a triumph—but within limits that make her seem more like a colored etching than a portrait.

Yet the lightness of Forster's characterizations probably stems more from his taste in prose than from anything else. It is a taste for the exquisitely chosen, the deft, the swift: the edge that cuts cleanly and summarily.[7] Forster's comedy and his lyricism alike seem the result of a love of concentrated style. Forster's texture is always thin, though not as a newspaper is, but thin like the taut and shining surface of a balloon, firm with the pressure of clear and intelligent purpose. Every word contributes its part to the final position of the scales; every word has its interest of intention and design.

Just for this reason, however, Forster's books leave unsatisfied the perhaps equally aesthetic hunger for what James called "solidity of specification," our desire to have, as it were, the world in a page. The characters, the objects, the places, in For-

[7] This is not to say, however, that Forster's style lacks a proportion consonant with his ideal of the self. It is as sensuous as it is intellectual, as comically shrewd as it is lyrical.

ster's novels rarely seem to have any weight of their own. Forster is so clear about what he wants to make of them that they threaten to be only surfaces; they have no reserves of mystery, of resistance to intention. *A Passage to India* apart, Forster can achieve ambiguity only by faking, as he does, I think, with Ruth Wilcox. "The intensely, stifling human quality of the novel," he writes in *Aspects of the Novel*, "is not to be avoided; the novel is sogged with humanity. . . ." But certainly his own novels are not sogged with it. They keep us at a little remove from the lives they portray—sharing the author's amusement, listening to his sermons, admiring his wit and dexterity, pursuing his intimations. In consequence, though Forster is, like Lawrence, a writer of imagination, not of thin fancy, his texture seems too crisp to be filling or richly nutritive. In point of adroitness, Forster can dance circles around George Eliot and Lawrence— each is so heavy, so solemn as a rule. All the same, we cannot but be impressed by their might and their patient labor; we are drawn in to share it, we respond to their struggle with the recalcitrant materials of human life.

The one novel in which Forster's thinness of specification seems scarely to matter is *A Passage to India*. Here it is redeemed by groping. Page by page, the texture is as haunted as it is confident; it is unsatisfied for all its poise. In keeping, there is here more complexity and mystery of design than in Forster's earlier work; we do not know quite where we are, where Forster is, where the truth can be found, if it can. The characters are quite as unmonumental, as hard to remember after a first reading, as the earlier ones; but in this instance they seem as large and substantial as their world will permit. Their smallness is not a result of Forster's art but a perplexing condition of life.

X. *Politics and the Spirit of Life*

"I criticize Russell, and Wells, and E. M. Forster," wrote Christopher Caudwell in *Studies in a Dying Culture* (1939), "because I believe they are the champions of unfreedom." In saying this, Caudwell doubtless knew that Forster, in his own eyes, was precisely a champion of freedom. Forster reviewed Caudwell's powerful and cogent book, but his mind was unchanged. He and Caudwell were both champions of freedom; it was simply that Forster wanted to preserve it while Caudwell wanted to create it.

To Caudwell, a Communist, liberty is "social co-operation." To Forster, an individualist, liberty is—well, he cannot quite define it: "as a conception it is negative"; but this much he can say, it has to do with being left alone. And is not "social co-operation," despite its name, likely to involve some coercion? Worse, might it not turn to grey what alone gives life its color, the imagination at play in the private life?

Forster, in short, does not quite know how to answer Caudwell. He only knows that Caudwell's faith in co-operation seems too simple—a noble but bullying faith, insensitive to the delicacies of the problem. To the plea for social planning, Forster had always given a start of enthusiasm, then found his approval sticking in his throat. He knew, and in *Howards End* he demonstrates, that a man born in economic chains cannot be free. Personal relations, culture, Romance—these things "stand upon money as upon islands." Men like Leonard Bast, a clerk in an insurance company, are "submerged." Leonard's "mind and his body had been alike underfed, because he was poor, and because he was modern they were always craving better food." What can be done for such a man? Until socialism comes, give him cash, suggests Margaret; "for it is the warp of civilization, whatever the woof may be." Leonard will not gain his soul until he gains a little of the world; as "an overworked clerk," he will never "explore the spiritual resources of this world" or "know the rarer joys of the body, or attain to clear and passionate intercourse with his fellows." But must we go so far as to reorganize society? Why not, instead, fix our eyes "on a few human beings, to see how, under present conditions, they could be made happier"? For the more *personal* help can be, the better. In fact, "doing good to humanity" is "useless." The "many-coloured efforts thereto" have resulted "in a universal grey."

For Forster, then, social effort is mistaken to the extent that it is impersonal. We lose our human character when we act for the sake of, or as a part of, a mass. "The complexion of his mind," Forster says pointedly of a character in *A Passage to India*, "turned from human to political." So, distrusting the group, Forster must fall back on unorganized philanthropy: helping "a few human beings." But how much good will this do? And how many are likely to do it? Forster himself was personally generous. "Throughout his life," writes P. N. Furbank, "he had one clear idea about money, that it was an opportunity to perform acts of loving-kindness." And Margaret Schlegel, as we noted, intends to "diminish her income by half during the next ten years." Yet Leonard Bast dies largely as a result of being, because poor, in poor health. How effective can unorganized philanthropy hope to be? Forster cannot have much hope, and hence is driven to write of Leonard almost with a note of objection that he exists, so great a problem does he pose.

One guessed him as the third generation, grandson to the shepherd or ploughboy whom civilization had sucked into the town; as one of the thousands who have lost the life of the body and failed to reach the life of the spirit. Hints of robustness survived in him, more than a hint of primitive good looks, and Margaret, noting the spine that might have been straight, and the chest that might have broadened, wondered whether it paid to give up the glory of the animal for a tail coat and a couple of ideas. Culture had worked in her own case, but during the last few weeks she had doubted whether it humanized the majority, so wide and so widening is the gulf that stretches between the natural and the philosophic man, so many the good chaps who are wrecked in trying to cross it.

Why is the gulf between the natural and the philosophic man wider now than before? Is this not a curious assertion? The truth is that Forster wants it to seem wide—too wide to cross. He *prefers* the natural to the philosophic man, Leonard as he was to Leonard as he wants to be. After all, the natural man is almost certain to be Romantic, while the philosophic man is likely to suffer from a cosmopolitanism of the mind. Forster describes Leonard at one point as being momentarily "the naïve and sweet-tempered boy . . . whom Nature had intended." And if Nature has her own plans for Leonard, why then give him money to stand on? Money may be "the warp of civilization"; but Nature did not intend Leonard for civilization. But there is no sending Leonard back, and Forster, frustrated, can scarcely portray his plight without an irony that seems a little unkind.

There are, then, two reasons why Forster cannot bring himself to share Caudwell's faith in a freedom to be gained by "social-co-operation" and "economic production": his inclination to leave social classes as they are, or rather were; and his distrust of social organization per se. His conservatism lies behind the first, his individualism behind the second, and his Romanticism (itself deeply conservative but favoring the personal) behind both. The conservatism was at length stared out of countenance, or at least out of speech, by the developments of the times; the individualism and the Romanticism were to last. Foster was to become more and more willing to admit that concerted social action needed to be taken; he was to remain as reluctant as ever to take it. In the essays gathered in *Abinger Havest* and *Two Cheers for Democracy*, socialism is generally regarded as an ominous if indefinite threat to the quality, the highest possibilities, of individual life.

The individual life had served Forster so well that he could not relinquish his allegiance to it; he could sooner tear out his own heart. Though not wealthy, he lived on inherited pounds and so, like Margaret, was free to become an individual: "an entity which," he says, "thinks for itself, says what it thinks, and acts according to its own considered standards. . . ." Could Forster have lived so happily, so "freely," under socialism or communism? Not nearly so well, he must have concluded. At least some such inference would seem to explain his holding back from communism even in the years of his greatest sympathy to it. In 1935 he states: ". . . I am not a Communist, though perhaps I might be one if I was a younger and a braver man, for in Communism I can see hope. It does many things which I think evil, but I know that it intends good." A year earlier also he had said that he was "too old for communism," and he had been specific about at least one of the evils: "the blood to be shed before its problematic victory." Yet what does all this add up to? The plea of age is not a noble one; nor, if hope can be seen in communism, is it enough to refer vaguely to its many evils. What is it, we wonder, that Forster is *not* saying about communism? Is it simply that he finds it alien to the atmosphere in which he and his friends became the individuals they are— alien, for example, to the Cambridge of his youth? Does he mean that if he were younger he would be the product of a different age and thus more likely to embrace social co-operation? Yet one senses from Forster's apologetic tone how dissatisfied he is with his loyalty to his past, a loyalty that lacks, after all, the self-evident largesse of socialistic compassion. But what can he do? He did not make the world; he grew up in it and it changed and then he did not know whether people of his kind really belonged. In 1944, he observes "how lost" some English writers "have been feeling during the last quarter of a century," in a world where "normal life" is a "life in factories and offices" and where "even farming has becomes scientific," where "insurance has taken the place of charity" and "status has given way to contract." And still other remarks of Forster's betray his feeling of being an anachronism in twentieth-century England.

Nonetheless, it is in the forties that Forster's attitude toward social planning becomes most sympathetic. We find him confessing in 1946, in "The Challenge of Our Time," that though the education he received was humane, "it was imperfect, inasmuch as we none of us realised our economic position." "We did not realise," he adds, "that all the time we were exploiting the poor of our own country and the backward races abroad, and getting bigger profits from our investments than we should." Now the "backward races," he says, "are kicking—and more power to their boots." As for the English poor, Forster has now worked up a tolerance for "planning." "We must have planning and ration books and controls, or millions of people will have nowhere to live and nothing to eat." It is hardly Caudwell's communism, nor even advanced socialism, but it is further than Forster had seemed ready to go when he wrote *Howards End*.

"We want the New Economy," he continues, "with the Old Morality." So, then, he is not foregoing a position, merely adding a new one. Yet he is apprehensive about this miscegenation. "We want planning for the body," he cautions, "and not for the spirit"—and then adds even more cautiously, "But the difficulty is this: where does the body stop and the spirit start?" "The doctrine of laisser-faire," he observes, "is the only one that seems to work in the world of the spirit. . . ." And obviously Foster has this spiritual freedom much more at heart than economic planning. This we could only have expected of him. In his new concern for social co-operation, he is not any the less a Romantic individualist than he was. Far from facing down his individualism, the twentieth century, with its mass movements, had only worked to justify it. More than ever did the individual seem threatened with extinction; more than ever did the individual seem worthier than any collective. The essays of the late thirties, the forties, and the fifties speak with horror of a civilization in which a "social conscience" has spread like a cancer, destroying individuality by disguising "the fear of the herd as loyalty towards the group," and persuading a man that "when he sacrifices himself to the State he is accomplishing a deed far more satisfying than anything which can be accomplished alone." They speak, too, of a time when not only fascism, Grundyism, bureaucratic encroachment, censorship, and conscription but communism, as well, menaces freedom from without, and all this just at a time when it has been ascertained beyond doubt that man's freedom is always and terribly menaced from within. Forster's sense of the enormity of the times and the fragility of the person, combined with the proven liberality of the formative influences of his youth, helped to confirm him in his distrust of "social co-operation" at the very time that his public conscience had at last made him side with social planning.

"We are here on earth not to save ourselves," Forster once wrote, "and not to save the community, but to save both." "In our trouble today," he added, we "look for a division which will render unto the community what is the community's and to the self what is the self's." It is a position between George Eliot's and Lawrence's and superior to theirs, I think, for being so. "I cannot shut myself up in a Palace of Art or a Philosophic Tower and ignore the masses and the misery of the world," Forster writes. "Yet I cannot throw myself into movements just because they are uncompromising, or merge myself in . . . my own country . . . as if that were the unique good." The distinction between the public and private conscience, the public and private spheres, is one that Caudwell does not make, and his position has, accordingly, both the strength and the dullness, the stolidity of the monolithic. Life being what it is, Forster's position is not the less but the more true for being difficult and complex. V. S. Pritchett notes that Forster's "apathy" really means "integrity" and that "one other writer of his generation, Boris Pasternak, has it, and has demonstrated its phenomenal spiritual strength." Pasternak and Forster alike located life—in the former's phrase, "the talent for life," in the latter's, "the Spirit of Life"—primarily in personal relations and the love of nature. Yet Pasternak is much less concerned with "what is the community's" than Forster. Forster alone among modern writers of comparable stature represents an attempt to keep the balance. Still, even he, as we have seen, has his bias, and falls, when he must fall, on the side of the private life.

To Forster, both the community and the individual are goods, but the individual is the greater good. The reason for this is the irrevocably subjective character of human life. We exist primarily as consciousnesses, only secondarily as social units. Forster agreed with George Moore that "by far the most valuable things, which we know or can imagine, are certain states of consciousness, which may be roughly described as the pleasures of human intercourse and the enjoyment of beautiful objects," and that "it is only for the sake of these things—in order that as much of them as possible may at some time exist— that any one can be justified in performing any public or private duty. . . ." If the community is a good, it is only because there are individuals in it. What else in it exists to be served? And the individuals in it can only be served if they are led, again in Moore's words, to "the greatest, and *by far* the greatest, goods we can imagine," namely "personal affections and aesthetic enjoyments." For Forster, in other words, the only useful end of public duty is the ensurance of the conditions of Romance.

So Forster falls, when he must, on the side of the private life.

In this respect, how different he is from George Eliot, who, even when it pained her, ratified public duty. The difference can be seen in these novelists' recorded reactions to *Antigone*. "Here lies the dramatic collision," writes George Eliot of Sophocles's play: "the impulse of sisterly piety which allies itself with reverence for the Gods, clashes with the duties of citizenship; two principles, both having their validity, are at war with each other." Uncharacteristically—for here she looks into Sophocles's work, not her own, and the contest is thus more equal—she goes on to imply that "the general" must adapt to the needs of the individual, not vice versa: ". . . the struggle between Antigone and Creon represents that struggle between elemental tendencies and established laws by which the outer life of man is gradually and painfully being brought into harmony with his inward needs." But, no, her partiality for the general, her fears for it, will not stay down: "Until this harmony is perfect, we shall never be able to attain a great right without also doing a wrong." A man who opposes "the rules which society has sanctioned . . . must not only dare to be right, he must also dare to be wrong—to shake faith, to wound friendship, perhaps, to hem in his own powers. Like Antigone, he may fall a victim to the struggle, and yet he can never earn the name of a blameless martyr any more than the society—the Creon he has defied, can be branded as a hypocritical tyrant." Let our protest for the right, she exhorts, "be seasoned with moderation and reverence": a formula that would have reduced Antigone to a harmless nuisance, a worrying friend of the State. Yet even this, of course, is liberal for George Eliot, a far more balanced position than she ordinarily felt free to endorse. If, on the other hand, Forster calls *Antigone* his "central faith," he has in mind a different reading of the play. Emulating the heroine, he writes: "I hate the idea of causes, and if I had to choose between betraying my country and betraying my friend, I hope I should have the guts to betray my country."

There was at least one case in Forster's life in which, if not his individualism, then his worship of the Spirit of Life involved him in a collision of loyalties. Just after World War II, the Ministry of Town and Country Planning announced that the agricultural land near London in which Forster had lived as a child had been commandeered for a satellite town of 60,000 people. The best agricultural land was taken; "ancient and delicate scenery" was obliterated. Yet people, Forster acknowledges, must have houses. ". . . I cannot equate the problem. It is a collision of loyalties. I cannot free myself from the conviction that something irreplaceable has been destroyed, and that a little piece of England has died as surely as if a bomb had hit it." What if the decision had been left to Forster? Perhaps fortunately for the 60,000 people, it was not. Or *was* it fortunate for them? It was also their ancient and delicate England that was lost.

The same sort of "collision of loyalties" had once divided Mr. Failing of *The Longest Journey*. "He loved poetry and music and pictures," Rickie says of him, "and everything tempted him to live in a kind of cultured paradise, with the door shut upon squalor. But to have more decent people in the world—he sacrificed everything to that." Of Failing's decency Forster, of course, has nothing but approval; but the Romantic in him speaks up through Rickie, who wonders if one need go quite so far as to sacrifice everything. After all, Rickie says, music and poetry "help"; and Jackson, one of the sheep of the novel, agrees. Balance between the community and the private is ever, in Forster, as far as one can go without relinquishing what makes any effort worth while. Toward Failing's socialism Forster is, in consequence, no more sympathetic than to the realm he saw depicted in the Soviet Pavilion at the Paris Exhibition of 1937: "a realm which is earnest, cheerful, instructive, constructive and consistent, but which has had to blunt some of the vagrant sensibilities of mankind and is consequently not wholly alive."

If Forster comes to terms with politics at all in his early nov-

els, it is with a socialism instinct with "the vagrant sensibilities"
—"the Socialism of Shelley and Blake." Who would guess from
Mr. Emerson's impassioned advocacies of love, truth, and the
holiness of direct desire, that he wrote for "the Socialistic
Press"? Who but one who still thinks of socialism as identical
with what it was in the blush of its youth? But, significantly, we
are told nothing else about Mr. Emerson's socialism. All the
rest, it would seem, is prose.

In the novels, the only follow-up to the Romantic socialism
of *A Room with a View* is the mystical internationalism of *A
Passage to India*. Like Arnold Toynbee, Forster entertains, in
this novel as in "Notes on the English Character," the possibility of an international character, a universal "religion" that will
transcend divisive creed. "Islam itself," concludes the Moslem
Aziz, "though true, throws cross-lights over the path to freedom.
The song of the future must transcend creed." Later, the Hindu
Godbole finds in one of Aziz's poems that Aziz "had skipped
over the mother-land . . . and gone straight to internationality."
"Ah, that is bhakti; ah, my friend, that is different and very
good. Ah, India, who seems not to move, will go straight there
while other nations waste their time." What interests Ralph
and Stella Moore in Hindusim in the last portion of the novel
is not its form but its spirit, a spirit of unifying and all-inclusive
love.

Forster's last novel to date is thus at the antipodes politically
from George Eliot's last novel, which encourages the separation
and diversity of national character. Lawrence, with his longing
for National Churches, also stands opposed to Forster in this
regard. Of the three, only Forster now seems abreast of the
problems of a divided world. Yet because of his political realism
—a realism at one with his Romanticism—Forster has very little
to say by way of help and little hope to offer. The problem is
simply too great. In truth, none of these writers can be said to
furnish a satisfactory politics. What separates Forster from the
others is that he knows, unhappily, the limitations of his own.

XI.   *A Passage to India:*
Beyond the Personal

In *A Passage to India* (1924), Romance, individuality, personal relations—the preeminent Forsterian values—falter and fail before a macrocosm that seems not so much indifferent as actively hostile to them. Gone is the glowing world of the earlier books, put out as if by a black gust from the Infinite—or, it may be, from Nothingness. In this book Forster's perspective alters radically, as when a telescope is turned around and looked into at the end that diminishes what it views. The human world shrinks, grows fragile, becomes confused, futile, lost. Here, with a prescience and daring at which we can only marvel, Forster has entered the contemporary world.

It is India of course that confronts and dwarfs Forster's values, and India has here a triple significance. It represents, first, the evil and confusion of Imperialism—of administration without love, of racism and its sordid rationalizations. It also represents, as James McConkey notes in *The Novels of E. M. Forster,* "the contemporary condition, the separation between all mankind and all earth." It is precisely that world without connection, peace, organic sanctity, in a word Romance, that Forster had foreseen in *Howards End*—only now in even deeper exile from the universe. "How can the mind take hold of such a country?" Forster writes. "Generations of invaders have tried, but they remain in exile. The important towns they build are only retreats, their quarrels the malaise of men who cannot find their way home. India knows their trouble. She knows the whole world's trouble, to its uttermost depth." True, Forster plays off against this India Wordsworth's Grasmere and the Hellenic coast—mentioning them with an almost audible gasp of relief that India is not in fact the whole world. But to no avail: when one is in India, India is indeed the world—and, in any case, it is India that is weighted with the future. Finally, Forster's India is an emblem of the macrocosm: a chaotic universe of total inclusion, equally hospitable to minerals, plants, and animals; the Hindu cosmos, confused because inclusive and inclusive because God is in everything, the unmanifested principle of all manifestation. Or, alternatively—for this is at once Forster's most skeptical and belief-hungry novel—India represents a nihilistic cosmos of insidious matter, of blind and ungenerous instinct: a world in which everything—love in a church, love in a cave— has a horrible and equal absence of value.

It is into this world that Forsterian Romance enters, as it were, in all innocence. And how sheltered, how romantic in the sense of fanciful, it seems by comparison. Here it finds that it cannot take root; it is totally unsuited. Romance depends, after all, upon beauty of place; but Chandrapore, where "the very wood seems made of mud, the inhabitants of mud moving," is not beautiful. Neither is the Indian sky. During the hot season, the sun returns "to his kingdom with power but without beauty—that was the sinister feature. If only there had been beauty!" At sunrise, at the Marabar—"look, the sun's rising," cries Adela Quested, "this'll be absolutely magnificent"—nothing happens: "It was as if virtue had failed in the celestial fount." Nor is there beauty in the countryside. It is "too vast to admit of excellence. In vain did each item in it call out, 'Come, come.' There was not enough god to go round." Even Mau, in Part III, though "as park-like as England," seems "queer." As for "distance and air," so magical in Forster's Italy and England, only at evening do they become congenial at Chandrapore, and then, just as Romance seems about to unfold its path to the Infinite, the mind awkwardly and wrenchingly overleaps it in worldless mysticism. Only Mrs. Moore finds any blessing here in matter. Observing the moon, she feels "caught in the shawl of night together with earth and all the other stars." "A sudden sense of unity, of kinship with the heavenly bodies, passed into the old woman and out. . . ." Even this is, however, slightly too abrupt for Romance. "Caught" has, after all, an unpleasant suggestion of entrapment, and certainly Mrs. Moore will come to hate her bondage to the world.

Romance blossoms in an atmosphere of tranquillity, but "there seemed no reserve of tranquillity to draw upon in India." "It was as if irritation exuded from the very soil." Then, too, Romance dreams on an image of permanence as a cloud floats on the calm surface of a lake. But in India the mere asking of what something is causes it "to disappear or to merge in something else." Romance is an intuition of the far in the near, the then in the now; but here everything seems "cut off at the roots," and "the spirit of the Indian earth . . . tries to keep men in compartments." Romance loves the distinctiveness of organic form; but in India the sun seems to boil and fry "all the glories of the earth into a single mess." Without mystery Romance cannot ignite, but Indian mystery is disconcertingly like muddle. Referring to "confusion" over whether a certain object is a twisted stump or a snake, Forster remarks, "nothing was explained, and yet there was no romance." Again, the Romantic self faces the unknown in time and space like a swimmer at the edge of the sea. But, in India, time and space appear either oppressive, suffocating and encircling like the "horrid" Marabar caves, or utterly dissolved, as in the soul mysticism of the Hindu ceremony in Part III. Like the London of *Howards End,* India is thus the negation of all Romance, but a far more unsettling negation, since India was not made by man.

Nor does individuality fare any better. In this novel, the loving tension that held the Forsterian Person in connection with the unseen has disintegrated, leaving the Person collapsed upon himself like a puppet, dwarfed and isolated, confined to his own poor, somehow artificial circle of rational light. There is a drying up, an internal shrinkage. The Person dwindles to a mere individual, not even certain that he has depths, though frightened of possible depths all the same, fearful, on the one hand, that they may swallow him and, on the other, that he should have explored them long ago. In India the individual, at least if he is British, stands not with but against the All, thin, uncomprehending, "cut off at the roots," afraid.

The truth is that even if India were Romantic, a Fielding or an Adela, liberated from the Anglo-Indian "herd" though they are, might yet fail to open into a Romantic self. Their foliage seems too sparse, their buds too few.[1] Rationality, dry intelligent self-possession, is their keynote. Both feel that everything worth knowing can be grasped and measured by the mind. Thus to Fielding, "a mystery is only a high-sounding term for a muddle." Everything he has learned has "helped him towards clarity"; he is "hard-bitten, good-tempered, intelligent." As for Adela, "her senses were abnormally inert and the only contact she anticipated was that of mind." Her instincts, she complains, never help her: "I can do this right, and that right; but when the two are put together they come wrong. That's the defect of my character." Her life is discursive in mode. If she travels, it must be with a plan. Like Fielding, she thinks that "all that is possible" has already broached her consciousness. Of these admirable but dessicated individualists Forster writes: "Perhaps life is a mystery, not a muddle; they could not tell. Perhaps the hundred Indias which fuss and squabble so tiresomely are one, and the universe they mirror is one. They had

[1] It may be that Romance, like Forster's Italy, is leagued with youth —that, like a fire that either dies or leaps a road, it either fades with age or moves on into mysticism.

not the apparatus for judging." Small because self-contained, in rejecting the "supernatural" they have left themselves only themselves.

Still, they are uneasy about their dryness. What if they have "missed" a universe of reality? Fielding, having "developed his personality, explored his limitations, controlled his passions," yet comes to feel that "he ought to have been working at something else the whole time,—he didn't know what, never would know, and that was why he felt sad." He senses that clarity has "prevented him from experiencing something else." In England, doubtless that "something else" would be presented as Romance; but Romance, again, is not an option in India, and Fielding is arraigned for closing out, not the organic intimations of Romance, but the dissolving, preformal waters of mysticism. The world he and Adela have missed lies—the word had appeared derangingly at the close of *Howards End*—"behind." "Not for them was an infinite goal behind the stars, and they never sought it. But wistfulness descended on them now, as on other occasions; the shadow of the shadow of a dream fell over their clear-cut interests, and objects never seen again seemed messages from another world."

So it is that in *A Passage to India,* the Western individual, bereft by the disappearance of Romance, and skeptical of "an infinite goal behind the stars," appears, even to himself, a purposeless or futile "end." Though Adela and Fielding stand upright and undaunted in the vastness of the cosmos, they nonetheless see themselves, and we see them, as "dwarfs talking, shaking hands and assuring each other that they stood on the same footing of insight."

In consequence, there is a reversal, here, of the characteristic function of Forster's plot. In the earlier novels, the plot is a vehicle for the self-development of the characters; here it imposes, by contrast, a discovery of self-limitations. Measuring the characters, India finds nearly all of them wanting. So Fielding comes to wonder "whether he was really and truly successful as a human being." Mrs. Moore, crumpled by a "vision" of universal sameness brought on by the Marabar caves, utterly fails as a human being; she retires into a cave of her own. As for the delightful Aziz, "imprisonment had made channels for his character, which would never fluctuate as widely now as in the past." Adela, it is true, develops. "Although her hard schoolmistressy manner remained," reflects Fielding, "she was no longer examining life, but being examined by it; she had become a real person." Yet Adela develops, only to limits that dismay even her by their meagerness: "Disaster had shown her her limitations. . . ." She has discovered her depths—but what shallow depths they are! They seem able to yield only the hallucination of a sexual assault (if so much). Adela concludes that she's not really "fit for personal relationships." Only Professor Godbole, a Hindu, seems adequate to India; and this he achieves by effacing himself—by ceasing to think or act as an individual at all.

Trammeled thus with a new and acute sense of individual limits, Forster becomes openly disillusioned with personal relationships. Two dwarfs talking together, shaking hands—these hardly add up to the "personal intercourse" that, according to *Howards End,* "alone . . . hints at a personality beyond our daily vision." Indeed, because the personal itself seems insignificant in India, here the unseen will not be linked with "a personality" at all: it will seem faceless and, to the Westerners, the more terrible for that. The personal, here, is dry; the waters of the Absolute are not in it. "What is the use of personal relationships," asks Adela, "when everyone brings less and less to them?" "Clarity," it seems, makes the heart arid. Adela, having discovered that she doesn't really like Indians, questions: "Do I like anyone, though?" Fielding, who is sapless, "seasoned," wishes that, like Aziz, "he too could be carried away on waves of emotion." He concludes, "I shall not really be intimate with this fellow, nor with anyone." In fact he does develop an intimacy with Aziz—but the relationship is then blighted, on the one side by Indian suspiciousness, on the other by British of-ficialism. When Fielding temporarily returns to England, land of Romance, "tender romantic fancies that he thought were dead for ever" burst out when he sees "the buttercups and daisies of June." He marries Mrs. Moore's daughter, Stella; and yet "he was not quite happy about his marriage." As for Mrs. Moore, "she felt increasingly (vision or nightmare?) that, though people are important, the relations between them are not, and that in particular too much fuss has been made over marriage. . . ."

A strange, desolate book to come from a man who was later to write: ". . . my books emphasize the importance of personal relationships and the private life, for I believe in them." The barrier to personal relationships set up by Anglo-Indian offi-cialism accounts a little for this striking anomaly; but chiefly the cause lies, as implied, in the death of Romance. In the earlier novels, the Person derives his entire significance from Romance—a world that he has, nonetheless, himself opened up or projected. But from what can he acquire significance in anti-Romantic India? Here the individual seems stranded from all spiritual importance; indeed, he is not even certain that there is a sea from which to be stranded. For Forster, value had formerly lain in the personal—in the vertical dimension of the "I." *There* had stood reality, *there* had been the glowing justifi-cation for life. But here, where the personal has shrunk and seems so stricken—where are value and reality to be found?

The novel is uncertain. Forster's mind is on the rack between a horrified skepticism as to whether spirit exists at all and piqued interest in an Absolute Spirit that, incomprehensible and vast, seems scarcely less appalling than the absence of spirit itself. The alternatives are staggering; yet Forster manages them with consummate subtlety and poise, and the novel is, in consequence, one of the most fascinating ever written.

These antithetical possibilities are concentrated in, indeed obtruded by, the Marabar caves. On the one hand, the caves, together with what happens in them, seem to assert, nastily, that as personalities, as spiritual beings, individuals do not exist, that only a snub-nosed instinct is real and enduring. The circular caves, everywhere reflecting their own darkness, unaltered by time, indistinguishable and isolated from one another, sealed off from the overarching and unifying sky, "horrid, stuffy," suggest some frightening, Freudian chamber of blind instinct, a dark, illicit core of life.[2] Mrs. Moore's "vision," which follows a nightmarish experience in one of the caves, where she is nearly suffocated, figuratively snuffs out her spirit, which thenceforward can see in everything only caves. Although the emptiness of the caves makes them seem symbols of the void, Mrs. Moore's "vision" is actually suggested by something dynamic, the cave's circularly writhing and all-reducing echo. It is a vision of "something very old and very small. Before time, it was before space also. Something snub-nosed, incapable of generosity—the undying worm itself."

Mrs. Moore enters the cave a remarkably spiritual woman; she leaves it to become "sunk in apathy and cynicism." She has virtually entered, it would seem, the heart of her own being, which, like the caves, proves "older than all spirit": she has encountered the "snub-nosed" horror of primordial instinct. Contrary to the usual view, what withers her as a "priestess" is not a metaphysical but a psychological horror—and yet, since the latter negates everything metaphysical, it has the force of both. She comes to see that the core of the self is indifferent to distinctions made by the spirit. As the echo reduces all sounds to "boum"—"a Marabar cave can hear no sound but its own"—so an irremediable selfishness finds "pathos, piety, courage . . . identical, and so is filth." In relation to it, the distinctions of the

[2] The association of the caves with the timeless unconscious has been made by others. See especially *E. M. Forster: The Perils of Humanism,* by Frederic C. Crews, Chapter Ten (New Jersey: Princeton University Press, 1962). Crews, however, gives a somewhat different account of the psychological import of the caves.

spirit are like the party that with its "varied forms and colours" disappears into a cave, leaving only "the small black hole," gaping. Such distinctions are, like these colors and forms, "sucked in like water down a drain." The caves of our instinctual nature, like the Marabar caves, are "flesh of the sun's flesh," and "no water has ever covered them." Water, the primitive symbol of a preformal spirit that refreshingly dissolves and cleanses and unifies, will seem to be ubiquitous in Part III, the "Hindu" portion of the book. Here, in Part II, "Caves," only a few puddles lie about, and even the wells on the plain below the caves disperse but "a feeble flow of water."

"Visions are supposed to entail profundity," Forster comments, and adds, unpleasantly, "but—Wait till you get one, dear reader! The abyss also may be petty, the serpent of eternity made of maggots. . . ." The "also" here is characteristic of the pervading doubleness of the book. Well, let us be as uncertain as Forster that Mrs. Moore's vision lays bare the heart of human life. But let us ask, all the same, how she comes to have it. Evidently it forms the culmination of her growing resentment against demands too long made upon her spirit—a backlash into "apathy and cynicism." Too much has been asked of her; she will henceforth give nothing at all. Mrs. Moore has brought Adela to India so that she may get to know better her son Ronny, a Chandrapore official whom the girl is expected to marry. And what do they do? They bicker. " '. . . I really can't have'—she tapped the cushion beside her—'so much quarreling and tiresomeness.' " That her altruism should be wasted! Does she not have—or could she not have had, if only her children had allowed it—a life of her own? On the train to the caves, she remarks: "It is the children who are the first consideration. Until they are grown up, and married off. When that happens one has again the right to live for oneself. . . ." She adds: "If one has not become too stupid and old." At this point she hands "her empty cup to the servant." She is dried out, she has given too much, she will not give any more. "She had brought Ronny and Adela together by their mutual wish, but really she could not advise them further." She falls asleep ("She was in rather low health, and ought not to have attempted the expedition, but had pulled herself together in case the pleasure of the others should suffer") and dreams of "her other children who were wanting something, Stella and Ralph, and she was explaining to them that she could not be in two families at once."

This, then, is the "mood of the last two months" that takes "form at last" after the experience in the cave. Mrs. Moore's snub-nosed resentment, as if released by the deaf, self-referring echo, swallows her altruism, which now seems to her insincere, a mere "dream." An ugly selfishness—why had she not seen it before?—is the only reality. "God is love," she had said, but in her heart there writhes—and must it not always have writhed? —the undying worm. Henceforth "a sort of resentment" will emanate from her. "It is time," she declares, "I was left in peace." "No doubt you expect me to die," she ungenerously observes to Adela, "but when I have seen you and Ronny married, and seen the other two and whether they want to be married— I'll retire then into a cave of my own." Indeed, she has already withdrawn from the lighted area of the spirit. When she speaks —"Oh, how tedious . . . trivial"—her mind seems to move "from a great distance and out of darkness." She will not testify for Aziz, even though certain that he is innocent; for, like all "good, happy, small people," Aziz does "not exist." As for marriage, "the human race would have become a single person centuries ago if marriage was any use"—if love were real. "And all this rubbish about love, love in a church, love in a cave, as if there is the least difference, and I held up from my business over such trifles!"

For Adela, too, the evil of the caves is psychological; she, too, walks into them as if into her own hidden core. There her instincts, usually inert, suddenly flare up, proving snub-nosed, ungenerous. Aziz has assaulted her! He must pay! Yet, Forster intimates, is it not her own desire for which he must pay? Ordinarily fair-minded—Mrs. Moore praises her for this quality—Adela seems to succumb to what one of the Indians calls the Anglo-Indians' "secret thoughts about our character." [3] Unable consciously to admit desire, she perhaps imputes it to Aziz, in whom, in consequence, it appears ugly. "In some vague way," she feels, ". . . she was leaving the world worse than she found it. She felt that it was her crime. . . ." Like Mrs. Moore, Adela seems thus to let loose within herself, and on others, an ungenerous power. Contemplating the accusation, the trial, the furor, Fielding feels that "a mass of madness had arisen and tried to overwhelm them all; it had to be shoved back into its pit somehow. . . ."

The echo—the buzzing—in Adela's head, lingering on after the experience in the cave, will last only so long as she persists in being ungenerous. The old, fair-minded Adela, however thinly spiritual, had known, like Mrs. Moore, that Aziz was "good." And does not Mrs. Moore still know it? "Only Mrs. Moore," Adela feels, could drive the echo back "to its source and seal the broken reservoir." She even imagines Mrs. Moore to say that Aziz "never did it" and, hearing this, gasps "as if she had risen to the surface of the water." "My echo's better," she observes.

It is not until the trial, however, that Adela emerges from her cave into the air, the daylight of fair-mindedness. She is struck by the "aloofness" of a punka wallah, a physically magnificent Indian who, nourished on Chandrapore garbage, "scarcely knew that he existed"; he "seemed apart from human destinies." His example of self-forgetting rebukes "the narrowness of her sufferings." Under cross-examination, Adela then forgets herself long enough to see into the "essential life" of Aziz. "A new and unknown sensation" overcomes her. ". . . she returned to the Marabar Hills, and spoke from them across a sort of darkness to Mr. McBryde. The fatal day recurred . . . but now she was of it and not of it at the same time. . . ." As "the airs from

---

[3] Forster does not allow us altogether to discount the possibility that Adela may indeed have been assaulted; a guide is suspected.

the punkah behind her" waft over her, she tries to "see" Aziz follow her into the cave. "She failed to locate him." The echo, symbol of snub-nosed self-enclosure, disappears. Spirit surfaces, "sees." And so it is that Adela's experience both confirms and contradicts Mrs. Moore's. Instinct is real, her story seems to say, but so is spirit.

On the dark side, then, the caves represent a radical denial of spirit. Spirituality, they say, is a "dream"; the good, happy, small people enclose an everlasting hell of petty selfishness. There is no help for the species, no help for life. Yet (so sounds another voice in the novel) what if the "undying worm" itself is an illusion, evil merely the negation of what alone is everlasting? Throughout the book, the evil depicted is that of division—division between body and spirit, between individuals, between sects and races, division between man and nature. And what if division itself is ultimately the evil of separation from undifferentiated Godhead, the only reality?

The caves seem to represent this possibility, too. Forster was later to say that Mrs. Moore's vision was "the Hindu vision with its back turned." She experienced, that is to say, not God's timeless and infinite presence, but precisely his absence. Westerner that she is, unadept, anthropocentric, she failed to discern infinite Godhead in stone, and her spirit collapsed, shocked by the void. Yet "absence," observes the Hindu Godbole, "is not nonexistence"; ". . . absence implies presence, . . . and we are therefore entitled to repeat, 'Come, come, come, come.'" "So you thought an echo was India," mock the coconut palms that Mrs. Moore sees as her boat sails from Bombay; "you took the Marabar caves as final?"

Perhaps recklessly, in view of his doubts, Forster goes even further, associating the caves with God's presence—indeed, he makes of them a symbol of Brahma. For example, it is said of the caves that "nothing attaches to them," and in Part III "a wild and beautiful saint" praises "God without attributes—thus did she apprehend Him." Then the caves are described as representing a "renunciation" more complete than Buddha's; and this also would seem to ally them with the Absolute Spirit, which, in the Hindu view, is irreducible—"non-sensuous, non-psychic, purely spiritual reality," as Aldous Huxley describes it in *Time Must Have a Stop*. Of course, to the Western mind, such a God is difficult to distinguish from nothing at all—like the black cave hole that gapes where the varied forms and colors "had momentarily functioned."

The "bubble-shaped" caves are described as mirroring their "own darkness in every direction infinitely." And if there is indeed only one Spirit in the world, so must it mirror itself. The novel reminds us that stones, too, are spiritual to the Hindu, since God is everywhere, except in evil. The birth of Shri Krishna in Part III, for instance, is said to annihilate "all sorrow . . . , not only for Indians, but for foreigners, birds, caves, railways, and the stars." In the same section, Godbole attempts unity with a stone and fails, but only, it is suggested, because his attempt was too conscious. On the polished surface of the caves, two flames, the reflections of a lighted match, will "touch one another, kiss, expire." Stone, then, is not an obstacle to union; spirit will meet itself despite the illusion of matter.

Not only might God be in the stone; the hills that contain the caves are made symbols of the God in which everything has being. According to the Hindu ceremony in Part III, the "whole universe" can be loved; and the Marabar hills give portents of totality. Though twenty miles off, they move upon Chandrapore at sunset—"if the sunset had lasted long enough, they would have reached the town." As Fielding gazes at them from the civil station, "they seemed to move graciously towards him like a queen, and their charm became the sky's. At the moment they vanished they were everywhere . . . and the whole universe was a hill." [4] At another time, too, "the fists and fingers of the Marabar" appear to "swell until they included the whole night sky."

[4] See Wilfred Stone, *The Cave and the Mountain* (Stanford: Stanford University Press, 1966), Chapter Twelve, for an account of Forster's later discovery that the Hindu temple symbolizes "The World Mountain," its cavelike central cell a place where the individual can be alone with God.

It should also be mentioned that Fielding associates the caves' echo with a "universe"—it is as large as that—that he has missed. " . . . the mosque missed it too," he reflects. Like Western culture, Islam holds the self precious, discouraging the abandonment of personality. Yet the looming hills seem to hint that the only real world lies entirely outside the "I" and its mode of history. The empty caves are full of God, Fielding only of himself.

The deluge of rain in Part III—"The air was thick with religion and rain"—and the association there of water with union and love, confirms our suspicion that Forster, in this novel, is seeking, for all his skepticism, to emulate a Hindu vision of the world. To such straits, to such daring, has India driven him. In *Howards End,* the ideal of the Person had continued to glow, even in the denouement, like a leaf in the light of the ultimate; but here, by contrast, the light glances off of it, obliterating it, and Forster is forced to look elsewhere for significance. Frustrated as a Romantic, he aspires to become a mystic instead, though almost gasping in the new, rarefied air, and all uncertain that it is healthy for human beings: Godbole, after all, is very queer, and troublesomely irresponsible-seeming in his attitude toward individual responsibility. However that may be, balked in his love for the personal, Forster, because incurably idealistic, here tries to make an ideal of the universal, reaching into it to test its density, its depths.

And yet, of course, to long for a universal principle of reality is not necessarily to find it, and it is difficult to tell where Forster stops teasing and intimidating his limited Westerners and himself begins to believe his own elaborate religious symbolism. His novel does not say that God exists, nor even that he is absent; but neither does it claim that He does *not* exist. Probably it does not know what to say, but I think that nonetheless it is trying hard to say, through its religious intimations, what God in India would be like, if man were so fortunate as to find him. At the least, man in India seems entitled to repeat, "Come, come, come, come."

So it is that psychology and metaphysics combine in Forster's

novel to call the personal into question. ". . . Psychology,"
Forster was later to write, "has split and shattered the idea of a
'Person,' and has shown that there is something incalculable in
each of us, which may at any moment rise to the surface and
destroy our normal balance. We don't know what we are like."
And as for the universe, what do we really know about it?
Thus, if there is uncertainty within the self, so is there uncertainty outside it. Forster has described the modern mood as
"obscure and minatory," and in *A Passage to India* psychology
and metaphysics are both. Between a doubtful cosmos and a
doubtful subterranean psyche, the individual moves imperiled,
as if running rapids under a lowering sky. From both above and
below there seem to come demands that he justify his thin, conscious, isolated existence. More, that he even exists is called into
question, menaced as he seems to be, on the one side, by a universal sameness of instinct and, on the other, by a universal
sameness of spirit. The personal self may be no more than a
phantom, a momentary smoke above the fire of undying evil or,
on the other hand, blown from off the eternal Godhead. In any
case, it is embattled; it is unsatisfied; it is uncertain. What can
it do? It has no clear knowledge of the reality that surrounds it.
In Fielding and Adela, it holds on, miserably conscious of its
own littleness and ineptitude.

Is it possible that Forster's earlier values merely suffered a
bad dream in India? Can it be that they were not permanently
damaged, not *traumatized*? Surely it would be surprising if they
were not. Yet even in this novel Forster does not so much
abandon proportion as hold it in abeyance. The "Greek" ideal
waits, as it were, on the sidelines, to see how the "Indian" ideal
of a self-extinguishing unity will fare with Forster, or Forster
with it. It is there, for instance, in the reference to the Mediterranean as the "human norm"—Fielding finding in Venice, as if
rediscovering a forgotten possibility, a "harmony between the
works of man and the earth that upholds them," a "civilization
that has escaped muddle, the spirit in a reasonable form, with

flesh and blood subsisting." The Greek ideal is implicit, too, in the mutual criticism that the British and Indian national characters are made to cast on one another, the first appearing aridly ordered and rational, the second unreliably emotional. The novel leaves us to infer that a mean—a keeping of proportion between the head and the heart, the practical motive and the soul—would be ideal. And yet, would it be to much avail in vast and menacing India? Could the ideal of proportion ever take root there? "Abandon yourself," cry the landscape, the sky. "Have done with illusion, become one with the All!"

Bad dream or not, *A Passage to India* is Forster's greatest work, for here alone was he challenged beyond his certitudes, drawn out into the ambiguities of experience, heroically to plumb them, risk them, expose them, yet with no loss, rather a gain, in poise and skill. Nothing about the book is more remarkable than Forster's own Brahma-like inclusiveness, his way of being immanent and transcendent in it at once, detached and yet a voice calling "come" to the nature of man and the world. "Extraordinarily satisfying," his friend T. E. Lawrence wrote to him, ". . . in the multiplicity of its effects & cross-lights & bearings." The "picture," he added, "a cloud might have painted, of man in India."

Afterword

Man has always existed primarily as a problem to himself, needing to be both animal and spiritual and, as if that were not perplexity enough, strapped also with an imaginative or spiritual hunger in perpetual excess of the world. For Western man the problem became intensified or, simply, was renewed, with the dwindling power of Christianity to answer his perplexities and release his soul. Probably Christianity had itself been invented not only to restore to each man a lost protector, a father (as Freud argued in *The Future of an Illusion*), but to authorize and give the individual an absolute value in the universe. Thanks to Christianity, Western man, for about two thousand years, was relieved of the burden of having to create his own purpose. Here was a trellis of steel for the terrible ivy of the spirit; here it could climb and, so it seemed, live forever. Here, too, was an authoritative settlement of the rival claims of the spirit and the flesh. The solution passed down was stringent; it required man to take the axe to himself. Nonetheless, it gave both the individual and the universe a meaning.

What unites the three novelists discussed in this book, different as they are, is the post-Christian need to forge a new principle of significance in the human being. The work of each is an impassioned protest against living a life without a deep, a sacred, an authorized meaning. The thought of being a self without an *idea* of the self, more, without its consecration to something transcendent, brought a terrible heart-sinking to each; it could not be borne. Each took upon himself the task of becoming a new author of human character—above all, of finding the point where the self could join with something universal and bask in its glory.

For George Eliot, the new "universal" was the "divinely-guided whole" of the community. Here, it seemed, was a purity from self, a refuge from turbulent egoism, a hallowed permanence, a *being*, comparable to the one lost in God; to enjoy it the individual had but to identify with the community—to become a "social self." Yet this was not to prove a satisfactory solution. As George Eliot's novels themselves betray, the community cannot quite make good the lives sacrificed to it. It constitutes a cold parent and lover, despite its power to confer esteem. Nor, closely examined, does it seem so glorious after all: in truth, as in *Middlemarch,* it appalls. What it takes away, moreover, can come to seem, as in the case of Maggie Tulliver, more like actual *being* than anything it has to offer. All in all, the identification of the individual with society proves hard to make, the "social self" a form of torture as well as of "larger life." George Eliot's scheme failed to make tolerable sense of the existence of the body, or to counter adequately the persistence of the ego. It closed out flesh from value, and since flesh will not be so easily denied, it condemned itself to at least partial futility. In sum, while perpetuating the Christian prejudice against the body, George Eliot's ideal of the self failed to provide a satisfactory substitute for Christianity's immense compensations to the spirit.

Where the individual in George Eliot has just so much value as the community, in Lawrence he has the value of organic life; but this, too, is conceived as a divinely-guided whole, an infinite reality, with all the enduringness that we associate with sacred *being*. Just here, in the sphere that George Eliot equated with nothingness, Lawrence found, with headlong conviction, the living hierophany of God. Conversely, it was the social and conscious life, the life of principle and self-giving, that he himself was to equate with nothingness.

Was Lawrence more successful than George Eliot at finding a new significance for the self? How doubtful this is. His scheme is beneficent, certainly, to the creaturely self; but how prescriptive it is for the Spirit, and how few will be able to follow the prescription. To find in the "body of the world" a "palpable" otherness, mystic, marvelous—this is too much to require of any human being, except perhaps Lawrence himself. Nor shall we easily submerge our minds in our blood. Lawrence's own mind, of course, kept popping up, finding the box of instinct too small. Naturally enough, Lawrence tried to found a religion on his own experiences, but these were the experiences of an exceptional being. His world is eccentric, a magnificent world apart.

"Man lives, and ought to live," writes Forster, "in a complex world, full of conflicting claims. . . ." And in his tolerance of our stubborn complexities, Forster differs from both these other novelists. Forsterian Romance is essentially a realm of balanced connections: a world that binds but does not constrict, a world fit for both the body and the spirit. Unlike the social self, the personal self is free to delight in a kinship with time and space, with an organic world that not only pleases the senses but indefinitely extends the soul. Unlike the vital self, on the other hand, it may also enjoy its own personal dimension, its private history, its treasury of associations and affections. It is not required to turn its back on itself. An inner world, it yet greets the outer world with "profound vivacity." In contrast to the other novelists, Forster, at least in his early work, does not wish to merge the self in some impersonal infinite. He wants it held, at most, in tension with the opened-up modes of its own experience, with endless time, with endless space.

Forster, all the same, seems to have felt some discontent with proportion and connection. This was only in small part because they are easier to achieve for some than for others, some being blessed by nature to attain them. For even when they are attained, even when the Romantic environment is still intact, they do not seem always to satisfy him. So proportion in *Howards End* falls off almost into a withdrawal of the soul from the immediate world. The truth is that even Forster's ideal of the Person had to struggle against that spiritual hunger for the ultimate which, as I began by saying, forms a perennial human problem. In *A Passage to India,* this hunger proved too much for it, weakened as it was by its uprootedness from Romantic England.

These, then, are the chief architects of the self among English writers since Jane Austen. They brought to the enormous challenge of designing a momentous human character three different temperaments, though all were alike idealistic; and the results are as disparate as they could possibly be. Fortunately, the literary greatness of these novelists, though inseparable, as it happens, from their idealism, proved independent of their models of the self; or we should feel forced to chop and choose among them, and be the poorer for it. Indeed, if we have *Middlemarch* and *Women in Love* and *A Passage to India,* it is despite their authors' ideals of human character—but not despite their common desire to discover a consuming significance for our life on earth.

Index